LANGUAGE, COUNTER-MEMORY, PRACTICE

Selected Essays and Interviews

MICHEL FOUCAULT

✘

LANGUAGE, COUNTER-MEMORY, PRACTICE

Selected Essays
and Interviews

Edited with an Introduction by
DONALD F. BOUCHARD

Translated from the French by
DONALD F. BOUCHARD
and SHERRY SIMON

Cornell University Press

ITHACA, NEW YORK

First published 1977 by Cornell University Press
First printing, Cornell Paperbacks, 1980

Printed in the United States of America

Library of Congress Cataloging-in-Publication Data
(For library cataloging purposes only)

Foucault, Michel.
  Language, counter-memory, practice.

  Includes bibliographical references and index.
  CONTENTS Language and the birth of "literature." A preface to transgression.
Language to infinity The father's "no." Fantasia of the library. [etc.]
  1 Languages—Philosophy—Collected works. 2. Literature—Philosophy—
Collected works 3. Difference (Philosophy)—Collected works. I. Title
P106.F67   401   77–4561
ISBN-13: 978-0-8014-9204-4 (pbk. : alk paper)

Cornell University Press strives to use environmentally responsible suppliers and materials to the fullest extent possible in the publishing of its books. Such materials include vegetable-based, low-VOC inks and acid-free papers that are also either recycled, totally chlorine-free, or partly composed of nonwood fibers. For further information, visit our website at www.cornellpress.cornell.edu.

Paperback printing   20 19 18 17 16 15 14 13 12

Thought is no longer theoretical. As soon as it functions it offends or reconciles, attracts or repels, breaks, dissociates, unites or reunites; it cannot help but liberate and enslave. Even before prescribing, suggesting a future, saying what must be done, even before exhorting or merely sounding an alarm, thought, at the level of its existence, in its very dawning, is in itself an action—a perilous act.

Foucault

The fact is that every writer *creates* his own precursors. His work modifies our conception of the past, as it will modify the future.

Borges

Preface

This collection arose out of the desire to come to terms with the already considerable accomplishment of Michel Foucault. I had hoped that an examination of his essays on the writers who have influenced him would resolve the difficulties of his books. Not unexpectedly, the essays reveal some continuity of intention and the persistence of certain preoccupations, but hardly the security of an origin. What could have served in the past as solid foundations had become, through Foucault's archaeological retrospective, an open site: the clearing away of a new space for investigation and the opening of new questions. Where I sought a guide to the perplexity of Foucault's language and an understanding of the often lyrical enterprise that sustains his historical perspective, I witnessed instead the emergence of a form of language that questions present experience.

The seven essays that make up the major portion of this book reflect Foucault's attitudes toward language. Taken together, they exhibit the complexity and variety of the experience of language, the insistence of those questions generated by language. Yet, because of the richness of Foucault's response to language, I faced a number of practical difficulties in selecting essays. This was especially true for the first group of essays in which Foucault's sense of language evolves out of the detailed analysis of literary authors and their works. My working principle—to which I have made exceptions—was to omit essays dealing with authors whose works are unavailable in translation: hence the absence of Foucault's essays on Maurice Blanchot and Pierre Klossowski ("La Pensée du dehors" and "La Prose d'Actéon"). Moreover, the attitude informing those two essays is fully represented by the lead essay, "A Preface to Transgression." I can only hope that if my choices appear arbitrary at times, the range and importance of the essays that are included will offset the omissions. Following the essays, a brief concluding section records Foucault's most recent activities at the Collège de France and his involvement in penal reform.

In choosing a title, I adopted the descriptive labels that identify the three separate sections: each is meant to gain force and precision from its contextual relation to the other two. According to Foucault, the historical experience of language underwent a fundamental shift toward the end of the eighteenth century, when language took on a life of its own and became an "objectivity." This new form of language compelled a series of compensations, the two most important being the creation of the modern human sciences and the birth of "literature" as a distinctive language in its own right. In fact, it is within literature that language finds itself embodied for the first time, and the writer now finds himself subjected to its alien logic. The human sciences, on the other hand, arise from the elision of this "literary" experience of language and from the subjection of language for the purpose of determining the nature of human identity, or for the fabrication of human memory. In developing a totally opposed relationship to language, literature has been transformed, since the nineteenth century, into a counter-memory; and the subjects that naturally evolve from this language manifest the history of our otherness: violence, transgression, madness, sexuality, death, and finitude. In the second section of essays, Foucault examines the ways in which this experience of language penetrates into the domain of discursive thought. Our understanding of counter-memory evolves in a practical fashion from Foucault's reconsideration of the nature of the author, from Nietzsche's exploration of the "long hieroglyphic record" of man's moral past, and from Gilles Deleuze's "reversal of Platonism." While counter-memory may superficially appear to be a form of negation, it becomes—with Foucault, Nietzsche, and Deleuze—the affirmation of the particularities that attend any practice, and perhaps the activity that permits new practices to emerge. *Language, Counter-Memory, Practice* is the name of an action that defines itself, that recognizes itself in words—in the multiplication of meaning through the practice of vigilant repetitions.

The task of translating these essays began in a straightforward way, but because of unexpected detours and often belated recognitions, it too experienced its own multiplication—of possibilities, debts, sources, meanings, cross references, friendly assistance. Throughout the preparation of the book, I have profited from Michel Foucault's advice and assistance. Without his generosity, I doubt that it could have been completed. Bernhard Kendler, at Cornell University Press, has my appreciation for his patience and direction throughout the different stages of my understanding of Foucault, as does Lisa Turner for the final editing of the manuscript. Peter Ohlin, Donald Theall, and David Williams, colleagues at McGill University, were always available for discussion and advice. Eugene Vance, at the University of Montreal, helped with an especially troublesome essay. Eugenio Donato, at SUNY at Buffalo, initially proposed this project and he is largely responsible for my original interest in Foucault. My wife, Bebeann, helped with the final draft of the manuscript and in countless other ways.

The McGill Graduate Faculty Fund provided a grant that assisted me in preparing the manuscript, and a Canada Council Fellowship afforded me the leisure to complete the book.

DONALD F. BOUCHARD

Montreal, Quebec

Contents

Introduction   15

PART I
LANGUAGE AND THE BIRTH OF "LITERATURE"

A Preface to Transgression   29
Language to Infinity   53
The Father's "No"   68
Fantasia of the Library   87

PART II
COUNTER-MEMORY: THE PHILOSOPHY OF DIFFERENCE

What Is an Author?   113
Nietzsche, Genealogy, History   139
Theatrum Philosophicum   165

PART III
PRACTICE: KNOWLEDGE AND POWER

History of Systems of Thought   199
Intellectuals and Power   205
Revolutionary Action: "Until Now"   218

Index   235

LANGUAGE, COUNTER-MEMORY, PRACTICE

Selected Essays and Interviews

꙳

Introduction

Michel Foucault's reputation was established in the nineteen sixties, at a time when Structuralism became, in Roland Barthes' words, an essential "activity" of French intellectual thought.[1] The publication of *The Order of Things* was seen, in this context, as one of many signs that structuralism had come of age.[2] In its brief history dating from the turn of the century, it had achieved early successes in linguistics, ethnology, and psychoanalysis, in precisely those sciences of man which evolved as structural disciplines at their most rigorous level; and during the sixties, it appeared revitalized if for no other reason than its having found a fertile soil in France. It extended its range and seemed to promise, through the application of sound methods, an even more general integration of the "human sciences": in the cultural and literary studies of Barthes, in the work of the *Tel Quel* group, in *Critique*, and in the publication of a series of apparently structuralist texts such as *De la grammatologie* and *L'écriture et la différence*. Foucault's task, it seemed, was to

1. Roland Barthes, "The Structuralist Activity," *European Literary Theory and Practice*, ed. Vernon W. Gras (New York: Dell Publishing, 1973), pp. 157–163.
2. See Edward Said, "Abecedarium Culturae: Structuralism, Absence, Writing," *Tri-Quarterly*, 20 (1971), 35–41. This essay in a substantially revised form, which modifies and extends Said's understanding of Foucault, is now an important chapter of *Beginnings: Methods and Intentions* (New York: Basic Books, 1975). See also Said's "An Ethics of Language," *Diacritics*, 4 (1974), 28–37.

subdue structuralism's most resistant foe: thus, those histories
that are not history, the historical trilogy that Foucault, in a
play on words, called archaeology—*Madness and Civilization,
The Birth of the Clinic,* and *The Order of Things.*³ Given this
contextual domain, this revitalized cultural space, it now seems
quite natural that some were led to speak of the consolidation
of the human sciences as an active possibility.

This is no longer the case, however; the goal of integration
has undergone an ironic dispersal and those who were thought
to be the major structuralists are now the center of sectarian
aspirations, at the extreme an authoritative voice binding together
a group of dedicated disciples.⁴ The novelty of this intellectual
experience of the sixties is that it has not had to await its fate at
the hands of subsequent generations—the traditional manner in
which movements decline—for the structuralists were the first to
disown their allegiance. For all its possibilities, structuralism was
stillborn and to know it now is to seize its character as an instantaneous transformation. Nietzsche would, of course, have
said that it appeared in "the hour of the shortest shadow."

From Foucault's point of view, the most significant effect of
this experience is that it separates us from the past. Structuralism
stands as a cleavage within the very tradition that was expected
to culminate in a new and revitalized science, and its present
sign is discontinuity. Foucault's analysis of the human sciences
in *The Order of Things* concerns the short history of Western

3. *Madness and Civilization: A History of Insanity in the Age of
Reason,* trans. Richard Howard (New York: Pantheon Books, 1965);
The Birth of the Clinic: An Archaeology of Medical Perception,
trans. A. M. Sheridan Smith (New York: Pantheon Books, 1973);
The Order of Things: An Archaeology of the Human Sciences (New
York: Pantheon Books, 1970). For Foucault's discussion of his sense
of archaeology, see *The Archaeology of Knowledge,* trans. A. M.
Sheridan Smith (New York: Pantheon Books, 1972), p. 131; and
"Entretien avec J.-J. Brochier," *Magazine Littéraire,* No. 28 (April–
May 1969).
4. Hayden V. White, "Foucault Decoded: Notes from Under-
Ground," *History and Theory,* 12, No. 1 (1971), 53.

man's infatuation with his language, the possibilities of constructing a language capable of fully representing the world; or
stated somewhat differently, it concerns three attempts since the
late Middle Ages at imposing a human reality onto an indifferent
world; and it is this discontinuous series which evolved in our
most recent experience as the dream of the human sciences. On
this basis, Foucault supplies a distinctive reading of the French
intellectual experience of the sixties, where structuralism is now
seen as the last attempt at representing the things of the world
to consciousness—"as if the world were made to be read by
man."[5] In this failure, Foucault locates another form of history:
not the slow progress of consciousness or the steady forging of
new tools which will finally reveal our identity, but a transgressive history; not the order of things, but the surface disorder of
things to the degree that they are spoken. Foucault, in short,
has written the genealogy of the human sciences and, like
Nietzsche, has given us the opportunity to question the "value
of our values."[6]

In his clarification of the human sciences and his archaeological
descent to the various historical layers of labor, life, and language from the Renaissance to our day, Foucault has shown
the something *other* which was said.[7] Setting aside the profound
intentions of an author, the creativity of genius, or the autonomy
of tradition, Foucault points to the work of historical accidents,
abrupt interruptions, and the play of surfaces. It is in this sense
that he speaks of his primary working method as reversal and of
the immediate consequences of this stand as the demarcation of
a field of study which is recognized for its discontinuity, specificity, and exteriority.[8] Further, these working principles disclose

5. *L'Ordre du discours* (Paris: Gallimard, 1971). Foucault's in-
augural lecture at Collège de France has been translated by Rupert
Swyer as *The Discourse on Language* and serves as an appendix to
The Archaeology of Knowledge.
6. *The Genealogy of Morals,* Preface, 3.
7. *The Archaeology of Knowledge,* pp. 131, 138–140.
8. *L'Ordre du discours,* pp. 53–55.

the constant distance which he maintained in relation to the structuralist enterprise, since they require the rejection of deep structure and of any significance that might be seen as inherent either in the world or in consciousness. In this light, *The Order of Things* must be read as the ironic title of a profound disorder in much the same sense as *The Genealogy of Morals* is an "immoral" reflection on the bloodshed that was historically justified by the traditional piety of the good. These transgressive texts were intended as a diagnosis, but diagnosis, by definition, implies recuperation: the particular recuperation of another tradition and of other voices which have remained silent for so long, "naturalized" as they were through the language of reason. This genealogical recovery also serves as the justification of this collection, since Foucault's essays, as well as the variety of the last section of this book, concern that other tradition which evolved side by side with the guarded optimism of the human sciences.

To keep to the rhetoric of the sixties, this tradition to which all of Foucault's essays are devoted can be characterized as a counter-culture, made up for the most part of individuals (to use Nietzsche's celebrated description of himself) who were born posthumously: Sade, Hölderlin, Flaubert, and, of particular importance to Foucault, Nietzsche. As a group held together by no formal ties, these authors experienced what was perhaps the most perplexing reality of the nineteenth century; they came to realize, in their work as in their life, that it is no longer the sleep of reason which breeds monsters and which liberates that Other of ourselves, but the attentiveness of scholarship, an insomniac knowledge, and the gray patience of genealogy. From these authors Foucault has come to discern the madness that attends the most lucid moments of the human sciences, and it is for this reason that they have been given such prominence throughout his histories as those excessive signs of the disorder of our understanding. If we seek a single figure to represent this group, it can only be found in the manner in which they present themselves to us, in the role of the mad philosopher who no longer stands behind his words as their implicit support in the implied profundity of philosophical language.[9] Rather, as Foucault writes in his essay on transgression, language—decidedly the language of Sade, Hölderlin, Flaubert, and Nietzsche—is no longer, in its simplest sense, the expression of a thought and, in the loss of the rhetorical basis of language, expression becomes a simultaneous exposure to madness and death. With the emergence of the mad philosopher, philosophical expression is subjected to the potential paralysis of a self-reflexive language.

This language, like the language that preceded the new science and Cartesian certainty of the seventeenth century, is devoted to enigma, "conceit," and paradox; and it stands in much the same relationship to the representative language of science in the nineteenth century as metaphysical wit did to the *Novum Organum*. Nevertheless, there are substantial differences between the two responses—to the imperatives of a scientific program. For the effect of two centuries of thought has been to destroy the foundation of Renaissance language. Foucault's privileged authors live within the rupture of this tradition, with the fact of a fundamental absence of either an original language which they might recapture in their speech or an original author (authority) who will comfort them in their quest. In short, the position of language as experienced by these authors is determined by the dazzling fact of God's disappearance, a fact which is at once the basis of sadism, of the crippling certainty of Hölderlin's *Empedocles*, of the monstrous apparitions in Flaubert's *Temptation*, or of Nietzsche's frenzied signature of "Antichrist-Dionysus."

It is to this experience that the first four essays of the collection are directed, and if we seek a convenient label to subsume the variety of Sade, Hölderlin, Flaubert, and Nietzsche, it can only be that of "literature":

The word is of recent date, as is also, in our culture, the isolation of a particular language whose peculiar mode of being is "literary." This is because at the beginning of the nineteenth century, at a time when

9. See below "A Preface to Transgression," pp. 41–43.

language was burying itself within its own density as an object and allowing itself to be traversed, through and through, by knowledge, it was also reconstituting itself elsewhere, in an independent form, difficult of access, folded back upon the enigma of its own origin and existing wholly in reference to the pure act of writing. Literature becomes progressively more differentiated from the discourse of ideas, and encloses itself within a radical intransitivity; it becomes detached from all the values which were able to keep it in general circulation during the Classical age (taste, pleasure, naturalness, truth), and creates within its own space everything that will ensure a ludic denial of them (the scandalous, the ugly, the impossible).[10]

In the most obvious sense, "literature" is a reversal, but its effect extends far beyond the merely local rebellion of certain nineteenth-century artists against an older tradition for it implies the recovery of language "in its own being." To this new (old) reality of language the essays of the first section are directed; each of them is organized in such a way as to depict the particular reversal affected by literature.

In these essays, it is less a question of new themes (although in a superficial sense the themes of sexuality, death, madness, and their debilitating knowledge may strike the reader as particularly original, at least in Foucault's handling of the subject) than of the specific discontinuity Foucault unravels from what have traditionally appeared as unchanging facts of human existence. As in *Madness and Civilization*, all of Foucault's essays follow the same procedure: what was thought to be a unitary concept or what was approached as if it were a concept capable of uniting a wide variety of cases taken from different times is shown, as the essay progresses, to reveal not the comparatist fact of identity but the difference of times: not the slow evolution of a human reality which we are only now beginning to appreciate owing to our increasing knowledge, but the disunity of concepts within history.[11] For this reason the authors dealt with in the first essays can be described as living within a state of

10. *The Order of Things*, p. 300.
11. *The Archaeology of Knowledge*, pp. 21–63; for a detailed discussion of this theme, see Angèle Kremer-Marietti, *Michel Foucault* (Paris: Editions Seguers, 1974), pp. 85–96.

permanent rupture and their speech can be said to arise from the void, the impossibility of language, and *l'absence d'oeuvre*.[12] The universal language of representation and mediation is, for them, a past and irretrievable condition; or as Foucault writes in the first essay of the collection, speech no longer finds recourse in the "limitless" possibilities of language. In the disappearance of a limitless discourse, authors such as Bataille encounter their own language as a practical limit and, from this, the impossibility of their own speech. Opposed to the possibilities of a growing science, these first essays inaugurate a reign of impossibilities.

This reflection, largely the product of the early sixties, is the basis of Foucault's more general arguments in his books and in the essays that form the middle section of this collection. They also can be said to follow from the reign of impossibilities. "What Is an Author?" concerns the curious fact of a text without an author; it reverses the ordinary priority of author over text through the argument that the role of the author is the product of a particular discursive function, that the author (like the concepts of sexuality, death, and madness) is not a constant through time, that the "author" has known countless invasions on its domain. This latter statement leads, in turn, to the recognition of Marx and Freud in their modern position as "initiators of discursive practices," yet another authorial function. In a complementary essay of the same period, Foucault argued that Nietzsche, Marx, and Freud are responsible for originating a new form of interpretation in our time: both the infinite task of interpretation and the threatened disappearance of the interpreter (author), since, as Nietzsche suspected, "to perish through absolute knowledge might constitute a part of the basis of being."[13] Furthermore, the new role of interpretation implies that the sign is a mask for a previous interpretation which does not give itself as such; "once a simple and benevolent nature," it now

12. "La folie, l'absence d'oeuvre," *Histoire de la folie à l'age classique,* rev. ed. (Paris: Gallimard, 1972), pp. 575–582.
13. *Beyond Good and Evil,* II, 39.

contains "an ambiguous and rather suspicious form of malice and ill will."[14]

This sense of interpretation and the manner in which it underscores the new role of the author underlies Foucault's analysis in "Nietzsche, Genealogy, History," the second essay of the middle group. Here, too, the principle of reversal is of particular importance in Nietzsche's own reevaluation of his earlier stand on the subject of history or his ideas concerning the nature of the origin, but it is also the discovery of genealogy as the internal principle of history, that is, as the particular interpretation built into any historical sign that says "something altogether different."[15] Where history depicts the continuity of times and the inevitable progress of the will to truth, where it finds a constant support in metaphysical illusion, genealogy points to the inequality of forces as the source of values or the work of *ressentiment* in the production of the objective world. Nietzsche's deconstruction of history reveals the passions at the heart of reason and the "pathos of distance" in which signs originate. In his reversal and reinterpretation of nineteenth-century philosophy, Nietzsche revived the ancient controversy between the Apollonian and the Dionysian. Or as he writes in *The Genealogy:* "Plato versus Homer: that is the complete, the genuine antagonism" (III, 25).

In "Theatrum Philosophicum," the last essay of the second group, this issue is taken up again in a review of Gilles Deleuze's *Différence et répétition* and *Logique du sens.* Its objective is immediately stated: "Which philosophy has not tried to overturn Platonism?"[16] In Deleuze, Foucault perceives the re-creation of an implicit genealogical method: "He carefully reintroduces the barely perceptible omissions, knowing full well that they imply a fundamental negligence." And in this reevaluation, he re-creates the earlier encounter between Socrates and the Sophists, between the belief in permanent and immaterial truths and the philosophy

14. "Nietzsche, Freud, Marx," *Nietzsche* (Cahiers de Royaumont, Philosophie VI, 1967), pp. 190–191.
15. See below "Nietzsche, Genealogy, History," p. 142.
16. See below "Theatrum Philosophicum," p. 166.

of events that occur on the surfaces of bodies—all those elements that Platonism rejected as the simulacrum of false knowledge. On the one hand, a philosophy (the origin of any possible metaphysical system) which stands above history and literature as its truth and, on the other, the thought of events that crossed Mediterranean culture for a millennium, of those events in its literature and history: battles, uncertain victories, poisoned queens, invasions, "the endlessly exemplary Actium, the eternal event." Because of Deleuze's return to the genealogical roots of Platonism, Foucault maintains that it is now possible to reposition philosophy in our time—more than that, "perhaps one day this century will be known as Deleuzian." The philosophy of truth and identity, and the institutions and pedagogy which serve as its handmaidens, will be replaced by the philosophy of difference, a philosophy which arises "through the looking glass" and through a perspectival reversal into new sense. (*Logique du sens* is an extended meditation upon *Through the Looking Glass*.) "Theatrum Philosophicum" is a sustained analysis of Deleuze's two books, but it also records Foucault's agreement with Deleuze's objective: "Let us pervert good sense and allow thought to play outside of the ordered table of resemblances." As a positive imperative, he affirms a thought "as intensive irregularity—disintegration of the subject."

What began as a reign of impossibilities has become, at once, the reevaluation of past traditions and the real possibility of the present. The "literary" insights of the turn of the nineteenth century have led, through Nietzsche, Marx, and Freud, to a reformulation of the thought of our time. As a movement of thought still in the process of emerging, it can nevertheless be recognized for its emphasis on singularity (in which Foucault locates the basis of the "concrete studies" that make up this collection) and in its opposition to any thought which is comparatist by nature: that is, which would establish the implicit similarity of different times and which points, in effect, to the operation of consciousness as the informing principle of the world's meaning. If it achieves its singular status, it is because it remains faithful to its genealogical roots.

The last section arises from a somewhat less formal context: a course description of Foucault's first year at Collège de France, a discussion with Deleuze, and a political interview conducted by *Actuel*. The reader will notice a continuity of purpose from the essays to the last section, but just as important, he should also appreciate the extent to which Foucault's thought presupposes a reorientation of the ordinary way we conceive of the connection between theory and practice. For Foucault, theory is not necessarily a prelude to practice, nor is practice the ground from which theory is elaborated. The two are firmly linked, as demonstrated in *The Order of Discourse*.[17] Theory is the exclusive domain of a particular group and constitutes the active principle through which others, of a different persuasion, are excluded from the "fellowship." This active ingredient of theoretical practice goes largely unnoticed since a discursive group only sanctions the expression of the *same* thing. But Foucault's purpose, constructed out of the disclosure of this unvoiced practice, is to enlarge the existing field of discourse and, in so doing, produce altogether different statements. The obvious political implications of the last section derive from Foucault's recognition that the desire for knowledge is always an "interested" desire[18] within the recent emergence of the interrelated domain of "power-knowledge."[19]

The publication of *Surveiller et punir* in 1975 attests to the continuing vitality of Foucault's position.[20] At first sight, the book seems essentially to mark a return to the preoccupations of *Madness and Civilization* as it describes the transformation of punishment in the eighteenth and nineteenth centuries. Both books are concerned with the birth of that institutional configuration in

17. *L'Ordre du discours*, pp. 11–18.
18. See below "History of Systems of Thought: Summary of a Course given at Collège de France," p. 203.
19. See below "Intellectuals and Power," p. 215.
20. *Surveiller et punir* (Paris: Gallimard, 1975).

which knowledge and power were joined and where the political dimension of knowledge inscribed within nineteenth-century forms of punishment assured that a prisoner would literally learn not to repeat his mistake. In this political history of punishment, theory and practice inhere in the body of a development, both as the changing order of an institution and the institutionalized order imposed upon the body of a convict. But this latter objective is also the basis of Foucault's inauguration of a new perspective. In *Surveiller et punir*, Foucault breaks with his earlier archaeological stance in order to establish a real genealogy, that is, a process that "poses the problem of power and of the body (of bodies), that poses problems beginning from the imposition of power upon bodies."[21]

In Foucault, then, we find this constant interpenetration of theory and practice in terms of both his subject matter and method: it begins with the enigma of language which implies a certain theoretical stance, but always in the awareness of its practical implications—Sade's imprisonment, Hölderlin's madness; it is elaborated in a larger discursive context with the analyses of Nietzsche, Marx, and Freud and secures a number of allies in Bataille, Beckett, Blanchot, Borges, Artaud, Klossowski, and Deleuze, but always, again, with an emphasis on the practice imposed by this position, whether in the *writing* of literature, in the concern voiced by Freud with respect to the concrete demands of the psychoanalytic session, or in the new theater in which philosophy now finds itself; it gains strength to voice this awareness of so many authors without a name; it deploys this genealogical development and, in doing so, secures its own position and evolves as a clarification of purpose in *The Order of Discourse* and *The Archaeology of Knowledge*. Foucault's essays record this concrete history; they assume the patrimony of his genealogical forebears. If this group now speaks to us, if we approach this difficult position with confidence, it is because Foucault's name can be added to our genealogical ancestry.

21. François Ewald, "Anatomie et corps politiques," *Critique*, No. 343 (1975), p. 1229.

PART I

❧

LANGUAGE AND
THE BIRTH OF
"LITERATURE"

⌁

A Preface to Transgression

We like to believe that sexuality has regained, in contemporary experience, its full truth as a process of nature, a truth which has long been lingering in the shadows and hiding under various disguises—until now, that is, when our positive awareness allows us to decipher it so that it may at last emerge in the clear light of language. Yet, never did sexuality enjoy a more immediately natural understanding and never did it know a greater "felicity of expression" than in the Christian world of fallen bodies and of sin. The proof is its whole tradition of mysticism and spirituality which was incapable of dividing the continuous forms of desire, of rapture, of penetration, of ecstasy, of that outpouring which leaves us spent: all of these experiences seemed to lead, without interruption or limit, right to the heart of a divine love of which they were both the outpouring and the source returning upon itself.[1] What characterizes modern sexuality from Sade to Freud is not its having found the language of its logic or of its natural process, but rather, through the violence done by such languages, its having been "denatured"—cast into

This essay first appeared in "Hommage à Georges Bataille," in *Critique*, Nos. 195–196 (1963), pp. 751–770; it is reprinted here by permission of *Critique*. Bataille is especially important to Foucault, who has assisted in the publication of Bataille's *Oeuvres complètes* (Paris: Gallimard, 1973); and has been a frequent contributor and editorial consultant to *Critique*, a journal founded by Bataille. (All notes in this essay are supplied by the editor.)
    1. For Bataille's analysis of Christian mysticism, see *Eroticism*, trans. Mary Dalwood (London: John Calder, 1962), pp. 117–128, 221–264.

an empty zone where it achieves whatever meager form is bestowed upon it by the establishment of its limits. Sexuality points to nothing beyond itself, no prolongation, except in a frenzy which disrupts it.[2] We have not in the least liberated sexuality, though we have, to be exact, carried it to its limits: the limit of consciousness, because it ultimately dictates the only possible reading of our unconscious; the limit of the law, since it seems the sole substance of universal taboos; the limit of language, since it traces that line of foam showing just how far speech may advance upon the sands of silence. Thus, it is not through sexuality that we communicate with the orderly and pleasingly profane world of animals; rather, sexuality is a fissure[3]—not one which surrounds us as the basis of our isolation or individuality, but one which marks the limit within us and designates us as a limit.

Perhaps we could say that it has become the only division possible in a world now emptied of objects, beings, and spaces to desecrate. Not that it proffers any new content for our age-old acts; rather, it permits a profanation without object, a profanation that is empty and turned inward upon itself and whose instruments are brought to bear on nothing but each other. Profanation in a world which no longer recognizes any positive meaning in the sacred—is this not more or less what we may call transgression? In that zone which our culture affords for our gestures and speech, transgression prescribes not only the sole manner of discovering the sacred in its unmediated substance, but also a way of recomposing its empty form, its absence, through which it becomes all the more scintillating. A rigorous language, as it arises from sexuality, will not reveal the secret of man's natural being, nor will it express the serenity of anthropological truths, but rather, it will say that he exists without God; the speech given to sexuality is contemporaneous, both in time and in structure, with that through which we announced to our-

2. See below in this essay, p. 50, for a discussion of the nonrepresentational nature of the language of sexuality.
3. See *The Order of Things*, p. 314.

selves that God is dead. From the moment that Sade delivered its
first words and marked out, in a single discourse, the boundaries
of what suddenly became its kingdom, the language of sexuality
has lifted us into the night where God is absent, and where all
of our actions are addressed to this absence in a profanation
which at once identifies it, dissipates it, exhausts itself in it, and
restores it to the empty purity of its transgression.[4]

There indeed exists a modern form of sexuality: it is that which
offers itself in the superficial discourse of a solid and natural
animality, while obscurely addressing itself to Absence, to this
high region where Bataille placed, in a night not soon to be
ended, the characters of *Eponine:*

In this strained stillness, through the haze of my intoxication, I seemed
to sense that the wind was dying down; a long silence flowed from the
immensity of the sky. The priest knelt down softly. He began to sing
in a despondent key, slowly as if at someone's death: *Miserere mei
Deus, secondum misericordiam magnam tuam.* The way he moaned
this sensuous melody was highly suspicious. He was strangely con-
fessing his anguish before the delights of the flesh. A priest should
conquer us by his denials but his efforts to humble himself only made
him stand out more insistently; the loveliness of his chant, set against
the silent sky, enveloped him in a solitude of morose pleasures. My
reverie was shattered by a felicitous acclamation, an infinite acclamation already on the edge of oblivion. Seeing the priest as she emerged
from the dream which still visibly dazed her senses, Eponine began
to laugh and with such intensity that she was completely shaken;
she turned her body and, leaning against the railing, trembled like a
child. She was laughing with her head in her hands and the priest,
barely stifling a clucking noise, raised his head, his arms uplifted,
only to see a naked behind: the wind had lifted her coat and, made
defenseless by the laughter, she had been unable to close it.[5]

Perhaps the importance of sexuality in our culture, the fact
that since Sade it has persistently been linked to the most profound decisions of our language, derives from nothing else than
this correspondence which connects it to the death of God. Not
that this death should be understood as the end of his historical

4. See Nietzsche, *The Gay Science,* 108.
5. *Oeuvres,* III, 263–264.

reign or as the finally delivered judgment of his nonexistence, but as the now constant space of our experience. By denying us the limit of the Limitless, the death of God leads to an experience in which nothing may again announce the exteriority of being, and consequently to an experience which is *interior* and *sovereign*. But such an experience, for which the death of God is an explosive reality, discloses as its own secret and clarification, its intrinsic finitude, the limitless reign of the Limit, and the emptiness of those excesses in which it spends itself and where it is found wanting. In this sense, the inner experience is throughout an experience of the *impossible* (the impossible being both that which we experience and that which constitutes the experience). The death of God is not merely an "event" that gave shape to contemporary experience as we now know it: it continues tracing indefinitely its great skeletal outline.

Bataille was perfectly conscious of the possibilities of thought that could be released by this death, and of the impossibilities in which it entangled thought. What, indeed, is the meaning of the death of God, if not a strange solidarity between the stunning realization of his nonexistence and the act that kills him? But what does it mean to kill God if he does not exist, to kill God *who has never existed?* Perhaps it means to kill God both because he does not exist and to guarantee he will not exist—certainly a cause for laughter: to kill God to liberate life from this existence that limits it, but also to bring it back to those limits that are annulled by this limitless existence—as a sacrifice; to kill God to return him to this nothingness he is and to manifest his existence at the center of a light that blazes like a presence—for the ecstasy; to kill God in order to lose language in a deafening night and because this wound must make him bleed until there springs forth "an immense alleluia lost in the interminable silence"[6]—and this is communication. The death of God does not restore us to a limited and positivistic world, but to a world exposed by the experience of its limits, made and unmade by that excess which transgresses it.

6. *Eroticism*, p. 271.

Undoubtedly it is excess that discovers that sexuality and the death of God are bound to the same experience; or that again shows us, as if in "the most incongruous book of all," that "God is a whore."[7] And from this perspective the thought that relates to God and the thought that relates to sexuality are linked in a common form, since Sade to be sure, but never in our day with as much insistence and difficulty as in Bataille. And if it were necessary to give, in opposition to sexuality, a precise definition of eroticism, it would have to be the following: an experience of sexuality which links, for its own ends, an overcoming of limits to the death of God. "Eroticism can say what mysticism never could (its strength failed when it tried): God is nothing if not the surpassing of God in every sense of vulgar being, in that of horror or impurity; and ultimately in the sense of nothing."[8]

Thus, at the root of sexuality, of the movement that nothing can ever limit (because it is, from its birth and in its totality, constantly involved with the limit), and at the root of this discourse on God which Western culture has maintained for so long—without any sense of the impropriety of "thoughtlessly adding to language a word which surpasses all words"[9] or any clear sense that it places us at the limits of all possible languages— a singular experience is shaped: that of transgression. Perhaps one day it will seem as decisive for our culture, as much a part of its soil, as the experience of contradiction was at an earlier time for dialectical thought. But in spite of so many scattered signs, the language in which transgression will find its space and the illumination of its being lies almost entirely in the future.

It is surely possible, however, to find in Bataille its calcinated roots, its promising ashes.

Transgression is an action which involves the limit, that narrow zone of a line where it displays the flash of its passage, but

---

7. Ibid., p. 269; and on excess, pp. 168–173.
8. Ibid.
9. Ibid.

perhaps also its entire trajectory, even its origin; it is likely that transgression has its entire space in the line it crosses. The play of limits and transgression seems to be regulated by a simple obstinacy: transgression incessantly crosses and recrosses a line which closes up behind it in a wave of extremely short duration, and thus it is made to return once more right to the horizon of the uncrossable. But this relationship is considerably more complex: these elements are situated in an uncertain context, in certainties which are immediately upset so that thought is ineffectual as soon as it attempts to seize them.

The limit and transgression depend on each other for whatever density of being they possess: a limit could not exist if it were absolutely uncrossable and, reciprocally, transgression would be pointless if it merely crossed a limit composed of illusions and shadows. But can the limit have a life of its own outside of the act that gloriously passes through it and negates it? What becomes of it after this act and what might it have been before? For its part, does transgression not exhaust its nature when it crosses the limit, knowing no other life beyond this point in time? And this point, this curious intersection of beings that have no other life beyond this moment where they totally exchange their beings, is it not also everything which overflows from it on all sides? It serves as a glorification of the nature it excludes: the limit opens violently onto the limitless, finds itself suddenly carried away by the content it had rejected and fulfilled by this alien plenitude which invades it to the core of its being. Transgression carries the limit right to the limit of its being; transgression forces the limit to face the fact of its imminent disappearance, to find itself in what it excludes (perhaps, to be more exact, to recognize itself for the first time), to experience its positive truth in its downward fall?[10] And yet, toward what is transgression un-

10. This can serve as a description of Foucault's technique in *Madness and Civilization* and also as the basis, in *The Order of Things*, of his statement that "modern thought is advancing towards that region where man's Other must become the same as himself" (p. 328).

leashed in its movement of pure violence, if not that which imprisons it, toward the limit and those elements it contains? What bears the brunt of its aggression and to what void does it owe the unrestrained fullness of its being, if not that which it crosses in its violent act and which, as its destiny, it crosses out in the line it effaces?

Transgression, then, is not related to the limit as black to white, the prohibited to the lawful, the outside to the inside, or as the open area of a building to its enclosed spaces. Rather, their relationship takes the form of a spiral which no simple infraction can exhaust. Perhaps it is like a flash of lightning in the night which, from the beginning of time, gives a dense and black intensity to the night it denies, which lights up the night from the inside, from top to bottom, and yet owes to the dark the stark clarity of its manifestation, its harrowing and poised singularity; the flash loses itself in this space it marks with its sovereignty and becomes silent now that it has given a name to obscurity.

Since this existence is both so pure and so complicated, it must be detached from its questionable association to ethics if we want to understand it and to begin thinking from it and in the space it denotes; it must be liberated from the scandalous or subversive, that is, from anything aroused by negative associations.[11] Transgression does not seek to oppose one thing to another, nor does it achieve its purpose through mockery or by upsetting the solidity of foundations; it does not transform the other side of the mirror, beyond an invisible and uncrossable line, into a glittering expanse. Transgression is neither violence in a divided world (in an ethical world) nor a victory over limits (in a dialectical or revolutionary world); and exactly for this reason, its role is to measure the excessive distance that it opens at the heart of the limit and to trace the flashing line that causes the limit to arise. Transgression contains nothing negative, but affirms limited being—affirms the limitlessness into which it leaps as it opens this zone to existence for the first time. But

11. *The Order of Things*, pp. 327–328.

correspondingly, this affirmation contains nothing positive: no content can bind it, since, by definition, no limit can possibly restrict it. Perhaps it is simply an affirmation of division; but only insofar as division is not understood to mean a cutting gesture, or the establishment of a separation or the measuring of a distance, only retaining that in it which may designate the existence of difference.[12]

Perhaps when contemporary philosophy discovered the possibility of nonpositive affirmation, it began a process of reorientation whose only equivalent is the shift instituted by Kant when he distinguished the *nihil negativum* and the *nihil privatium*—a distinction known to have opened the way for the advance of critical thought. This philosophy of nonpositive affirmation is, I believe, what Blanchot was defining through his principle of "contestation."[13] Contestation does not imply a generalized negation, but an affirmation that affirms nothing, a radical break of transitivity. Rather than being a process of thought for denying existences or values, contestation is the act which carries them all to their limits and, from there, to the Limit where an ontological decision achieves its end; to contest is to proceed until one reaches the empty core where being achieves its limit and where the limit defines being. There, at the transgressed limit, the "yes" of contestation reverberates, leaving without echo the hee-haw of Nietzsche's braying ass.[14]

Thus, contestation shapes an experience that Bataille wanted to circumscribe through every detour and repetition of his work,

12. See *The Archaeology of Knowledge*, pp. 130–131; and below, "Theatrum Philosophicum," pp. 181–187. See also Mark Seems, "Liberation of Difference: Toward a Theory of Antiliterature," *NLH*, 5 (1973), 121–134.

13. For a discussion of this term, see Bataille's *L'Expérience intérieure*, in *Oeuvres*, V, 24, 143, 221; and Foucault's study of Blanchot, "La Pensée du dehors," *Critique*, No. 229 (1966): "We must transform reflexive language. It should not point to an inner confirmation, a central certainty where it is impossible to dislodge it, but to the extreme where it is always contested" (p. 528).

14. *Thus Spoke Zarathustra*, Part Four, "The Awakening."

an experience that has the power "to implicate (and to question) everything without possible respite"[15] and to indicate, in the place where it occurs and in its most essential form, "the immediacy of being."[16] Nothing is more alien to this experience than the demonic character who, true to his nature, "denies everything." Transgression opens onto a scintillating and constantly affirmed world, a world without shadow or twilight, without that serpentine "no" that bites into fruits and lodges their contradictions at their core. It is the solar inversion of satanic denial. It was originally linked to the divine, or rather, from this limit marked by the sacred it opens the space where the divine functions. The discovery of such a category by a philosophy which questions itself upon the existence of the limit is evidently one of the countless signs that our path is circular and that, with each day, we are becoming more Greek.[17] Yet, this motion should not be understood as the promised return to a homeland or the recovery of an original soil which produced and which will naturally resolve every opposition. In reintroducing the experience of the divine at the center of thought, philosophy has been well aware since Nietzsche (or it should undoubtedly know by now) that it questions an origin without positivity and an opening indifferent to the patience of the negative.[18] No form of dialectical movement, no analysis of constitutions and of their transcendental ground can serve as support for thinking about such an experience or even as access to this experience. In our day, would not the instantaneous play of the limit and of transgression be the essential test for a thought which centers on the "origin," for that

15. *L'Expérience intérieure*, in *Oeuvres*, V, 16, and also 347.
16. Ibid., p. 60: "A project is not only a mode of existence implied by action, necessary to action; it is rather existence within a paradoxical form of time—the postponement of life to a later of time. . . . The inner experience denounces this intermission; it is being without delay."
17. Cf. *The Order of Things*, p. 342.
18. For an extended discussion of the "origin," see below "Nietzsche, Genealogy, History"; and on contradiction, see *The Archaeology of Knowledge*, pp. 151–155.

form of thought to which Nietzsche dedicated us from the beginning of his works and one which would be, absolutely and in the same motion, a Critique and an Ontology, an understanding that comprehends both finitude and being?

What possibilities generated this thought from which everything, up until our time, has seemingly diverted us, but as if to lead us to the point of its returning? From what impossibilities does it derive its hold on us? Undoubtedly, it can be said that it comes to us through that opening made by Kant in Western philosophy when he articulated, in a manner which is still enigmatic, metaphysical discourse and his reflection on the limits of reason. However, Kant ended by closing this opening when he ultimately relegated all critical investigations to an anthropological question; and undoubtedly, we have subsequently interpreted Kant's action as the granting of an indefinite respite to metaphysics, because dialectics substituted for the questioning of being and limits the play of contradiction and totality.[19] To awaken us from the confused sleep of dialectics and of anthropology, we required the Nietzschean figures of tragedy, of Dionysus, of the death of God, of the philosopher's hammer, of the Superman approaching with the steps of a dove, of the Return. But why, in our day, is discursive language so ineffectual when asked to maintain the presence of these figures and to maintain itself through them? Why is it so nearly silent before them, as if it were forced to yield its voice so that they may continue to find their words, to yield to these extreme forms of language in which Bataille, Blanchot, and Klossowski have made their home, which they have made the summits of thought?[20]

The sovereignty of these experiences must surely be recognized

19. For Bataille's analysis of Hegel, see Oeuvres, I, 177–190. Cf. Karl Popper's "What Is Dialectics," in Conjectures and Refutations (London: Routledge & Kegan Paul, 1975), pp. 312–335.

20. In connection with this passage, see "La Pensée du dehors," p. 524; and also Foucault's essay on Klossowski: "La Prose d'Actéon," Nouvelle Revue Française, No. 135 (1964).

some day, and we must try to assimilate them: not to reveal their truth—a ridiculous pretension with respect to words that form our limits—but to serve as the basis for finally liberating our language. But our task for today is to direct our attention to this nondiscursive language, this language which, for almost two centuries, has stubbornly maintained its disruptive existence in our culture; it will be enough to examine its nature, to explore the source of this language that is neither complete nor fully in control of itself, even though it is sovereign for us and hangs above us, this language that is sometimes immobilized in scenes we customarily call "erotic" and suddenly volatized in a philosophical turbulence, when it seems to lose its very basis.

The parcelling out of philosophical discourse and descriptive scenes in Sade's books is undoubtedly the product of complex architectural laws. It is quite probable that the simple rules of alternation, of continuity, or of thematic contrast are inadequate for defining a linguistic space where descriptions and demonstrations are articulated, where a rational order is linked to an order of pleasures, and where, especially, subjects are located both in the movement of various discourses and in a constellation of bodies. Let us simply say that this space is completely covered by a language that is discursive (even when it involves a narrative), explicit (even when it denotes nothing), and continuous (especially at the moment that the thread passes from one character to another): a language that nevertheless does not have an absolute subject, that never discovers the one who ultimately speaks and incessantly maintains its *hold* on speech from the announcement of the "triumph of philosophy" in Justine's first adventure to Juliette's corpseless disappearance into eternity.[21] Bataille's language, on the other hand, continually breaks down at the center of its space, exposing in his nakedness, in the inertia of ecstasy, a visible and insistent subject who had tried to keep language at arms length, but who now finds himself thrown by it, exhausted, upon the sands of that which he can no longer say.

21. See *Eroticism*, pp. 185–196.

How is it possible to discover, under all these different figures, that form of thought we carelessly call "the philosophy of eroticism," but in which it is important to recognize (a less ambitious goal, but also more central to our understanding) an essential experience for our culture since Kant and Sade—the experience of finitude and being, of the limit and transgression? What natural space can this form of thought possess and what language can it adopt? Undoubtedly, no form of reflection yet developed, no established discourse, can supply its model, its foundation, or even the riches of its vocabulary. Would it be of help, in any case, to argue by analogy that we must find a language for the transgressive which would be what dialectics was, in an earlier time, for contradiction? Our efforts are undoubtedly better spent in trying to speak of this experience and in making it speak from the depths where its language fails, from precisely the place where words escape it, where the subject who speaks has just vanished, where the spectacle topples over before an upturned eye—from where Bataille's death has recently placed his language. We can only hope, now that his death has sent us to the pure transgression of his texts, that they will protect those who seek a language for the thought of the limit, that they will serve as a dwelling place for what may already be a ruined project.

In effect, do we not grasp the possibility of such thought in a language which necessarily strips it of any semblance of thought and leads it to the very impossibility of language? Right to this limit where the existence of language becomes problematic? The reason is that philosophical language is linked beyond all memory (or nearly so) to dialectics; and the dialectic was able to become the form and interior movement of philosophy from the time of Kant only through a redoubling of the millenary space from which philosophy had always spoken. We know full well that reference to Kant has invariably addressed us to the most formative elements of Greek thought: not to recapture a lost experience, but to bring us closer to the possibility of a nondialectical language. This age of commentary in which we live, this historical redoubling from which there seems no escape, does not indicate the velocity of our language in a field now devoid of new philosophical objects, which must be constantly recrossed in a forgetful and always rejuvenated glance. But far more to the point, it indicates the inadequacy, the profound silence, of a philosophical language that has been chased from its natural element, from its original dialectics, by the novelties found in its domain. If philosophy is now experienced as a multiple desert, it is not because it has lost its proper object or the freshness of its experience, but because it has been suddenly divested of that language which is historically "natural" to it. We do not experience the end of philosophy, but a philosophy which regains its speech and finds itself again only in the marginal region which borders its limits: that is, which finds itself either in a purified metalanguage or in the thickness of words enclosed by their darkness, by their blind truth. The prodigious distance that separates these alternatives and that manifests our philosophical dispersion marks, more than a disarray, a profound coherence. This separation and real incompatibility is the actual distance from whose depths philosophy addresses us. It is here that we must focus our attention.

But what language can arise from such an absence? And above all, who is the philosopher who will now begin to speak? "What of us when, having become sobered, we learn what we are? Lost among idlers in the night, where we can only hate the semblance of light coming from their small talk."[22] In a language stripped of dialectics, at the heart of what it says but also at the root of its possibilities, the philosopher is aware that "we are not everything;" he learns as well that even the philosopher does not inhabit the whole of his language like a secret and perfectly fluent

22. This passage is taken from the Preface to *L'Expérience intérieure*, in *Oeuvres*, V, 10.

god. Next to himself, he discovers the existence of another language that also speaks and that he is unable to dominate, one that strives, fails, and falls silent and that he cannot manipulate, the language he spoke at one time and that has now separated itself from him, now gravitating in a space increasingly silent. Most of all, he discovers that he is not always lodged in his language in the same fashion and that in the location from which a subject had traditionally spoken in philosophy—one whose obvious and garrulous identity has remained unexamined from Plato to Nietzsche—a void has been hollowed out in which a multiplicity of speaking subjects are joined and severed, combined and excluded.[23] From the lessons on Homer to the cries of a madman in the streets of Turin,[24] who can be said to have spoken this continuous language, so obstinately the same? Was it the Wanderer or his shadow? The philosopher or the first of the nonphilosophers? Zarathustra, his monkey, or already the Superman? Dionysus, Christ, their reconciled figures, or finally this man right here? The breakdown of philosophical subjectivity and its dispersion in a language that dispossesses it while multiplying it within the space created by its absence is probably one of the fundamental structures of contemporary thought. Again, this is not the end of philosophy, but rather, the end of the philosopher as the sovereign and primary form of philosophical language. And perhaps to all those who strive above all to maintain the unity of the philosopher's grammatical function—at the price of the coherence, even of the existence of philosophical language—we could oppose Bataille's exemplary enterprise: his desperate and relentless attack on the preeminence of the philosophical subject as it confronted him in his own work, in his experience and his language which became his private torment, in the first reflected torture of that which speaks in philosophical language—in the dispersion of stars that encircle

23. Cf. *Eroticism*, pp. 274–276.
24. The reference is, of course, to the beginning of Nietzsche's madness in Turin in the late fall of 1888.

a median night, allowing voiceless words to be born. "Like a flock chased by an infinite shepherd, we, the bleating wave, would flee, endlessly flee from the horror of reducing being to totality."[25]

It is not only the juxtaposition of reflective texts and novels in the language of thought that makes us aware of the shattering of the philosophical subject. The works of Bataille define the situation in far greater detail: in the constant movement to different levels of speech and a systematic disengagement from the "I" who has begun to speak and is already on the verge of deploying his language and installing himself in it: temporal disengagements ("I was writing this," or similarly "in retrospect, if I return to this matter"), shifts in the distance separating a speaker from his words (in a diary, notebooks, poems, stories, meditations, or discourses intended for demonstration), an inner detachment from the assumed sovereignty of thought or writing (through books, anonymous texts, prefaces to his books, footnotes). And it is at the center of the subject's disappearance that philosophical language proceeds as if through a labyrinth, not to recapture him, but to test (and through language itself) the extremity of its loss. That is, it proceeds to the limit and to this opening where its being surges forth, but where it is already completely lost, completely overflowing itself, emptied of itself to the point where it becomes an absolute void—an opening which is communication: "at this point there is no need to elaborate; as my rapture escapes me, I immediately reenter the night of a lost child, anguished in his desire to prolong his ravishment, with no other end than exhaustion, no way of stopping short of fainting. It is such excruciating bliss."[26]

This experience forms the exact reversal of the movement which has sustained the wisdom of the West at least since the time of Socrates, that is, the wisdom to which philosophical language promised the serene unity of a subjectivity which would

25. *L'Expérience intérieure*, in *Oeuvres*, V, 48.
26. Ibid., p. 68.

triumph in it, having been fully constituted by it and through it. But if the language of philosophy is one in which the philosopher's torments are tirelessly repeated and his subjectivity is discarded, then not only is wisdom meaningless as the philosopher's form of composition and reward, but in the expiration of philosophical language a possibility inevitably arises (that upon which it falls—the face of the die; and the place into which it falls—the void into which the die is cast): the possibility of the mad philosopher. In short, the experience of the philosopher who finds, not outside his language (the result of an external accident or imaginary excercise), but at the inner core of its possibilities, the transgression of his philosophical being; and thus, the non-dialectical language of the limit which only arises in transgressing the one who speaks. This play of transgression and being is fundamental for the constitution of philosophical language, which reproduces and undoubtedly produces it.

Essentially the product of fissures, abrupt descents, and broken contours, this misshapen and craglike language describes a circle; it refers to itself and is folded back on a questioning of its limits—as if it were nothing more than a small night lamp that flashes with a strange light, signalling the void from which it arises and to which it addresses everything it illuminates and touches. Perhaps, it is this curious configuration which explains why Bataille attributed such obstinate prestige to the Eye.[27] Throughout his career (from his first novel to *Larmes d'Eros*), the eye was to keep its value as a figure of inner experience: "When at the height of anguish, I gently solicit a strange absurdity, an eye opens at the summit, in the middle of my skull."[28] This is because the eye, a small white globe that encloses its darkness, traces a limiting circle that only sight can cross. And

27. Cf. Roland Barthes, "La Métaphor de l'oeil," *Essais Critique* (Paris: Editions du Seuil, 1964), pp. 238–244.

28. *L'Expérience intérieure*, in *Oeuvres*, V, 92.

the darkness within, the somber core of the eye, pours out into the world like a fountain which sees, that is, which lights up the world; but the eye also gathers up all the light of the world in the iris, that small black spot, where it is transformed into the bright night of an image. The eye is mirror and lamp: it discharges its light into the world around it, while in a movement that is not necessarily contradictory, it precipitates this same light into the transparency of its well. Its globe has the expansive quality of a marvellous seed—like an egg imploding towards the center of night and extreme light, which it is and which it has just ceased to be. It is the figure of being in the act of transgressing its own limit.

The eye, in a philosophy of reflection, derives from its capacity to observe the power of becoming always more interior to itself. Lying behind each eye that sees, there exists a more tenuous one, an eye so discreet and yet so agile that its all-powerful glance can be said to eat away at the flesh of its white globe; behind this particular eye, there exists another and, then, still others, each progressively more subtle until we arrive at an eye whose entire substance is nothing but the transparency of its vision. This inner movement is finally resolved in a nonmaterial center where the intangible forms of truth are created and combined, in this heart of things which is the sovereign subject.[29] Bataille reverses this entire direction: sight, crossing the globular limit of the eye, constitutes the eye in its instantaneous being; sight carries it away in this luminous stream (an outpouring fountain, streaming tears and, shortly, blood), hurls the eye outside of itself, conducts it to the limit where it bursts out in the immediately extinguished flash of its being. Only a small white ball, veined with blood, is left behind, only an exorbitated eye to which all sight is now denied. And in the place from which sight had once passed, only a cranial cavity remains, only this black globe which the uprooted eye has made to close upon its sphere, depriving it of vision, but offering to this absence the spectacle of that in-

29. Cf. *The Birth of the Clinic*, pp. 107–108.

destructible core which now imprisons the dead glance. In the distance created by this violence and uprooting, the eye is seen absolutely, but denied any possibility of sight: the philosophizing subject has been dispossessed and pursued to its limit; and the sovereignty of philosophical language can now be heard from the distance, in the measureless void left behind by the exorbitated subject.

But perhaps the eye accomplishes the most essential aspect of its play when, forced from its ordinary position, it is made to turn upwards in a movement that leads it back to the nocturnal and starred interior of the skull and it is made to show us its usually concealed surface, white and unseeing: it shuts out the day in a movement that manifests its own whiteness (whiteness being undoubtedly the image of clarity, its surface reflection, but for this very reason, it cannot communicate with it, nor communicate it); and the circular night of the iris is made to address the central absence which it illuminates with a flash, revealing it as night. The upturned orb suggests both the most open and the most impenetrable eye: causing its sphere to pivot, while remaining exactly the same and in the same place, it overturns day and night, crosses their limit, but only to find it again on the same line and from the other side; and the white hemisphere that appears momentarily at the place where the pupil once opened is like the being of the eye as it crosses the limit of its vision—when it transgresses this opening to the light of day which defined the transgression of every sight. "If man did not imperiously close his eyes, he would finally be unable to see the things worth seeing."[30]

But what we need to see does not involve any interior secret or the discovery of a more nocturnal world. Torn from its ordinary position and made to turn inwards in its orbit, the eye now only pours its light into a bony cavern. This turning up of

30. An aphorism (from René Char) used at the beginning of *Méthode de méditation*, in *Oeuvres*, V, 192.

its globe may seem a betrayal of "la petite mort,"[31] but more exactly, it simply indicates the death that it experiences in its natural location, in this springing up in place which causes the eye to rotate. Death, for the eye, is not the always elevated line of the horizon, but the limit it ceaselessly transgresses in its natural location, in the hollow where every vision originates, and where this limit is elevated into an absolute limit by an ecstatic movement which allows the eye to spring up from the other side. The upturned eye discovers the bond that links language and death at the moment that it acts out this relationship of the limit and being; and it is perhaps from this that it derives its prestige, in permitting the possibility of a language for this play. Thus, the great scenes that interrupt Bataille's stories invariably concern the spectacle of erotic deaths, where upturned eyes display their white limits and rotate inwards in gigantic and empty orbits. *Bleu du ciel* gives a singularly precise outline of this movement: early in November, when the earth of a German cemetery is alive with the twinkling light of candles and candle stubs, the narrator is lying with Dorothy among the tombstones; making love among the dead, the earth around him appears like the sky on a bright night. And the sky above forms a great hollow orbit, a death mask, in which he recognizes his inevitable end at the moment that pleasure overturns the four globes of flesh, causing the revolution of his sight. "The earth under Dorothy's body was open like a tomb, her belly opened itself to me like a fresh grave. We were struck with stupor, making love on a starred cemetery. Each light marked a skeleton in a grave and formed a wavering sky as perturbed as our mingled bodies. I unfastened Dorothy's dress, I dirtied her clothes and her breast with the fresh earth which was stuck to my fingers. Our bodies trembled like two rows of clattering teeth."[32]

31. *Eroticism*, p. 170: "Pleasure is so close to ruinous waste that we refer to the moment of climax as a 'little death.' "
32. *Oeuvres*, III, 481.

But what might this mean at the heart of a system of thought? What significance has this insistent eye which appears to encompass what Bataille successively designated *the inner experience, the extreme possibility, the comic process,* or simply *meditation?*[33] It is certainly no more metaphoric than Descartes' phrasing of the "clear perception of sight" or this sharp point of the mind which he called *acies mentis.*[34] In point of fact, the upturned eye has no meaning in Bataille's language, can have no meaning since it marks its limit. It indicates the moment when language, arriving at its confines, overleaps itself, explodes and radically challenges itself in laughter, tears, the overturned eyes of ecstasy, the mute and exorbitated horror of sacrifice, and where it remains fixed in this way at the limit of its void, speaking of itself in a second language in which the absence of a sovereign subject outlines its essential emptiness and incessantly fractures the unity of its discourse. The enucleated or upturned eye marks the zone of Bataille's philosophical language, the void into which it pours and loses itself, but in which it never stops talking—somewhat like the interior, diaphanous, and illuminated eye of mystics and spiritualists that marks the point at which the secret language of prayer is embedded and choked by a marvellous communication which silences it. Similarly, but in an inverted manner, the eye in Bataille delineates the zone shared by language and death, the place where language discovers its being in the crossing of its limits: the nondialectical form of philosophical language.

This eye, as the fundamental figure of the place from which Bataille speaks and in which his broken language finds its uninterrupted domain, establishes the connection, prior to any form of discourse, that exists between the death of God (a sun

33. These concepts are opposed to Hegel's philosophy of work and encourage "non-discursive existence, laughter, ecstasy" (*Oeuvres,* V, 96).

34. With respect to this reference to Descartes' "Third Meditation," see *Oeuvres,* V, 123–126.

that rotates and the great eyelid that closes upon the world),
the experience of finitude (springing up in death, twisting the
light which is extinguished as it discovers that the interior is an
empty skull, a central absence), and the turning back of language upon itself at the moment that it fails—a conjunction which
undoubtedly has no other equivalent than the association, well
known in other philosophies, of sight to truth or of contemplation to the absolute. Revealed to this eye, which in its pivoting
conceals itself for all time, is the being of the limit: "I will never
forget the violent and marvellous experience that comes from
the will to open one's eyes, facing what exists, what happens."[35]

Perhaps in the movement which carries it to a total night, the
experience of transgression brings to light this relationship of
finitude to being, this moment of the limit which anthropological
thought, since Kant, could only designate from the distance and
from the exterior through the language of dialectics.

The twentieth century will undoubtedly have discovered the
related categories of exhaustion, excess, the limit, and transgression—the strange and unyielding form of these irrevocable
movements which consume and consummate us. In a form of
thought that considers man as worker and producer—that of
European culture since the end of the eighteenth century—con-
sumption was based entirely on need, and need based itself
exclusively on the model of hunger. When this element was
introduced into an investigation of profit (the appetite of those
who have satisfied their hunger), it inserted man into a dialectic
of production which had a simple anthropological meaning: if
man was alienated from his real nature and immediate needs
through his labor and the production of objects with his hands,
it was nevertheless through its agency that he recaptured his essence and achieved the indefinite gratification of his needs. But
it would undoubtedly be misguided to conceive of hunger as

35. *Eroticism*, p. 266.

that irreducible anthropological factor in the definition of work, production, and profit; and similarly, need has an altogether different status, or it responds at the very least to a code whose laws cannot be confined to a dialectic of production. The discovery of sexuality—the discovery of that firmament of indefinite unreality where Sade placed it from the beginning, the discovery of those systematic forms of prohibition which we now know imprison it, the discovery of the universal nature of transgression in which it is both object and instrument—indicates in a sufficiently forceful way the impossibility of attributing the millenary language of dialectics to the major experience that sexuality forms for us.[36]

Perhaps the emergence of sexuality in our culture is an "event" of multiple values: it is tied to the death of God and to the ontological void which his death fixed at the limit of our thought; it is also tied to the still silent and groping apparition of a form of thought in which the interrogation of the limit replaces the search for totality and the act of transgression replaces the movement of contradictions. Finally, it involves the questioning of language by language in a circularity which the "scandalous" violence of erotic literature, far from ending, displays from its first use of words. Sexuality is only decisive for our culture as spoken, and to the degree it is spoken: not that it is our language which has been eroticized now for nearly two centuries. Rather, since Sade and the death of God, the universe of language has absorbed our sexuality, denatured it, placed it in a void where it establishes its sovereignty and where it incessantly sets up as the Law the limits it transgresses. In this sense, the appearance of sexuality as a fundamental problem marks the transformation of a philosophy of man as worker to a philosophy based on a being who speaks; and insofar as philosophy has traditionally maintained a secondary role to knowledge and work, it must be admitted, not as a sign of crisis but of essential structure, that it is now secondary to language. Not that philosophy is now fated to a role of

36. Ibid., pp. 275-276; cf. *The Order of Things*, pp. 221-226.

repetition or commentary, but that it experiences itself and its limits in language and in this transgression of language which carries it, as it did Bataille, to the faltering of the speaking subject. On the day that sexuality began to speak and to be spoken, language no longer served as a veil for the infinite; and in the thickness it acquired on that day, we now experience finitude and being. In its dark domain, we now encounter the absence of God, our death, limits, and their transgression. But perhaps it is also a source of light for those who have liberated their thought from all forms of dialectical language, as it became for Bataille, on more than one occasion, when he experienced the loss of his language in the dead of night. "What I call night differs from the darkness of thoughts: night possesses the violence of light. Yes, night: the youth and the intoxication of thinking."[37]

Perhaps this "difficulty with words" that now hampers philosophy, a condition fully explored by Bataille, should not be identified with the loss of language that the closure of dialectics seemed to indicate. Rather, it follows from the actual penetration of philosophical experience in language and the discovery that the experience of the limit, and the manner in which philosophy must now understand it, is realized in language and in the movement where it says what cannot be said.

Perhaps this "difficulty with words" also defines the space given over to an experience in which the speaking subject, instead of expressing himself, is exposed, goes to encounter his finitude and, under each of his words, is brought back to the reality of his own death: that zone, in short, which transforms every work into the sort of "tauromachy" suggested by Leiris, who was thinking of his own action as a writer, but undoubtedly also of Bataille.[38] In any event, it is on the white beach of an arena (a gigantic eye) where Bataille experienced the fact—crucial

37. *Le Coupable,* in *Oeuvres,* V, 354; cf. pp. 326–327, 349.
38. See M. Leiris, *Manhood,* trans. Richard Howard (London: Jonathan Cape, 1968): "The bull's keen horn . . . gives the torero's art a human reality, prevents it from becoming no more than the vain grace of a ballerina."

for his thought and characteristic of all his language—that death *communicated with communication* and that the uprooted eye, a white and silent sphere, could become a violent seed in the night of the body, that it could give substance to this absence of which sexuality has never stopped speaking and from which it is made to speak incessantly. When the horn of the bull (a glittering knife that carries the threat of night, and an exact reversal of the image of light that emerges from the night of the eye) penetrates the eyeball of the toreador, who is blinded and killed, Simone performs an act we have come to expect: she swallows a pale and skinless seed and returns to its original night the luminous virility which has just committed murder. The eye is returned back to its night, the globe of the arena turns upwards and rotates; but it is the moment when being necessarily appears in its immediacy and where *the act which crosses the limit touches absence itself:* "Two globes of the same color and consistency were simultaneuously activated in opposite directions. A bull's white testicle had penetrated Simone's black and pink flesh; an eye had emerged from the head of the young man. This coincidence, linked until death to a sort of urinary liquefaction of the sky, gave me Marcelle for a moment. I seemed, in this ungraspable instant, to touch her."[39]

39. *Histoire de l'oeil*, in *Oeuvres*, I, 57.

Language to Infinity

Writing so as not to die, as Blanchot said,[1] or perhaps even speaking so as not to die is a task undoubtedly as old as the word. The most fateful decisions are inevitably suspended during the course of a story. We know that discourse has the power to arrest the flight of an arrow in a recess of time, in the space proper to it. It is quite likely, as Homer has said, that the gods send disasters to men so that they can tell of them, and that in this possibility speech finds its infinite resourcefulness; it is quite likely that the approach of death—its sovereign gesture, its prominence within human memory—hollows out in the present and in existence the void toward which and from which we speak. But the *Odyssey*, which affirms this gift of language in death, tells the inverted story of how Ulysses returns home: it repeats, each time death threatened him and in order to ward off its dangers, exactly how (by what wiles and intrigues) he had succeeded in maintaining this imminence that returns again the moment he begins to speak, in the form of a menacing gesture

This essay appeared originally in *Tel Quel*, No. 15 (1963), pp. 44–53. It is reproduced here by permission of this journal. (All footnotes, with the exception of note 14, are the editor's.)

1. This theme is the focus of Française Collin's recent book on Blanchot, *Maurice Blanchot et la question de l'écriture* (Paris: Gallimard, 1971). For instance: "Death is at the heart of Blanchot's writing and, for Blanchot, at the heart of any writing" (p. 49); see also pp. 150–159 and all of Chapter 4. "Négatif et négativité" (pp. 190–221). Foucault has devoted an essay to Blanchot: "La Pensée du dehors," *Critique*, No. 229 (1966), pp. 523–546.

or a new danger. And when, as a stranger among the Phaeacians, he hears in another's voice the tale, already a thousand years old, of his own history, it is as if he were listening to his own death:[2] he covers his face and cries, in the gesture of a woman to whom the dead body of a hero is brought after a battle. Against this speech which announces his death and which arises from deep within the new *Odyssey* as from an older time, Ulysses must sing the song of his identity and tell of his misfortunes to escape the fate presented to him by a language before language. And he pursues this fictive speech, confirming and dissipating its powers at the same time, into this space, which borders death but is also poised against it, where the story locates its natural domain. The gods send disasters to mortals so that they can tell of them, but men speak of them so that misfortunes will never be fully realized, so that their fulfillment will be averted in the distance of words, at the place where they will be stilled in the negation of their nature. Boundless misfortune, the resounding gift of the gods, marks the point where language begins; but the limit of death opens before language, or rather within language, an infinite space. Before the imminence of death, language rushes forth, but it also starts again, tells of itself, discovers the story of the story and the possibility that this interpenetration might never end.[3] Headed toward death, language turns back upon itself; it encounters something like a mirror; and to stop this death which would stop it, it possesses but a single power: that of giving birth to its own image in a play of mirrors that has no limits. From the depths of the mirror where it sets out to arrive anew at the point where it started (at death), but so as finally to escape death, another language can be heard—the image of actual language, but as a miniscule, interior, and virtual model; it is the song of the bard who had already sung of Ulysses before

2. *The Odyssey*, Book VIII.
3. This is one of the structures of language which defines fantastic literature for Borges; see *Labyrinths* (New York: New Directions, 1967), p. xviii.

the *Odyssey* and before Ulysses himself (since Ulysses hears the song), but who will also sing of him endlessly after his death (since, for the bard, Ulysses is already as good as dead); and Ulysses, who is alive, receives this song as a wife receives her slain husband.

Perhaps there exists in speech an essential affinity between death, endless striving, and the self-representation of language. Perhaps the figure of a mirror to infinity erected against the black wall of death is fundamental for any language from the moment it determines to leave a trace of its passage. Not only since the invention of writing has language pretended to pursue itself to infinity; but neither is it because of its fear of death that it decided one day to assume a body in the form of visible and permanent signs. Rather, somewhat before the invention of writing, a change had to occur to open the space in which writing could flow and establish itself, a change, symbolized for us in its most original form by Homer, that forms one of the most decisive ontological events of language: its mirrored reflection upon death and the construction, from this reflection, of a virtual space where speech discovers the endless resourcefulness of its own image and where, it can represent itself as already existing behind itself, already active beyond itself, to infinity. The possibility of a work of language finds its original fold in this duplication. In this sense, death is undoubtedly the most essential of the accidents of language (its limit and its center): from the day that men began to speak toward death and against it, in order to grasp and imprison it, something was born, a murmuring which repeats, recounts, and redoubles itself endlessly, which has undergone an uncanny process of amplification and thickening, in which our language is today lodged and hidden.[4]

(An hypothesis that is hardly indispensable: alphabetical writing is already, in itself, a form of duplication, since it represents not the signified but the phonetic elements by which it is

4. See above, "Transgression," pp. 47–48.

signified; the ideogram, on the other hand, directly represents the signified, independently from a phonetic system which is another mode of representation. Writing, in Western culture, automatically dictates that we place ourselves in the virtual space of self-representation and reduplication;[5] since writing refers not to a thing but to speech, a work of language only advances more deeply into the intangible density of the mirror, calls forth the double of this already doubled writing, discovers in this way a possible and impossible infinity, ceaselessly strives after speech, maintains it beyond the death which condemns it, and frees a murmuring stream. This presence of repeated speech in writing undeniably gives to what we call a work of language an ontological status unknown in those cultures where the act of writing designates the thing itself, in its proper and visible body, stubbornly inaccessible to time.)

Borges tells the story of a condemned writer to whom God grants, at the precise instant of his execution, another year of life to complete the work he had begun.[6] Suspended between life and death, this work is a drama where everything is necessarily repeated: the end (as yet unfinished) taking up word for word the (already written) beginning, but in such a way as to show the main character, whom we know and who has spoken since the first scenes, to be not himself but an imposter. And during this impending death, during the year which passes while a drop of rain streaks the condemned man's cheek, as the smoke of his last cigarette disappears, Hladik writes—but with words that no one will be able to read, not even God—the great, invisible labyrinth of repetition, of language that divides itself and becomes its own mirror. When the last epithet is found (also the first since the drama began again), the volley of rifle fire, released less than a second before, strikes his silence at the heart.

I wonder if it is not possible to construct or, at the very least,

5. Cf. Jacques Derrida, *De la grammatologie* (Paris: Editions de Minuit, 1967).

6. "The Secret Miracle," in *Labyrinths*, pp. 88–94.

to outline from a distance an ontology of literature beginning from these phenomena of self-representation in language; such figures, which seemingly belong to the level of guile or entertainment, conceal, that is, betray the relationship that language establishes with death—with this limit to which language addresses itself and against which it is poised. It would be necessary to begin with a general analysis of all the forms of reduplication of language to be found in Western literature. These forms, there is no reason to doubt, are of a limited number and it should be possible to list them in their entirety. Their often extreme discretion, the fact that they are occasionally hidden and surface through what seems chance or inadvertance, should not deceive us; or rather we must recognize in them the very power of illusion, the possibility for language (a single stringed instrument) to stand upright as a work. The reduplication of language, even if it is concealed, constitutes its being as a work, and the signs that might appear from this must be read as ontological indications.

These signs are often imperceptible, bordering on the futile. They manage to present themselves as faults—slight imperfections at the surface of a work: we might say that they serve as an involuntary opening to the inexhaustible depths from which they come to us. I am reminded of an episode in *The Nun* where Suzanne's mother explains the history of a letter to Suzanne (its composition, hiding place, attempted theft, and finally its custody by a friend who was able to deliver it)—of precisely this letter in which she explains to her correspondent etc.[7] Proof, to be sure, that Diderot was distracted, but, more importantly, a sign that language is speaking of itself, that the letter is not the letter, but the language which doubles it within the same system of reality (because they speak at the same time, use the same words, and identically share the same body; language is the letter's flesh and blood); and yet, language is also absent, but not as a result of

7. *The Nun*, trans. Leonard Tancock (London: Folio Society, 1922).

the sovereignty we ascribe to a writer; rather, it renders itself absent by crossing the virtual space where language is made into an image of itself and transgresses the limit of death through its reduplication in a mirror. Diderot's "blunder" is not the result of his eagerness to intervene, but is due to the opening of language to its system of self-representation: the letter in *The Nun* is only an analogue of a letter, resembling it in every detail with the exception of being its imperceptibly displaced double (this displacement made visible only because of a tear in the fabric of language). In this lapsus (in the exact sense of the word), we find a figure which is quite similar to—but exactly the inverse of—that found in *The Arabian Nights,* where an episode recounted by Scheherazade tells why she was obliged for a thousand and one nights, etc. In this context, the mirrored structure is explicitly given: at its center, the work holds out a mirror (*"psyche"*: a fictive space, a real soul) where it appears like a miniature of itself and preceding itself, since it tells its own story as one among the many wonders of the past, among so many other nights. And in this privileged night, so much like the others, a space is opened which seems to be that in which it merely forms an insignificant aberration, and it reveals the same stars in the same sky. We could say that there is one night too many, that a thousand would have been enough; we could say, inversely, that a letter is missing in *The Nun* (the one that should tell the history of the letter so that it would no longer be required to tell of its own adventure). It seems clear, in any event, that in the same dimension there exists, from the one, a missing day and, from the other, one night too many: the fatal space in which language speaks of itself.

It is possible that in every work language is superimposed upon itself in a secret verticality, where the double is exactly the same as the thin space between—the narrow, black line which no perception can divulge except in those fortuitous and deliberately confusing moments when the figure of Scheherazade surrounds itself with fog, retreats to the origins of time, and arises infinitely reduced at the center of a brilliant, profound, and virtual disc. A work of language is the body of language crossed by death in order to open this infinite space where doubles reverberate. And the forms of this superimposition, essential to the construction of any work, can undoubtedly only be deciphered in these adjacent, fragile, and slightly monstrous figures where a division into two signals itself; their exact listing and classification, the establishment of the laws which govern their functioning or transformations, could well lead to a formal ontology of literature.

It seems to me that a change was produced in the relationship of language to its indefinite repetition at the end of the eighteenth century—nearly coinciding with the moment in which works of language became what they are now for us, that is literature.[8] This is the time (or very nearly so) when Hölderlin became aware, to the point of blindness, that he could only speak in the space marked by the disappearance of the gods and that language could only depend on its own power to keep death at a distance.[9] Thus, an opening was traced on the horizon toward which our speech has ceaselessly advanced.

For a long time—from the advent of the Homeric gods to the remoteness of the divine in the fragment of *Empedocles*—speaking so as not to die had a meaning now alien to us. To speak of heroes or as a hero, to desire to construct something like a work, to speak so that others speak of it to infinity, to speak for "glory," was indeed to move toward or against this death maintained by language; to speak as a sacred orator warning of death, to threaten men with this end beyond any possible glory, was also to disarm death and promise immortality. In other words, every work was intended to be completed, to still itself in a silence where the infinite Word reestablished its supremacy.[10] Within a work, lan-

8. See *The Order of Things*, pp. 300, 306.
9. See below, "The Father's 'No,'" pp. 31, 86.
10. Cf. above, "Transgression," pp. 32–33, and the chapter entitled "The Place of the King" in *The Order of Things*, pp. 325–359.

guage protected itself against death through this invisible speech, this speech before and after any possible time from which it made itself into its self-enclosed reflection. The mirror to infinity, to which every language gives birth once it erects itself vertically against death, was not displayed without an evasion: the work placed the infinite outside of itself—a real and majestic infinity in which it became a virtual and circular mirror, completed in a beautifully closed form.

Writing, in our day, has moved infinitely closer to its source, to this disquieting sound which announces from the depths of language—once we attend to it—the source against which we seek refuge and toward which we address ourselves. Like Kafka's beast, language now listens from the bottom of its burrow to this inevitable and growing noise.[11] To defend itself it must follow its movements, become its loyal enemy, and allow nothing to stand between them except the contradictory thinness of a transparent and unbreakable partition. We must ceaselessly speak, for as long and as loudly as this indefinite and deafening noise—longer and more loudly so that in mixing our voices with it we might succeed—if not in silencing and mastering it—in modulating its futility into the endless murmuring we call literature. From this moment, a work whose only meaning resides in its being a self-enclosed expression of its glory is no longer possible.

The date of this transformation is roughly indicated by the simultaneous appearance at the end of the eighteenth century of the works of Sade and the tales of terror. It is not their common predilection for cruelty which concerns us here; nor is it the discovery of the link between literature and evil, but something more obscure and paradoxical at first sight: these languages which are constantly drawn out of themselves by the overwhelming, the unspeakable, by thrills, stupefaction, ecstasy, dumbness, pure violence, wordless gestures, and which are calculated with the greatest economy and precision to produce effects (so that

11. "The Burrow" in *The Complete Stories*, ed. Nahum M. Glatzer (New York: Schocken Books, 1971), pp. 325–359.

they make themselves as transparent as possible at this limit of language toward which they hurry, erasing themselves in their writing for the exclusive sovereignty of that which they wish to say and which lies outside of words)—these languages very strangely represent themselves in a slow, meticulous, and infinitely extended ceremony. These simple languages, which name and give one to see, are curiously double.

Undoubtedly, it would still take a long time to understand the language of Sade as it exists for us today: I am not referring to the possible meaning of this prisoner's purpose in endlessly writing books that could not be read (somewhat on the order of Borges' character who boundlessly extends the second of his death through the language of a repetition which is addressed no one); but to the nature of these words in the present and to the existence in which they prolong their life to our day. This language's claim to tell all is not simply that of breaking prohibitions, but of seeking the limits of the possible; the design, in a systematically transformed network, of all the branchings, insertions, and overlappings which are deduced from the human crystal in order to give birth to great, sparkling, mobile, and infinitely extendable configurations; the lengthy passage through the underground of nature to the double lightning flash of the spirit (the first, derisive and dramatic, which blasts Justine, and the second, invisible and absolutely slow, which—in the absence of a charnel house—causes Juliette to disappear into a kind of eternity asymptotic to death)[12]—these elements designate the project of subjecting every possible language, every future language, to the actual sovereignty of this unique Discourse which no one, perhaps, will be able to hear. Through so many bodies consummated in their actual existence, this Saturnian language devours all eventual words, all those words which have yet to be born. And if each scene in its visible aspect is doubled by a demonstration which repeats it and gives it value as a universal element, it is because what is being consumed in this second

12. See Maurice Blanchot, "Sade," in *The Marquis de Sade* (New York: Grove Press, 1965), pp. 37–72.

discourse, and upon another mode, is not all future languages, but every language that has been effectively pronounced: everything, before Sade and in his time, that could have been thought, said, practiced, desired, honored, flouted, or condemned in relation to man, God, the soul, the body, sex, nature, priests, or women finds itself meticulously repeated (from this arise the interminable enumerations on the historical or ethnographic level which do not support Sade's reasoning, but delineate the space where his reason functions)—thus, repeated, combined, dissociated, reversed, and reversed once again, not in view of a dialectical reward, but toward a radical exhaustion. Saint-Fond's wonderful negative cosmology, the punishment which reduces it to silence, Clairville thrown into a volcano, the wordless apotheosis of Juliette are moments which register the calcination of every language. Sade's impossible book stands in the place of every book—of all these books which it makes impossible from the beginning to the end of time. Under this obvious pastiche of all the philosophies and stories of the eighteenth century, beneath this immense double which is not without analogy to *Don Quixote*, the totality of language finds itself sterilized by the single and identical movement of two inseparable figures: the strict, inverted repetition of what has already been said and the simple naming of that which lies at the limit of what we can say.

The precise object of "sadism" is not the other, nor his body, nor his sovereignty: it is everything that might have been said. Furthermore and still somewhat at a distance, it is the mute circle where language deploys itself:[13] to a world of captive readers, Sade, the captive, denies the possibility of reading. This is done so effectively that if we asked to whom the works of Sade were addressed (and address themselves today), there is only one answer: no one. The works of Sade inhabit a strange limit, which they, nevertheless, persist in transgressing—or rather which they transgress because of the fact that they speak: they deny themselves the space of their language—but by confiscating

13. See above, "Transgression," pp. 39, 50.

it in a gesture of repetitive appropriation; and they evade not
only their meaning (a meaning constructed at every turn), but
their possible being; the indecipherable play of ambiguity within
them is nothing but the serious sign of this conflict which forces
them to be the double of every language (which, in their repetition, they set to fire) and of their own absence (which they
constantly manifest). These works could and should, in a strict
sense, continue without interruption, in a murmuring which has
no other ontological status than that of a similar conflict.

In spite of appearances, the simplicity of the novels of terror
achieves much the same ends. They were meant to be read and
were in effect: *Coelina or The Child of Mystery* sold 1.2 million
copies from its publication in 1798 to the Restoration. This
means that every person who knew how to read, and had read
at least one book in his life, had read *Coelina*. It was The
Book—an absolute text whose readership exactly corresponded to
the total domain of possible readers. It was a book without a
future, without a fringe exposed to deaf ears, since almost in-
stantaneously and in a single movement it was able to achieve
its goal. Historical conditions were necessary to foster this new
phenomenon (as far as I know, it has never been repeated). It
was especially necessary that the book possess an exact functional
efficiency and that it coincide, without any screening or alteration, without dividing itself into two, with its objective which
was very simply to be read. But novels of this type were not
meant to be read at the level of their writing or in the specific
dimensions of their language; they wished to be read for the
things they recounted, for this emotion, fear, horror, or pity
which words were charged to communicate, but only through
their pure and simple transparency. Language should acquire the
thinness and absolute seriousness of the story; in making itself
as gray as possible, it was required to transmit an event to its
docile and terrorized reader, to be nothing but the neutral element of pathos. That is to say that it never offered itself in its
own right; that there was no mirror, wedged into the thickness
of its discourse, which might open the unlimited space of its

own image. Rather, it erased itself between the things it said and the person to whom it spoke, accepting with absolute seriousness and according to the principle of strict economy its role as horizontal language, its role of communication.

Yet, these novels of terror are accompanied by an ironic movement which doubles and divides them, and which is not the result of historical repercussions or an effect of tedium. In a phenomenon quite rare in the history of literary language, satire in this instance is exactly contemporaneous with the situation it parodies.[14] It is as if two twin and complementary languages were born at once from the same central source: one existing entirely in its naivety, the other within parody; one existing solely for the reader's eyes, the other moving from the reader's simpleminded fascination to the easy tricks of the writer. But in actuality, these two languages are more than simply contemporaneous; they lie within each other, share the same dwelling, constantly intertwine, forming a single verbal web and, as it were, a forked language that turns against itself from within, destroying itself in its own body, poisonous in its very density.

The naive thinness of the story is perhaps firmly attached to a secret annihilation, to an internal struggle which is the very law of its development, proliferation, and inexhaustible flora. This "too-muchness" functions somewhat like the excess in Sade, but the latter proceeds to the simple act of naming and to the recovery of all language while the former relies on two different figures. The first is an ornamental superabundance, where nothing is shown without the explicit, simultaneous, and contradictory indication of all its attributes at once: it is not a weapon that shows itself under a word and cuts through it, but an inoffensive and complete panoply (let us call this figure, after an often repeated episode, the effect of the "bloody skele-

14. A text like Bellin de Labordière's *Une nuit anglaise* (*An English Night*) was meant to have the same relation to tales of terror as *Don Quixote* had to chivalric romances; but it is their exact contemporary—FOUCAULT.

ton": the presence of death is manifested by the whiteness of the rattling bones and, at the same time, on this smooth skeleton, by the dark and contradictory streaks of blood). The second figure is that of a "wavelike succession to infinity": each episode must follow the preceding one in keeping with the simple but absolutely essential law of increment. It is necessary to approach always closer to the moment when language will reveal its absolute power, by giving birth, through each of its feeble words, to terror; but this is the moment in which language inevitably becomes impotent, when its breath is cut short, when it should still itself without even saying that it stops speaking. Language must push back to infinity this limit it bears with itself, and which indicates, at once, its kingdom and its limit. Thus, in each novel, an exponential series of endless episodes; and then, beyond this, an endless series of novels. The language of terror is dedicated to an endless expense, even though it only seeks to achieve a single effect. It drives itself out of any possible resting place.

Sade and the novels of terror introduce an essential imbalance within works of language: they force them of necessity to be always excessive and deficient. Excessive because language can no longer avoid multiplying itself—as if struck from within by a disease of proliferation; it is always beyond the limit in relation to itself; it only speaks as a supplement starting from a displacement such that the language from which it separates itself and which it recovers is the one that appears useless and excessive, and that deserves to be expunged; but as a result of the same shift, it sheds, in turn, all ontological weight; it is at this point excessive and of so little density that it is fated to extend itself to infinity without ever acquiring the weight that might immobilize it. But does this not also imply that it suffers a deficiency, or rather that it is struck by the wound of the double? That it challenges language to reproduce it in the virtual space (in the real transgression) of the mirror, and to create a new mirror in the first, and again another, and always to infinity? The actual infinity of illusion which forms, in its vanity, the thickness of a work—that absence in the interior from which the work paradoxically erects itself.

∾

Perhaps that which we should rigorously define as "literature" came into existence at precisely the moment, at the end of the eighteenth century, when a language appeared that appropriates and consumes all other languages in its lightning flash, giving birth to an obscure but dominant figure where death, the mirror and the double, and the wavelike succession of words to infinity enact their roles.

In "The Library of Babel,"[15] everything that can possibly be said has already been said: it contains all conceived and imagined languages, and even those which might be conceived or imagined; everything has been pronounced, even those things without meaning, so that the odds of discovering even the smallest formal coherence are extremely slight, as witnessed by the persevering search of those who have never been granted this dispensation. And yet standing above all these words is the rigorous and sovereign language which recovers them, tells their story, and is actually responsible for their birth: a language which is itself poised against death, because it is at the moment of falling into the shaft of an infinite Hexagon that the most lucid (and consequently the last) of the librarians reveals that even the infinity of language multiplies itself to infinity, repeating itself without end in the divided figures of the Same.[16]

This configuration is exactly the reverse of that found in classical Rhetoric. Rhetoric did not enunciate the laws or forms of a language; it established the relationship between two forms of speech: the first, mute, indecipherable, fully present to itself, and absolute; the other, garrulous, had only to voice this first speech according to forms, operations, and conjunctions whose space measured its distance from the first and inaudible text. For finite creatures and for men who would die, Rhetoric ceaselessly re-

15. *Labyrinths*, pp. 51–58.
16. See *The Order of Things*, pp. 328, 334.

peated the speech of the Infinite that would never come to an end. Every figure of rhetoric betrayed a distance in its own space, but in signaling the first speech it lent the provisional density of a revelation to the second: it showed. The space of language today is not defined by Rhetoric, but by the Library: by the ranging to infinity of fragmentary languages, substituting for the double chain of Rhetoric the simple, continuous, and monotonous line of language left to its own devices, a language fated to be infinite because it can no longer support itself upon the speech of infinity. But within itself, it finds the possibility of its own division, of its own repetition, the power to create a vertical system of mirrors, self images, analogies. A language which repeats no other speech, no other Promise, but postpones death indefinitely by ceaselessly opening a space where it is always the analogue of itself.

Libraries are the enchanted domain of two major difficulties. They have been resolved, we know, by mathematicians and tyrants (but perhaps not altogether). There is a dilemma: either all these books are already contained within the Word and they must be burned, or they are contradictory and, again, they must be burned. Rhetoric is a means of momentarily postponing the burning of libraries (but it holds out this promise for the near future, that is, for the end of time). And thus the paradox: if we make a book which tells of all the others, would it or would it not be a book itself? Must it tell its own story as if it were a book among others? And if it does not tell its story, what could it possibly be since its objective was to be a book? Why should it omit its own story, since it is required to speak of every book? Literature begins when this paradox is substituted for the dilemma; when the book is no longer the space where speech adopts a form (forms of style, forms of rhetoric, forms of language), but the site where books are all recaptured and consumed: a site that is nowhere since it gathers all the books of the past in this impossible "volume" whose murmuring will be shelved among so many others—after all the others, before all the others.

The Father's "No"

The *Hölderlin Jahrbuch* has been extremely important; since 1946, it has managed with admirable patience to dislodge Hölderlin's texts from the accumulated weight of a half-century of interpretations obviously inspired by the disciples of Stefan George. Freidrich Gundolf's analysis of *The Archipelago* stands as an excellent example of this latter approach,[1] given its emphasis on the sacred, circular presence of nature, the visible proximity of the gods who metamorphose into lovely bodies, their cyclical emergence within history, and their ultimate return heralded by the fleeting presence of the Child—the eternal and perishable guardian of fire. Caught up in the lyricism of a fulfilling time, all of these themes served to stifle what Hölderlin had announced in the vitality of a rupture. Following the thematics of Stefan George, the young hero of "The Fettered River," torn from the stupefied bank in a theft that exposes him to the boundless violence of the gods, is transformed into a tender, soft, and

This essay first appeared in *Critique*, No. 178 (1962), pp. 195–209. It is a review of Jean Laplanche's *Hölderlin et la question du père* (Paris: P.U.F., 1961), a book that, unfortunately, has yet to be translated into English. Its significance, however, extends far beyond the critique it supplies of Laplanche's book, since it offers an especially clear example of Foucault's understanding of the relationship between literature and madness, the theme which implicitly informs the analyses of *Madness and Civilization*. The essay is reproduced here by permission of *Critique*. (All footnotes have been supplied by the editor.)

1. In *Dichter und Helder* (Heidelberg, 1921).

promising child. The hymn commemorating cyclical process had silenced Hölderlin's words, the hard words that divide time. It was obviously necessary to recapture his language at its source.

A number of studies (some rather early and others more recent) have significantly altered the traditional reference points of the Hölderlin chronology. Lange's simple scheme,[2] which placed all the "obscure" texts (like the *Grund Zum Empedokles*) in a pathological calendar originating with the Bordeaux episode, was considerably modified some time ago; it was necessary to alter its dates so that the enigma of Hölderlin's madness could arise earlier than had been previously supposed (all the drafts of *Empedokles* were completed before Hölderlin left for France). But in an inverse sense, the obstinate erosion of meaning proliferated; Beissner tirelessly investigated the last hymns and the texts of madness; Liegler and Andreas Müller examined the successive configurations that developed from the same poetic core (*The Wanderer* and *Ganymede*).[3] The escarpment of mythic lyricism, the struggle at the limits of language from which it grows, its unique expression and perpetually open space, are no longer the last rays of light escaping from the growing darkness. They arise, on the level of meaning as in time, in that central and profoundly embedded point where poetry self-consciously discovers itself on the basis of its proper language.

Adolf Beck's clarifications with respect to the biography have also led to a whole series of reevaluations.[4] His studies bear in particular on two episodes: the return from Bordeaux (1802), and the eighteen-month period of Hölderlin's tutorship at Waltershauser from the end of 1793 to the middle of 1795 and the departure from Jena. This period is especially important for the light it sheds on relationships which were previously neglected

2. Heinrich Lange, *Hölderlin. Eine Pathographie* (Munich, 1942).
3. Freidrich Beissner, *Hölderlin; Reden und Aufsätze* (Weimar, 1961); L. Liegler, "Der Gefesselte Strom und Ganymed . . . ," *HJ*, 2 (1947), 62–77; A. Müller, "Die beiden Fassungen von Hölderlin's Elegie 'Der Wanderer'," *HJ*, 3 (1948–49), 103–31.
4. Beck has published many articles in the *Hölderlin Jahrbuch*.

or misunderstood. This is the time in which Hölderlin met Charlotte von Kalb, the period of his attachment to the unapproachable Schiller, of Fichte's influence, and of Hölderlin's abrupt return to his mother's house; but, most importantly, it is a time of strange anticipations, repetitions against the grain, of those experiences that dictate a future repetition in a muted form. Charlotte von Kalb obviously prefigures Diotima and Suzette Gontard; equally, Hölderlin's fervent attachment to Schiller, who observes, protects, and declares the Law from his infinite reserve, outlines from without and within the order of events the terrible presence of the "unfaithful" gods from whom Oedipus (because he dared infringe on their territory) will turn away through the gesture in which he blinds himself: "a traitor in the realm of the sacred."[5] Following the broken line of Hölderlin's adventures, was not his flight to Nürtingen—far from Schiller, Fichte's laws, and the already established godhead of Goethe who was unresponsive to Hölderlin's silence—one with the homecoming which will later be balanced against the categorical rejection of the gods? Yet other repetitions are introduced into the already dense situation at Jena—invariably at Jena—but these according to the simultaneity produced by mirrors: on the level of Hölderlin's dependencies, his now established intimacy with Wilhelmina Marianne Kirmes forms the double of the enchanted and inaccessible union in which, like gods, Schiller and Charlotte von Kalb are joined; the teaching position as a young tutor, which he accepts with enthusiasm and in which he showed himself rigorous and demanding to the point of cruelty, presents in relief the inverted image of the accessible and loving master he sought in Schiller but in whom he only found discrete concern, a constant, unbreachable distance, and deaf incomprehension.

5. Hölderlin's *Hyperion*, trans. William R. Trask (New York: Ungar, 1965), reflects his relationship to Schiller; see Michael Hamburger, *Friedrich Hölderlin: Poems and Fragments* (Ann Arbor: University of Michigan Press, 1967), pp. 4–7.

We are indeed fortunate that the *Hölderlin Jahrbuch* has remained alien to the babbling of psychologists—doubly fortunate that they have not seen fit to investigate its finding. The gods were with us; they removed the temptation of submitting Hölderlin and his madness to a stricter form of the traditional discourse which most psychologists (Karl Jaspers first and foremost)[6] perpetually repeat, if only as a product of their vanity: this approach, pursued to the very heart of madness, is based on the assumption that the meaning of a work, its themes and specific domain, can be traced to a series of events whose details are known to us. The question posed by this nonconceptual eclecticism, as it derives from "clinical" psychology, is whether a chain of significations can be formed to link, without discontinuity or rupture, an individual life to a life's work, events to words, and the mute forms of madness to the most essential aspects of a poem.

This possibility, which is particularly compelling from the moment it arises, must be reformulated. The traditional problem, concerned with the point at which a work ends and madness begins, is meaningless when posed in a context of uncertain dates and a maze of overlapping phenomena. Instead of assuming that a work collapses in the shadows of a pathological event once it achieves its secret truth, we are now compelled to follow the movement in which a work gradually discloses the open and extended space of schizophrenic existence. At this extreme limit, we find a revelation that no language could have expressed outside of the abyss that engulfs it and that no fall could have demonstrated if it were not at the same time a conquest of the highest peaks.

This is the direction taken by Jean Laplanche in his book. He begins by adopting the discreet style of a "psychobiography." From this opening, he crosses his chosen field diagonally and discovers, approaching his conclusion, the nature of the problem

6. For example, *Strindberg et Van Gogh* (Paris: Editions de Minuit, 1953).

which had informed his text from the start and from which it derived its prestige and mastery: how can language apply a *single and identical* discourse to poetry and madness? Which syntax functions *at the same time* on the level of declared meaning *and* on that of interpreted signification?

But, perhaps, in order to illuminate the particular powers of systematic inversion that animate Laplanche's text, we should at least pose—if not resolve—this question in its original form: what source gives rise to the possibility of this language and why, for the longest time, has it appeared so "natural" to us, that is, oblivious to its proper enigma?

As a Christianized Europe first began to name its artists, their lives were accorded the anonymity of heroic forms, as if the name could only adopt the colorless role of chronological memory within the cycle of perfect recommencements. Vasari's *Vite* sets as its goal the evocation of an immemorial past, and it proceeds according to an ordained and ritual order. Genius makes itself known from infancy, not in the psychological form of precocity, but by virtue of its intrinsic right to exist prior to its manifestation in specific accomplishments. Genius is not born, but appears without intermediary or duration in the rift of history; similar to the hero, the artist sunders time so as to reestablish its continuity with his own hands. The manifestation of genius, however, is accompanied by a series of vicissitudes: the most frequent episode concerns the passage from obscurity to recognition. Giotto was a shepherd sketching sheep on a rock when Cimabue found him and paid homage to his hidden majesty (as the prince in medieval tales, living among peasants who adopted him, is suddenly recognized by a mysterious mark). An apprenticeship follows this experience, but it is more symbolic than real since it can invariably be reduced to the singular and unequal confrontation between the master and his disciple—the older man thought he was giving everything away to a youngster who already possessed all the older man's powers. The clash that ensues reverses their relationship: the adolescent, set apart by a sign, transforms the master into a disciple, and the master, whose reign was merely a usurpation, suffers a symbolic death by virtue of the inviolable rights possessed by the anonymous shepherd. After Leonardo Da Vinci painted the angel in the *Baptism of Christ*, Verrochio abandoned his career and, similarly, the aging Ghirlandaio withdrew in favor of Michelangelo. The artist has yet to attain his full sovereignty; another secret test awaits him, but this one is voluntary. Like the hero who fights in black armor, his visor covering his face, the artist hides his work and reveals it only upon completion. This was Michelangelo's procedure with the *David* as it was with Uccello's fresco above the gates of San Tommaso. Finally, the artist receives the keys to the kingdom, the keys of creation, as he produces a world which is the double, the fraternal rival, of our own. In the instantaneous ambiguity of illusion, the painter assumes his proper place and his world takes on the reality of God's creation—the monsters painted by Leonardo on the roundel of Ser Piero are as horrifying as any found in nature. Through this return to nature, in the perfection of identity, a promise is fulfilled: man is freed, as the legend recounts that Filippo Lippi was actually liberated on the day he painted a supernatural resemblance of his master.

The Renaissance attitude towards the artist's individuality combined an epic perception which derived from the already archaic form of the medieval hero to the Greek themes of the initiatory cycle, and at their boundary appeared the ambiguous and overdetermined structures of enigma and discovery, of the intoxicating force of illusion, of a return to nature that is basically *other*, and of an access to new lands revealed as *the same*. The artist was able to emerge from the age-old anonymity of epic singers only by usurping the power and meaning of the same epic values. The heroic dimension passed from the hero to the one whose task it had been to represent him at a time when Western culture itself became a world of representations. A work no longer achieved its sole meaning as a monument, a memory engraved in stone which was capable of surviving the ravages of time; it now belonged to the legend it had once commemorated; it became in itself an "exploit" because it conferred eternal truth upon men and upon their ephemeral actions and also because it referred to the marvellous realm of the artist's life as its "natural" birthplace. The painter was the first subjective inflection of the hero. His self-portrait was no longer merely a marginal sign of the artist's furtive participation in the scene being represented, as a figure hidden at the corner of the canvas; it became, at the very center of the work, the totality of the painting where the beginning joins the ending in the absolute heroic transformation of the creator of heroes.

In this fashion, the artist was able to develop a relationship to himself within his work that the hero could never experience. The heroic mode became the primary manifestation—at the boundary of the things that appear and their representations, for oneself and for others—of the singleness of approach to the truth of the work. This was nevertheless a unity both precarious and ineradicable, and one which disclosed, on the basis of its essential constitution, the possibility of a series of dissociations. Among the most characteristic were: the "distraught hero" whose life or passions were continually in conflict with his work (this is Filippo Lippi who suffered from the torments of the flesh and, unable to possess the lady whose portrait he was painting, was forced to "stifle his passion"); the "alienated hero," losing himself in his work and also losing sight of the work itself (plainly Uccello who "could have been the most elegant and original painter since Giotto had he devoted to human and animal figures the time lost in his studies of perspective"); the "misunderstood hero," scorned by his peers (like Tintoretto who was banished by Titian and spurned throughout his life by the Venetian painters). These avatars, which gradually traced the dividing line between the artist's gestures and the exploits of heroes, give rise to the possibility of an ambiguous stance (maintained through a composite vocabulary) which embraces *both* the work and what the work is not. The space cleared in the decline of heroism, a space whose nature was suspected by the sixteenth century and one which our present culture cheerfully investigates in keeping with its basic forgetfulness, is ultimately occupied by the "madness" of the artist; it is a madness which identifies the artist to his work and which makes him different— from all those who remain silent—and it also situates the artist outside his work when it blinds him to the things he sees and makes him deaf to even his own words.[7] This state can no longer be understood as a Platonic ecstacy which protects him from il-lusion and exposes him to the radiant light of the gods, but as a subterranean relationship in which the work and what it is not construct their exteriority within the language of dark interiority. Given these conditions, it became possible to envisage the strange enterprise we call the "psychology of the artist," a procedure always haunted by madness even when the pathological dimen-sion is absent. It is inscribed on the beautiful heroic unity that gave names to the first painters, but as an index of their separa-tion, negation, and oblivion. The psychological dimension in our culture is the negation of epic perceptions. If we hope to under-stand the artists of the past, we can only do so by following this indirect and illusive path; only from the distance can we ap-preciate the older, mute alliance between the work and the "other" of the work whose tales of heroic rituals and immutable cycles were commemorated by Vasari.

❧

In keeping with our discursive understanding, we have tried to construct the language of this unity. But is it to be found? Has it been completely lost, or so fully incorporated in other dis-

7. Cf. Foucault, "La Folie, l'absence d'oeuvre," in the appendix to *Histoire de la folie à l'âge classique* (Paris: Gallimard, 1972). This text is a revised edition of *Folie et déraison* (Paris: Plon, 1961) and it is unavailable in English translation.

courses, in the monotony generated by discourses on "the relationship of art and madness," that it is nearly impossible to unravel? This unity is at the root of all the discourses that attack this problem, regardless of their tiresome repetitions (this applies to Jean Vinchon, Jean Fretet,[8] and many others): at the same time, it is constantly occulted, deliberately neglected, and scattered through these repetitions. It lies dormant within discourse and forced by it into stubborn oblivion. This unity can be given new life only through a rigorous and uncompromising discourse such as that developed by Laplanche, perhaps the only scion to be saved from a most inglorious dynasty. Laplanche's remarkable readings stress the multiplicity of problems and the renewed insistence raised by schizophrenia for psychoanalytic studies.

What is the precise point of saying that the place left empty by the Father is the *same* place which Schiller occupied in Hölderlin's imagination and which he subsequently abandoned, the *same* place made radiant by the unfaithful presence of the gods of the last texts prior to leaving the Hesperians under the royal law of institutions? More simply, what is this *same* figure outlined in the *Thalia-Fragment* before the actual meeting with Suzette Gontard which is then faithfully reproduced in the definitive version of Diotima? What is this "sameness" to which analysis is so readily drawn? Why is this "identity" so insistently introduced in every analysis; why does it seem to guarantee the easy passage between the work and what lies outside the work?

Of the numerous paths which lead to this "identity," Laplanche's analysis undoubtedly follows the most rewarding; he moves from one approach to another without ever losing his way, without wavering in his pursuit of this "sameness" which obsesses him with its inaccessible presence and its tangible absence. These paths form, as it were, three methodologically distinct but convergent approaches: the assimilation of themes in the imagination; an outline of the fundamental forms of experience; and finally, the dividing line along which Hölderlin's work and his

8. See, for example, Fretet, *L'Alienation poétique* (Paris, 1946).

life confront each other, where they are balanced, and where they become both possible and impossible in relation to each other.

1. The mythical forces, whose strange and penetrating vitality is experienced both inside and outside of Hölderlin's poetry, are those in which divine violence penetrates mortals to create a proximity in which they are illuminated and reduced to ashes; these are the forces of the Jungling, of a river at its source, contained and sealed by ice, winter, and sleep, which shatters its bonds in a single movement in order to find its profound and inviting homeland at a distance from itself, outside itself. Are they not *also* Hölderlin's forces as a child, forces confiscated out of avarice and withheld by his mother, forces of which he requested the "full and unimpaired use" as a paternal inheritance he could dispose of as he liked? And are they not *also* the forces Hölderlin opposed to those of his student in a struggle exacerbated by the recognition that they were mirror images? Hölderlin's experience is totally informed by the enchanted threat of forces that arose from within himself and from others, that were at once distant and nearby, divine and subterranean, invincibly precarious; and it is in the imaginary distances between these forces that their mutual identity and the play of their reciprocal symbolization are constructed and contested. Is the oceanic relationship of the gods to the unleashing of their new vitality the symbolic and luminous form of Hölderlin's relationship to the image of the mother, or its profound and nocturnal basis? These relationships are constantly being transposed.

2. This play of forces, without beginning or ending, is deployed within its natural space, one organised by the categories of proximity and distance. These categories regulated the immediately contradictory oscillations of Hölderlin's relationship to Schiller. In Jena, Hölderlin was exalted by his "closeness to truly great minds," but, in this profusion, he experienced states of despondency—a desertlike emptiness that distanced him from others and that created an internal and unbreachable gap within

himself. As a result of his own barrenness, he develops an abundant capacity to absorb the fertility of the others, of this other who, in maintaining his reserve, refuses to give of himself and deliberately keeps his distance. The departure from Jena becomes comprehensible in this context: Hölderlin left Schiller's vicinity because in being close to him, he felt that he held no value for his hero, that he remained infinitely distant from him. In trying to gain Schiller's affection, he was trying "to come closer to the Good"—that which is by definition out of reach. He left Jena to realise more closely this "attachment," which was degraded each time he tried to establish a link and made more distant by his approach. It is likely that this experience for Hölderlin was connected to that of the fundamental space in which the gods appear only to turn away. This space, in terms of its basic configuration, is that of the great circle of nature, the "divine All-in-One," but this perfect circle without fault or mediation only emerges in the now extinguished light of Greece; the gods are *here* only by being *there*. The genius of Hellas, "the first-born of lofty nature," must be located in the great return commemorated in *Hyperion* in its evocation of endless circles.[9] But in the *Thalia-Fragment,* which forms the first draft of the novel, Greece is no longer the land of glorious presence. When Hyperion leaves Melitus (visited for only a short time) to undertake a pilgrimage to the dead heroes on the banks of the Scamander, it too disappears and he is condemned to return to a native land where the gods are present and absent, visible and hidden, in the manifest reserve of the "supreme secret which gives life or death." Greece is the shore where gods and men intermingled, the land of mutual presence and reciprocal absence. From this derives its prestige as the land of light; it defines a distant luminosity (exactly opposed to Novalis' nocturnal proximity) which is traversed, like the flight of an eagle or a lightning flash, by the violence of an abduction that is both murderous and

9. See *Hyperion,* p. 23, for the "All-in-one"; and for the genius of Hellas, pp. 88–96.

loving. The light of Greece is an absolute distance which is destroyed and exalted by the imminent force of the assembled gods. Against the certain flight of all things near, against the threatening arrow of the most distant forces, what remedies are possible? Who will protect us? "Is space always to be this absolute and radiant departure, this abject volte-face?"[10]

3. The definitive wording of *Hyperion* is already a search for a fixed point; it seeks to anchor itself in the improbable unity of two beings as closely aligned as a figure and its reflection in a mirror. In this context, the limit assumes the shape of a perfect circle which includes all things, a state as circular and pure as Hölderlin's friendship with Suzette Gontard. The flight of the Immortals is arrested in the light that reflects two similar faces; the divine is trapped by a mirror and the dark threat of absence and emptiness is finally averted. Language now advances against this space whose opening summoned it and it attempts to obliterate this space by covering it with the lovely images of immediate presence. The work of art becomes a measure of what it is not in the double sense that it traverses the entire surface of this other world, and then limits it through its opposition. The work of art installs itself as joy of expression and averted madness. This is the period spent in Frankfurt as a tutor for the Gontard family, a time of shared tenderness and mutual understanding. But Diotima dies; Alabanda leaves in search of a lost homeland, Adamas in search of an impossible Arcadia. The dual relationship of the mirror has been shattered by a supreme and empty form, a form whose emptiness devours the fragile reflection, a form which is nothing in itself but which designates the *Limit* in all its aspects:[11] the inevitability of death, the unwritten law of human brotherhood, the inaccessible existence of mortals who were touched by the divine. In the pleasure of an artistic work, at the border of its language, a limit emerges whose function is to silence its language and bring the work to completion,

10. The *Thalia-Fragment* has not been translated into English.
11. Cf. above "Transgression," p. 52.

and this is the limit which formed the work against all that was not itself. The shape of this balance is that of a precipitous cliff where the work finds completion only through those elements it subtracts from itself.

The work is ruined by that which initially constituted it. The limit which balanced the dual existence with Suzette Gontard and the enchanted mirror of *Hyperion* emerges as a limit *in* life (Hölderlin's "unexplained" departure from Frankfurt) and as a limit *of* the work (Diotima's death and Hyperion's return to Germany "like homeless, blind Oedipus to the gates of Athens").[12]

We can now see that this enigma of "similarity," in which the work merges with all that it is not, assumes an exactly reversed form from that proposed by Vasari. It becomes situated at the very center of the work, in those forces which necessitate its destruction from the start. A work and its *other* can speak in the *same* language of the *same* things only on the basis of the limit of the work. Any discourse which seeks to attain the fundamental dimensions of a work must, at least implicitly, examine its relationship to madness: not only because of the resemblance between the themes of lyricism and psychosis, or because the structures of experience are occasionally isomorphous, but more fundamentally, because the work poses and transgresses the limit which creates, threatens, and completes it.[13]

The gravitational pull which the greatest platitudes seem to exert on the majority of psychologists has led them for several years to the study of "frustrations"; the involuntary fasting of rats serves as their infinitely fertile epistemological model. It is because of his double grounding in philosophy and psychoanalysis that Laplanche was able to direct his study of Hölderlin to a profound questioning of the negative, in which the Hegelian

12. *Hyperion*, p. 163.
13. See above "Transgression," p. 31.

repetition of Jean Hippolyte and the Freudian *repetition* of Jacques Lacan find themselves *repeated:* repeated, that is, by the very necessity of their destined itinerary and its conclusion.[14]

German prefixes and suffixes (*ab-, ent-, -los, un-, ver-*) are particularly well-suited (far better than in French) for expressing the specific forms of absence, hiatus, and distancing which are indispensible for the psychotic construction of the father's image and the weapons of virility. It is not a question of seeing in the father's "no" either a real or a mythical orphanage; nor does it imply the eradication of the father's characteristic traits. Hölderlin's case is apparently straightforward, but becomes extremely ambiguous if examined in depth. He lost his father at the age of two and his mother was remarried to Gock, the burghermaster, two years later. After five years, Gock died, leaving the child with delightful memories which were apparently unaffected even by the existence of a half-brother. On the level of Hölderlin's memories, the father's place was occupied by a distinct and positive figure, and only through death did it become partially obscured. Undoubtedly, the idea of absence will not be found in this interplay of presences and disappearances, but in a context where speech is linked to a particular speaker. Lacan, following Melanie Klein, has shown that the father, as the third party in the Oedipal situation, is not only the hated and feared rival, but the agent whose presence limits the unlimited relationship between the mother and child and whose first, anguished image emerges in the child's fantasy of being devoured.[15] Consequently, the father separates, that is, he is the one who protects when, in his proclamation of the Law, he links space, rules, and language within a single and major experience. At a stroke, he creates the distance along which will develop the scansion of presences and

14. See page 142 in Laplanche's text. Aside from his famous translation of Hegel's *Phenomenology of the Spirit,* Hyppolite has also written on Freud's "verneinung" (denial). See J. Lacan's response to this text in *Ecrits* (Paris: Editions du Seuil, 1966), pp. 369–400.

15. See *Ecrits,* pp. 114–20.

absences, the speech whose initial form is based on constraints, and finally, the relationship of the signifier to the signified which not only gives rise to the structure of language but also to the exclusion and symbolic transformation of repressed material. Thus it is not in alimentary or functional terms of deficiency that we understand the gap which now stands in the Father's place. To be able to say that he is missing, that he is hated, excluded, or introjected, that his image has undergone symbolic transmutations, presumes that he is not "foreclosed" (as Lacan would say) from the start and that his place is not marked by a gaping and absolute emptiness. The Father's absence, manifested in the headlong rush of psychosis, is not registered by perceptions or images, but relates to the order of the signifier. The "no" through which this gap is created does not imply the absence of a real individual who bears the father's name; rather, it implies that the father has never assumed the role of nomination and that the position of the signifier, through which the father names himself and, according to the Law, through which he is able to name, has remained vacant. It is toward this "no" that the unwavering line of psychosis is infallibly directed; as it is precipitated inside the abyss of its meaning, it evokes the devastating absence of the father through the forms of delirium and phantasms and through the catastrophe of the signifier.

Beginning with the period in Homburg, Hölderlin devoted himself to this absence, which is constantly elaborated in the successive drafts of *Empedocles*. At first, the tragic hymn sets out in search of the profound center of things, this central "Limitless" where all determinations are invalidated. To disappear into the fire of the volcano is to rejoin, at the point of its inaccessible and open hearth, the All-in-One—simultaneously, the subterranean vitality of stones and the bright flame of truth. But as Hölderlin reworked this theme, he modified the basic spatial relationships: the burning proximity of the divine (high and profound forge of chaos where all that has ended can begin anew) is transformed into the distant radiance of the unfaithful gods; Empedocles destroyed the lovely alliance by assuming the status of a mediator with divine powers. Thinking he had realised the "Limitless," he had, in fact, merely succeeded in driving the Limits further away in a transgression that stood for his entire existence and that was the product of his "handiwork." And in this definitive distancing of limits, the gods had already prepared their inevitable ruse; the blinding of Oedipus will now proceed with open eyes on this deserted shore where Language and the Law, in fraternal confrontation, await the garrulous parricide. In a sense, it is in language that the transgression occurs; Empedocles profanes the gods in proclaiming their existence and releases the arrow of absence to pierce the heart of things. Empedocles' language is opposed by the endurance of its fraternal enemy whose role is to create, in the interval of the limit, the pedestal of the Law which links understanding to necessity and determinations to their destiny. This positivity is not the result of an oversight; in the last draft, it reappears as an aspect of Manes' character in his absolute power of interrogation ("tell me who you are, tell me who I am")[16] and as the unshakable will to remain silent—he is a perpetual question without answer. And yet, having arisen from the depths of time and space, he acts as an unwavering witness to Empedocles' nature as the Chosen One, the definitive absence, the one through whom "all' things return again and future events have already achieved completion."[17]

Two extreme possibilities—the most allied and most opposed—are presented in this final and closely fought struggle. First, we are given the categorical withdrawal of the gods to their essential ether, the Hesperians in possession of the terrestial world, the effacement of the figure of Empedocles as the last Greek, the arrival from the depths of the Orient of the couple Christ-Dionysus, come to witness the tempestuous exit of the dying gods. Simultaneously, a zone is created where language loses

16. Hamburger, p. 355.
17. Ibid., p. 353.

itself in its extreme limits, in a region where language is most unlike itself and where signs no longer communicate, that region of an endurance without anguish: "Ein Zeichen sind wir, deutungslos. . . ."[18] The expansion of this final lyric expression is also the disclosure of madness. The trajectory that outlines the flight of the gods and that traces, in reverse, the return of men to their native land is indistinguishable from this cruel line that leads Hölderlin to the absence of the father, that directs his language to the fundamental gap in the signifier, that transforms his lyricism into delirium, his work into the absence of a work.

࿆

At the beginning of his book, Laplanche wonders if Blanchot, in his discussion of Hölderlin, had not rejected the possibility of extending the unity of meaning to the end of his analysis, if he had not prematurely appealed to the opaque event of madness or unquestioningly invoked the mute nature of schizophrenia.[19] In the name of a "unitary" theory, he criticizes Blanchot for introducing a breaking point, the absolute catastrophe of language, when it was possible to extend—perhaps indefinitely—the communication between the meaning of schizophrenic speech and the nature of the illness. But Laplanche is able to maintain this continuity only by excluding from language the enigmatic identity which permits it to speak at the same time of madness *and* of an artistic work. Laplanche has remarkable analytic powers: his meticulous and rapid discourse competently covers the domain circumscribed by poetic forms and psychological structures; this is undoubtedly the result of extremely rapid oscillations which permit the imperceptible transfer of analogical figures in both directions. But a discourse (similar to Blanchot's) which places itself within the grammatical posture of the "and"

18. "We are a meaningless sign. . . ."
19. M. Blanchot, "La folie par excellence," *Critique*, No. 45 (1951), pp. 99–118.

that joins madness *and* an artistic work, a discourse which investigates this indivisible unity and which concerns itself with the space created when these two are joined, is necessarily an interrogation of the Limit, understood as the line where madness becomes, in a precise sense, a perpetual rupture.

These two forms of discourse obviously manifest a profound incompatibility, even though an identical content is put to profitable use in either discourse; the simultaneous unravelling of poetic and psychological structures will never succeed in reducing the distance which separates them. Nevertheless, they are extremely close, perhaps as close as a possibility is to its realisation. This is because the *continuity of meaning* between a work and madness can only be realised if it is based on the *enigma of similarity,* an enigma which gives rise to the *absolute nature of the breaking point.* The dissolution of a work in madness, this void to which poetic speech is drawn as to its self-destruction, is what authorizes the text of a language common to both. These are not abstractions, but historical relationships which our culture must eventually examine if it hopes to find itself.

"Depression at Jena" is the term that Laplanche applies to Hölderlin's first pathological episode. We could allow our imagination to play on this depressing event: in keeping with the post-Kantian crisis, the disputes of atheism, Schlegel's and Novalis' speculations, the clamor of the Revolution which was understood as the promise of another world, Jena was certainly the arena where the fundamental concerns of Western culture abruptly emerged. The presence and absence of the gods, their withdrawal and imminence, defined the central and empty space where European culture discovered, as linked to a single investigation, the finitude of man and the return of time. The nineteenth century is commonly thought to have discovered the historical dimension, but it did so only on the basis of the *circle,* the spatial form which negates time, the form in which the gods manifest their arrival and flight and men manifest their return to their native ground of finitude. More than simply an event that affected our emotions, that gave rise to the fear of nothingness, the death of God profoundly influenced our language; the silence that replaced its source remains unpenetrable to all but the most trivial works.[20] Language thus assumes a sovereign position; it comes to us from elsewhere, from a place of which no one can speak, but it can be transformed into a work only if, in ascending to its proper discourse, it directs its speech towards this absence.[21] In this context, every work is an attempt to exhaust language; eschatology has become of late a structure of literary experience, and literary experience, by right of birth, is now of paramount importance. This was René Char's meaning: "When the dam built by men finally collapsed, torn along the giant fault line created by the abandonment of the gods, words in the distance, immemorial words, tried to resist the exorbitant thrust. In this moment was decided the dynasty of their meaning. I rushed to the very end of this diluvian night."[22]

In relation to this event, Hölderlin occupies a unique and exemplary position: he created and manifested the link between a work and the absence of a work, between the flight of the gods and the loss of language. He stripped the artist of his magnificent powers—his timelessness, his capacity to guarantee the truth and to raise every event to the heights of language. Hölderlin's language replaced the epic unity commemorated by Vasari with a division that is responsible for every work in our culture, a division that links it to its own absence and to its dissolution in the madness that had accompanied it from the beginning. He made it possible for us, positivist quadrupeds, to climb the slopes of an inaccessible summit which he had reached and which marked the *limit*, and, in doing so, to ruminate upon the psychopathology of poets.

20. See above "Transgression," pp. 32, 38, 50.
21. See above "Language to Infinity," p. 59.
22. "Seuil," in *Fureur et mystère* (Paris: Gallimard, 1962).

Fantasia of the Library

I

The Temptation of Saint Anthony was rewritten on three different occasions: in 1849, before *Madame Bovary*; in 1856, before
Salammbô; and in 1872, while Flaubert was writing *Bouvard et
Pécuchet*. He published extracts in 1856 and 1857. Saint Anthony
accompanied Flaubert for twenty-five or thirty years—for as
long, in fact, as the hero of the *Sentimental Education*. In these
twin and inverted figures, the old anchorite of Egypt, still
besieged by desires, responds through the centuries to a young
man of eighteen, seized by the apparition of Madame Arnoux
while travelling from Paris to Le Havre. Moreover, the evening
when Frédéric—at this stage, a pale reflection of himself—turns
away, as if in fear of incest, from the woman he continues to
love recalls the shadowed night when the defeated hermit learns
to love even the substance of life in its material form. "Temptation" among the ruins of an ancient world populated by spirits
is transformed into an "education" in the prose of the modern
world.

The Temptation was conceived early in Flaubert's career—
perhaps after attending a puppetshow—and it influenced all of
his works. Standing alongside his other books, standing behind

This essay originally appeared in *Cahiers Renaud-Barrault*, No. 59
(1967), pp. 7–30; it was also used as an introduction to the German
translation of *The Temptation* (*Insel Verlag*) by Anneliese Botond.
It is reprinted here by permission of Editions Gallimard. (Unless
otherwise indicated, all footnotes are supplied by the editor.)

them, *The Temptation* forms a prodigious reserve: for scenes of violence, phantasmagoria, chimeras, nightmares, slapstick. Flaubert successively transformed its inexhaustible treasure into the grey provincial reveries of *Madame Bovary*, into the sculpted sets of *Salammbô*, and into the eccentricities of everyday life in *Bouvard*. *The Temptation* seems to represent Flaubert's unattainable dream: what he wanted his works to be—supple, silky, delicate, spontaneous, harmoniously revealed through rapturous phrases—but also what they must never be if they were to see the light of day. *The Temptation* existed before any of Flaubert's books (its first sketches are found in *Mémoires d'un Fou*, *Rêve d'Enfer*, *Danse des Morts*, and, particularly, in *Smahr*),[1] and it was repeated—as ritual, purification, exercise, a "temptation" to overcome—prior to writing each of his major texts. Suspended over his entire work, it is unlike all his other books by virtue of its prolixity, its wasted abundance, and its overcrowded bestiary; and set back from his other books, it offers, as a photographic negative of their writing, the somber and murmuring prose which they were compelled to repress, to silence gradually, in order to achieve their own clarity. The entire work of Flaubert is dedicated to the conflagration of this primary discourse: its precious ashes, its black, unmalleable coal.

II

We readily understand *The Temptation* as setting out the formal progression of unconfined reveries. It would be to literature what Bosch, Breughel, or the Goya of the *Caprichos* were at one time to painting. The first readers (or audience) were bored by the monotonous progression of grotesques: Maxime Du Camp remarked: "We listened to the words of the Sphinx, the chimera, the Queen of Sheba, of Simon the Magician. . . . A bewildered, somewhat simpleminded, and, I would even say, foolish Saint Anthony sees, parading before him, different forms

1. Flaubert's juvenilia.

of temptation."[2] His friends were enraptured by the "richness of his vision" (François Coppée), "by its forest of shadows and light" (Victor Hugo), and by its "hallucinatory mechanism" (Hippolyte Taine). But stranger still, Flaubert himself invoked madness, phantasms; he felt he was shaping the fallen trees of a dream: "I spend my afternoons with the shutters closed, the curtains drawn, and without a shirt, dressed as a carpenter. I bawl out! I sweat! It's superb! There are moments when this is decidedly more than delirium." As the book nears completion: "I plunged furiously into *Saint Anthony* and began to enjoy the most terrifying exaltation. I have never been more excited."

In time, we have learned as readers that *The Temptation* is not the product of dreams and rapture, but a monument to meticulous erudition.[3] To construct the scene of the heresiarchs, Flaubert drew extensively from Tillemont's *Mémoires Ecclésiastiques*, Matter's four-volume *Histoire du gnosticisme*, the *Histoire de Manichée* by Beausobre, Reuss's *Théologie chrétienne*, and also from Saint Augustine and, of course, from Migne's *Patrologia* (Athanasius, Jerome, and Epiphanus). The gods that populate the text were found in Burnouf, Anquetil-Duperron, in the works of Herbelot and Hottinger, in the volumes of the *Univers Pittoresque*, in the work of the Englishman, Layard, and, particularly, in Creutzer's translation, the *Religions de l'Antiquité*. For information on monsters, he read Xivrey's *Traditions tératologiques*, the *Physiologus* re-edited by Cahier and Martin, Boaïstrau's *Histoires prodigieuses*, and the Duret text devoted to plants and their "admirable history." Spinoza inspired his metaphysical meditation on extended substance.[4] Yet, this list is far from exhaustive. Certain evocations in the text seem totally dominated by the machinery of dreams: for example, the

2. *Souvenirs littéraires* (Paris, 1882); Du Camp, who was among the first to listen to Flaubert's recitation, discouraged his efforts.

3. As a result of the remarkable studies by Jean Seznec—FOUCAULT.

4. Jacques Suffel, in a Preface to *The Temptation* (Paris: Garnier-Flammarion, 1967), p. 19, discusses Flaubert's preoccupation with *The Ethics*.

magisterial Diana of Ephesus, with lions at her shoulders and with fruits, flowers, and stars interlaced on her bosom, with a cluster of breasts, and griffins and bulls springing from the sheath which tightly encircles her waist. Nevertheless, this "fantasy" is an exact reproduction of plate 88 in Creutzer's last volume: if we observe the details of the print, we can appreciate Flaubert's diligence. Cybele and Atys (with his languid pose, his elbow against a tree, his flute, and his costume cut into diamond shapes) are both found in plate 58 of the same work; similarly, the portrait of Ormuz is in Layard and the medals of Oraios, Sabaoth, Adonaius, and Knouphus are easily located in Matter. It is indeed surprising that such erudite precision strikes us as a phantasmagoria. More exactly, we are astounded that Flaubert experienced the scholar's patience, the very patience necessary to knowledge, as the liveliness of a frenzied imagination.

Possibly, Flaubert was responding to an experience of the fantastic which was singularly modern and relatively unknown before his time, to the discovery of a new imaginative space in the nineteenth century. This domain of phantasms is no longer the night, the sleep of reason, or the uncertain void that stands before desire, but, on the contrary, wakefulness, untiring attention, zealous erudition, and constant vigilance. Henceforth, the visionary experience arises from the black and white surface of printed signs, from the closed and dusty volume that opens with a flight of forgotten words; fantasies are carefully deployed in the hushed library, with its columns of books, with its titles aligned on shelves to form a tight enclosure, but within confines that also liberate impossible worlds. The imaginary now resides between the book and the lamp. The fantastic is no longer a property of the heart, nor is it found among the incongruities of nature; it evolves from the accuracy of knowledge, and its treasures lie dormant in documents. Dreams are no longer summoned with closed eyes, but in reading; and a true image is now a product of learning:[5] it derives from words spoken in the past,

5. See above, "Language to Infinity," p. 61, for a similar under-

exact recensions, the amassing of minute facts, monuments reduced to infinitesimal fragments, and the reproductions of reproductions. In the modern experience, these elements contain
the power of the impossible.[6] Only the assiduous clamor created
by repetition can transmit to us what only happened once. The
imaginary is not formed in opposition to reality as its denial or
compensation; it grows among signs, from book to book, in the
interstice of repetitions and commentaries; it is born and takes
shape in the interval between books.[7] It is a phenomenon of the
library.

Both Michelet (in the *Sorcière*) and Edgar Quinet (in *Ahas-
vérus*) had explored these forms of erudite dreams, but *The
Temptation* is not a scholarly project which evolved into an
artistically coherent whole. As a work, its form relies on its location within the domain of knowledge: it exists by virtue of its
essential relationship to books. This explains why it may represent more than a mere episode in the history of Western imagination; it opens a literary space wholly dependent on the network
formed by the books of the past: as such, it serves to circulate
the fiction of books. Yet, we should not confuse it with apparently similar works, with *Don Quixote* or the works of Sade,
because the link between the former and the tales of knight-
errantry or between the *Nouvelle Justine* and the virtuous novels
of the eighteenth century is maintained through irony; and,
more importantly, they remain books regardless of their intention. *The Temptation*, however, is linked in a completely serious
manner to the vast world of print and develops within the recognizable institution of writing. It may appear as merely another
new book to be shelved alongside all the others, but it serves, in
actuality, to extend the space that existing books can occupy. It

standing of Sade's relationship to the learning of the eighteenth
century.

6. Cf. below "Nietzsche, Genealogy, History," p. 139, and "Theatrum Philosophicum," p. 169.

7. On the role of "repetition" in Foucault's thought, see below,
"Theatrum Philosophicum," pp. 186–196.

recovers other books; it hides and displays them and, in a single movement, it causes them to glitter and disappear. It is not simply the book that Flaubert dreamed of writing for so long; it dreams other books, all other books that dream and that men dream of writing—books that are taken up, fragmented, displaced, combined, lost, set at an unapproachable distance by dreams, but also brought closer to the imaginary and sparkling realization of desires. In writing *The Temptation,* Flaubert produced the first literary work whose exclusive domain is that of books: following Flaubert, Mallarmé is able to write *Le Livre* and modern literature is activated—Joyce, Roussel, Kafka, Pound, Borges. The library is on fire.

Déjeuner sur l'Herbe and *Olympia* were perhaps the first "museum" paintings, the first paintings in European art that were less a response to the achievement of Giorgione, Raphael, and Velasquez than an acknowledgement (supported by this singular and obvious connection, using this legible reference to cloak its operation) of the new and substantial relationship of painting to itself, as a manifestation of the existence of museums and the particular reality and interdependence that paintings acquire in museums. In the same period, *The Temptation* was the first literary work to comprehend the greenish institutions where books are accumulated and where the slow and incontrovertible vegetation of learning quietly proliferates. Flaubert is to the library what Manet is to the museum. They both produced works in a self-conscious relationship to earlier paintings or texts—or rather to the aspect in painting or writing that remains indefinitely open. They erect their art within the archive.[8] They were not meant to foster the lamentations—the lost youth, the absence of vigor, and the decline of inventiveness—through which we reproach our Alexandrian age, but to unearth an essential aspect of our culture: every painting now belongs within the squared and massive surface of painting and all literary

8. See Foucault's discussion of the "archive" in *The Archaeology of Knowledge,* pp. 126–31.

works are confined to the indefinite murmur of writing. Flaubert and Manet are responsible for the existence of books and paintings within works of art.

III

The presence of the book in *The Temptation*, its manifestation and concealment, is indicated in a strange way: it immediately contradicts itself as a book. From the start, it challenges the priority of its printed signs and takes the form of a theatrical presentation: the transcription of a text that is not meant to be read, but recited and staged. At one time, Flaubert had wanted to transform *The Temptation* into a kind of epic drama, a *Faust* capable of swallowing the entire world of religion and gods. He soon gave up this idea but retained within the text the indications marking a possible performance: division into dialogues and scenes, descriptions of the place of action, the scenic elements, and their modifications, blocking directions for the "actors" on stage—all given according to a traditional typographical arrangement (smaller type and wider margins for stage directions, a character's name in large letters above the speeches, etc.). In a significant redoubling, the first indicated setting—the site of all future modifications—has the form of a natural theater: the hermit's retreat has been placed "at the top of a mountain, on a platform rounded in the form of a half-moon and enclosed by large boulders." The text describes a stage which, itself, represents a "platform" shaped by natural forces and upon which new scenes will in turn impose their sets. But these indications do not suggest a future performance (they are largely incompatible with an actual presentation); they simply designate the specific mode of existence of the text. Print can only be an unobtrusive aid to the visible; an insidious spectator takes the reader's place and the act of reading is dissolved in the triumph of another form of sight. The book disappears in the theatricality it creates.

But it will immediately reappear within a scenic space. No

sooner have the first signs of temptation emerged from the
gathering shadows, no sooner have the disquieting faces appeared
in the night, than Saint Anthony lights a torch to protect himself
and opens a "large book." This posture is consistent with the
iconographic tradition: in the painting of Breughel the Younger,
the painting that so impressed Flaubert when he visited the
Balbi collection in Genoa and that he felt had incited him to
write *The Temptation,* the hermit, in the lower right-hand corner
of the canvas, is kneeling before an immense volume, his head
slightly bowed, and his eyes intent on the written lines. Surrounding him on all sides are naked women with open arms,
lean Gluttony stretching her giraffe's neck, barrel-like men
creating an uproar, and nameless beasts devouring each other; at
his back is a procession of the grotesques that populate the
earth—bishops, kings, and tyrants. But this assembly is lost on
the saint, absorbed in his reading. He sees nothing of this great
uproar, unless perhaps through the corner of his eye, unless he
seeks to protect himself by invoking the enigmatic powers of a
magician's book. It may be, on the contrary, that the mumbling
recitation of written signs has summoned these poor shapeless
figures that no language has ever named, that no book can contain, but that anonymously invade the weighty pages of the
volume. It may be, as well, that these creatures of unnatural
issue escaped from the book, from the gaps between the open
pages or the blank spaces between the letters. More fertile than
the sleep of reason, the book perhaps engenders an infinite brood
of monsters. Far from being a protection, it has liberated an
obscure swarm of creatures and created a suspicious shadow
through the mingling of images and knowledge. In any case,
setting aside this discussion of the open folio in Breughel's painting, Flaubert's Saint Anthony seizes his book to ward off the
evil that begins to obsess him and reads at random five passages
from Scriptures. But, by a trick of the text, there immediately
arises in the evening air the odors of gluttony, the scent of blood
and anger, and the incense of pride, aromas worth more than

their weight in gold, and the sinful perfumes of Oriental queens. The book—but not any book—is the site of temptation. Where the first passage read by the hermit is taken from the "Acts of the Apostles," the last four, significantly, come from the Old Testament[9]—from God's Scripture, from the supreme book.

The two earlier versions of *The Temptation* excluded the reading of sacred texts. Attacked by the canonical figures of evil, the hermit immediately seeks refuge in his chapel; goaded by Satan, the Seven Deadly Sins are set against the Virtues and, led by Pride, they make repeated assaults upon the protected enclosure. This imagery of the portal and the staging of a mystery are absent from the published text. In the final version, evil is not given as the property of characters, but incorporated in words. A book intended to lead to the gates of salvation also opens the gates of Hell. The full range of fantastic apparitions that eventually unfold before the hermit—orgiastic palaces, drunken emperors, unfettered heretics, misshapen forms of the gods in agony, abnormalities of nature—arise from the opening of a book, as they issued from the libraries that Flaubert consulted. It is appropriate, in this context, that Flaubert dropped from the definitive text the symmetrical and opposing figures of logic and the swine, the original leaders of the pageant, and replaced them with Hilarion, the learned disciple who was initiated into the reading of sacred texts by Saint Anthony.

The presence of the book in *The Temptation*, initially in a theatrical spectacle and then more prominently as the source of a pageant, which, in turn, obscures its presence, gives rise to an extremely complicated space. We are apparently presented with a frieze of colorful characters set against cardboard scenery; on the edge of the stage, in a corner, sits the hooded figure of the motionless saint. The scene is reminiscent of a puppet theater. As a child, Flaubert saw *The Mystery of Saint Anthony* performed numerous times by Père Legrain in his puppet theater;

9. Acts of the Apostles 10:11; Daniel 2:46; 2 Kings 20:13; 1 Kings 10:1—FOUCAULT.

he later brought Georges Sand to a performance. The first two versions of *The Temptation* retained elements from this source (most obviously, the pig, but also the personification of sin, the assault on the chapel, and the image of the virgin). In the definitive text, only the linear succession of the visions remains to suggest an effect of "marionnettes": sins, temptations, divinities, and monsters are paraded before the laconic hermit—each emerging, in turn, from the hellish confines of the box where they were kept. But this is only a surface effect constructed upon a staging in depth (it is the flat surface that is deceptive in this context).

As support for these successive visions, to set them up in their illusory reality, Flaubert arranged a limited number of stages, which extends, in a perpendicular direction, the pure and straightforward reading of the printed phrases. The first inter-section is the reader (1)—the actual reader of the text—and the book lies before him (1a); from the first lines (*it is in the Thebaid . . . the hermit's cabin appears in the background*) the text in-vites the reader to become a spectator (2) of a stage whose scenery is carefully described (2a); at center stage, the spectator sees the hermit (3) seated with his legs crossed: he will shortly rise and turn to his book (3a) from which disturbing visions will gradually escape—banquets, palaces, a voluptuous queen, and finally Hilarion, the insidious disciple (4). Hilarion leads the saint into a space filled with visions (4a); this opens a world of heresies and gods, and a world where improbable creatures proliferate (5). Moreover, the heretics are also capable of speech and recount their shameless rites; the gods recall their past glories and the cults that were devoted to them; and the monsters proclaim their proper bestiality. Derived from the power of their words or from their mere presence, a new dimension is realized, a vision that lies within that produced by the satanic disciple (5a), a vision that contains the abject cult of the Ophites, the miracles of Apollonius, the temptations of Buddha, and the ancient and blissful reign of Isis (6). Beginning as actual readers,

we successively encounter five distinct levels, five different orders
of language (indicated by *a*): that of the book, a theater, a
sacred text, visions, and visions that evolve into further visions.
There are also five series of characters, of figures, of landscapes,
and of forms: the invisible spectator, Saint Anthony in his retreat, Hilarion, the heretics, the gods and the monsters, and
finally, the shadows propagated by their speeches or through
their memories.

This organization, which develops through successive en-
closures, is modified by two others. (In actuality, it finds its confirmation and completion in two others.) The first is that of a
retrospective encasement. Where the figures on the sixth level
(visions of visions) should be the palest and least accessible to
direct perception, they appear forcefully on the scene, as dense,
colorful, and insistent as the figures that precede them or as
Saint Anthony himself. It is as if the clouded memories and
secret desires, which produced these visions from the first, have
the power of acting without mediation in the scenic space, upon
the landscape where the hermit pursues his imaginary dialogue
with his disciple, or upon the stage that the fictitious spectator is
meant to behold during the acting out of this semi-mystery. Thus,
the fictions of the last level fold back upon themselves, envelop
the figures from which they arose, quickly surpass the disciple
and the anchorite, and finish by inscribing themselves within the
supposed materiality of the theater. Through this retrospective
envelopment, the most ephemeral fictions are presented in the
most direct language, through the stage directions, indicated by
the author, whose task is an external definition of the characters.

This arrangement allows the reader (1) to see Saint Anthony
(3) over the shoulder of the implied spectator (2) who is an
accomplice to the dramatic presentation: the effect is to identify
the reader with the spectator. Consequently, the spectator sees
Anthony on the stage, but he also sees over his shoulder the
apparitions presented to the hermit, apparitions that are as substantial as the saint: Alexandria, Constantinople, the Queen of

Sheba, Hilarion. The spectator's glance dissolves into the hallucinated gaze of the hermit. Anthony then leans over Hilarion's shoulder, and sees with his eyes the figures evoked by the evil disciple; and Hilarion, through the arguments of the heretics, perceives the face of the gods and the snarling monsters, contemplates the images that haunt them. Developed from one figure to another, a wreath is constructed which links the characters in a series of knots independent of their proper intermediaries, so that their identities are gradually merged and their different perceptions blended into a single dazzling sight.

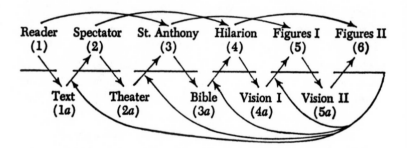

An immense distance lies between the reader and the ultimate visions that entrance the imaginary figures: orders of language placed according to degrees of subordination, relay-characters gazing over each other's shoulders and withdrawing to the depths of this "text-representation," and a population abounding in illusions. But two movements counter this distance: the first, affecting the different orders of language, renders the invisible elements visible through a direct style, and the second, which concerns the figures, gradually adopts the vision and the light fixed upon the characters and brings forward the most distant images until they emerge from the sides of the scene. It is this double movement that makes a vision actually tempting: the most indirect and encased elements of the vision are given with a brilliance compatible with the foreground; and the visionary, attracted by the sights placed before him, rushes into this simultaneously empty and overpopulated space, identifies himself with this figure of shadow and light, and begins to see, in turn, with unearthly eyes. The profundity of these boxed apparitions and the linear and naive succession of figures are not in any way contradictory. Rather, they form the perpendicular intersections that constitute the paradoxical shape and the singular domain of *The Temptation*. The frieze of marionnettes and the stark, colored surface of these figures who jostle one another in the shadows offstage are not the effects of childhood memories or the residue of vivid impressions: they are the composite result of a vision that develops on successive and gradually more distant levels and a temptation that attracts the visionary to the place he has seen and that suddenly envelops him in his own visions.

IV

The Temptation is like a discourse whose function is to maintain not a single and exclusive meaning (by excising all the others), but the simultaneous existence of multiple meanings. The visible sequence of scenes is extremely simple: first, the memories of the aging monk, the hallucinations and sins summarized by the figure of an ancient queen who arrives from the Orient (Chapters I and II); then, the disciple who initiates the rapid multiplication of heresies through his debate on Scripture (III and IV); followed by the emergence of the gods who successively appear on the stage (V); with the depopulation of the earth, Anthony is free to return to it guided by his disciple who has become both Satan and Knowledge, free to gauge its expanse and to observe the tangled and infinite growth of monsters (VI, VII). This visible sequence is supported by a number of underlying series.

1. Temptation is conceived in the hermit's heart; it hesitantly evokes his companions during his retreat and the passing caravans; from this, it extends into vaster regions: overpopulated Alexandria, the Christian Orient torn by theological conflicts, all

those Mediterranean civilizations ruled by gods who emerged from Asia, and, finally, the limitless expanses of the universe— the distant stars at night, the imperceptible cell from which life awakens. But this ultimate scintillation only serves to return the hermit to the material principle of his first desires. Having reached the limits of the world, the grand and tempting itinerary returns to its point of departure. In the first two versions of the text, the Devil explained to Anthony "that sins were in his heart and sorrows in his mind." These explanations are now inessential: pushed to the limits of the universe, the arching waves of the temptation return to those things that are nearest. In the minute organism where the primordial desires of life are awakened, Anthony recaptures his ancient heart, his badly controlled appetites, but no longer experiences their charged fantasies. Before his eyes, there lies the material truth. Under this red light, the larva of desire is gently formed. The center of temptation has not shifted: or rather, it has been displaced very slightly from the top to the bottom—passing from the heart to the sinews, from a dream to the cell, from a bright image to matter. Those things that haunted the imagination of the hermit from inside can now become the object of enraptured contemplation; and where he had pushed them aside in fear, they now attract and invite him to a dormant identification: "to descend to the very depths of matter, to become matter."[10] It is only in appearance that the temptation wrenches the hermit from his solitude and populates his field of vision with men, gods, and monsters, for, along its curved expanse, it gives rise to a number of distinct movements: a progressive expansion to the confines of the universe; a loop bringing desire back to its truth; a shift that causes a violent phantasm to subside in the soft repose of matter; a passage from the inside to the outside—from heartfelt nostalgia to the vivid spectacle of life; the transformation of fear into the desire for identification.

10. *The Temptation of Saint Anthony*, trans. Lafcadio Hearn (New York: Grosset & Dunlap, [No date]), p. 164.

2. Sitting on the doorstep of his cabin, the hermit is obsessed by the memories of an old man: formerly, isolation was less painful, work less tedious, and the river not as distant as now. He had enjoyed his youth—the young girls who congregated at the fountain—and also his retreat, and the opportunity for companionship, particularly with his favorite disciple. His memories flood back upon him in this slight wavering of the present at the hour of dusk. It is a total inversion of time: first, the images of twilight in the city humming with activity before dark—the port, shouting in the streets, the tambourines in the taverns; followed by Alexandria in the period of the massacres, Constantinople during the Council; this suddenly gives way to the heretics whose affronts originated with the founding of Christianity; behind them are the gods who once had a following of faithful and whose temples range from India to the Mediterranean; and finally, the appearance of figures as old as time itself—the distant stars, brute matter, lust and death, the recumbent Sphinx, chimeras, all those things that, in a single movement, create life and its illusions. Further, beyond this primordial cell from which life evolved, Anthony desires an impossible return to the passive state prior to life: the whole of his existence is consequently laid to rest where it recovers its innocence and awakens once again to the sounds of animals, the bubbling fountain, and the glittering stars. The highest temptation is the longing to be another, to be all others; it is to renew identifications and to achieve the principle of time in a return that completes the circle. The vision of Engadine approaches.[11]

An ambiguous figure—simultaneously a form of duration and eternity, acting as conclusion and a fresh start—introduces each stage of this return through time. The heresies are introduced by Hilarion—as small as a child and withered like an old man, as young as awakening knowledge and as old as well-pondered learning. Apollonius introduces the gods: he is familiar with

11. Engadine is an Alpine valley in Switzerland where Nietzsche spent his summers between 1879 and 1888.

their unending metamorphoses, their creation and death, but he is also able to regain instantly "the Eternal, the Absolute, and Being."[12] Lust and Death lead the dance of life because they undoubtedly control the end and new beginnings, the disintegration of forms and the origin of all things. The larva-skeleton, the eternal Thaumaturge, and the old child each function within the book as "alternators" of duration; through the time of history, myth, and the entire universe, they guarantee the hermit's recapture of the cellular principle of life. The night of *The Temptation* can greet the unchanged novelty of a new day, because the earth has turned back upon its axis.

3. The resurgence of time also produces a prophetic vision of the future. Within his recollections, Anthony encountered the ancient imagination of the Orient: deep within this memory, which no longer belongs to him, he saw a form arising that represented the temptation of the wisest of the kings of Israel—the Queen of Sheba. Standing behind her, he recognized in the shape of an ambiguous dwarf, her servant and his own disciple, a disciple who is indissociably linked to Desire and Wisdom. Hilarion is the incarnation of all the dreams of the Orient, but he possesses as well a perfect knowledge of Scriptures and their interpretation. Greed and science are united in him—covetous knowledge and damnable facts. This gnome increases in size throughout the course of the liturgy; by the last episode, he has become gigantic, "beautiful as an archangel and luminous as the sun." His kingdom now includes the universe as he becomes the Devil in the lightning flash of truth. Serving as an embryonic stage in the development of Western thought, he first introduces theology and its infinite disputes; then, he revives ancient civilizations and their gods whose rule was so quickly reduced to ashes; he inaugurates a rational understanding of the world; he demonstrates the movement of the stars and reveals the secret powers of life. All of European culture is deployed in this Egyptian night where the spector, the ancient history, of the Orient still haunts

12. *The Temptation*, p. 97.

the imagination: the theology of the Middle Ages, the erudition of the Renaissance, and the scientific bent of the modern period. *The Temptation* acts as a nocturnal sun whose trajectory is from east to west, from desire to knowledge, from imagination to truth, from the oldest longings to the findings of modern science. The appearance of Egypt converted to Christianity (and with it Alexandria) and the appearance of Anthony represent the zero point between Asia and Europe; both seem to arise from a fold in time, at the point where Antiquity, at the summit of its achievement, begins to vacillate and collapses, releasing its hidden and forgotten monsters; they also plant the seed of the modern world with its promise of endless knowledge. We have arrived at the hollow of history.[13]

The "temptation" of Saint Anthony is the double fascination exercised upon Christianity by the sumptuous spectacle of its past and the limitless acquisitions of its future. The definitive text excludes Abraham's God, the Virgin, and the virtues (who appear in the first two versions), but not to save them from profanation; they were incorporated in figures that represent them—in Buddha, the tempted god, in Apollonius the thaumaturge who resembles Christ, and in Isis the mother of sorrows. *The Temptation* does not mask reality in its glittering images, but reveals the image of an image in the realm of truth. Even in its state of primitive purity, Christianity was formed by the dying reflections of an older world, formed by the feeble light it projected upon the still grey shadows of a nascent world.

4. The two earlier versions of *The Temptation* began with the battle of the Seven Deadly Sins against the three theological virtues (Faith, Hope, and Charity), but this traditional imagery of the mysteries disappears in the published text. The sins appear only in the form of illusions and the virtues are given a secret existence as the organizing principles of the sequences. The endless revival of heresies places Faith at the mercy of over-

13. The "hollow of history" may represent Foucault's understanding of the "event"; see below, "Theatrum Philosophicum," pp. 172–176, for a discussion of this term.

powering error; the agony of the gods, which makes them disappear as glimmers of imagination, transforms Hope into a futile quest; and nature in repose or with its savage forces unleashed reduces Charity to a mockery. The three supreme virtues have been vanquished; and turning away from Heaven, the saint "lies flat on his stomach, and leaning upon his elbows, he watches breathlessly. Withered ferns begin to flower anew."[14] At the sight of this small palpitating cell, Charity is transformed into dazzling curiosity ("O joy! O bliss! I have seen the birth of life; I have seen motion begin."),[15] Hope is transformed into an uncontrollable desire to dissolve into the violence of the world ("I long to fly, to swim, to bark, to shout, to howl."),[16] and Faith becomes an identification with brute nature, the soft and somber stupidity of things ("I wish to huddle upon these forms, to penetrate each atom, to descend to the depths of matter—to become pure matter.").[17]

This book, which initially appears as a progression of slightly incoherent fantasies, can claim originality only with respect to its meticulous organization. What appears as fantasy is no more than the simple transcription of documents, the reproductions of drawings or texts, but their sequence conforms to an extremely complex composition. By assigning a specific location to each documentary element, it is also made to function within several simultaneous series.[18] The linear and visible sequence of sins, heresies, divinities, and monsters is merely the superficial crest of an elaborate vertical structure. This succession of figures, crowded like puppets dancing the farandole, also functions as: a trinity of canonical virtues; the geodesic line of a culture born in the dreams of the Orient and completed in the knowledge of the West; the return of History to the origin of time and the beginning of things; a pulsating space that expands to the outer limits

14. *The Temptation,* p. 163.
15. Ibid.
16. Ibid.
17. Ibid., p. 164.
18. See below, "Theatrum Philosophicum," p. 180, for a discussion of the importance of the concept of series.

of the universe and suddenly recedes to return to the simplest element of life. Each element and each character has its place not only in the visible procession, but in the organization of Christian allegories, the development of culture and knowledge, the reverse chronology of the world, and the spatial configurations of the universe.

In addition, *The Temptation* develops the encapsulated visions in depth as they recede, through a series of stages, to the distance; it constitutes a volume behind the thread of its speeches and under its line of successions. Each element (setting, character, speech, alteration of scenery) is effectively placed at a definite point in the linear sequence, but each element also has its vertical system of correspondences and is situated at a specific depth in the fiction. This explains why *The Temptation* can be the book of books: it unites in a single "volume" a series of linguistic elements that derive from existing books and that are, by virtue of their specific documentary character, the repetition of things said in the past. The library is opened, catalogued, sectioned, repeated, and rearranged in a new space; and this "volume" into which Flaubert has forced it is both the thickness of a book that develops according to the necessarily linear thread of its text and a procession of marionnettes that, in deploying its boxed visions, also opens a domain in depth.

V

Saint Anthony seems to summon *Bouvard et Pécuchet*, at least to the extent that the latter stands as its grotesque shadow, its tiny, yet boundless, double. As soon as Flaubert completed *The Temptation,* he began his last book. It contains the same elements: a book produced from other books; the encyclopedic learning of a culture; temptation experienced in a state of withdrawal; an extended series of trials; the interplay of illusions and belief. But the general shape is altered. First, the relationship of the Book to the indefinite series of all other books has changed. *The Temptation* was composed of fragments drawn from invisible volumes and transformed into a display of pure phantasms: only the Bible—the supreme Book—shows the sovereign presence of the written word in the text and on the center of its stage; it announced, once and for all, the powers of temptation possessed by the Book. Bouvard and Pécuchet are directly tempted by books, by their endless multiplicity, by the frothing of works in the grey expanse of the library. In *Bouvard et Pécuchet*, the library is clearly visible—classified and analysed. It can exert its fascination without being consecrated in *a* book or transformed into images. Its powers stem from its singular existence—from the unlimited proliferation of printed paper.

The Bible has become a bookstore, and the magic power of the image has become a devouring appetite for reading. This accounts for the change in the form of temptation. Saint Anthony had withdrawn into idle seclusion in his desire to avoid the disturbing presence of others; yet, neither a living grave nor a walled fortress are sufficient protection. He had exorcised every living form but they returned with a vengeance, testing the saint by their proximity but also by their remoteness. These forms surround him on every side, possess him, but disappear as he extends his hand. Their operation places the saint in a state of pure passivity: his only function was to localize them in the Book through happy memories or the force of imagination. All of his gestures, every word of compassion, and any show of violence, dissipate the mirage—proving that he had suffered a temptation (that only in his heart did an illusory image take on reality). Bouvard and Pécuchet, on the other hand, are indefatigable pilgrims: they try everything, they touch and are drawn to everything; they put everything to the test of their marginal industry. If they withdraw from the world as the Egyptian monk did, it is an active retreat, an enterprising use of their leisure where they summon, with constant recourse to their extensive reading, all the seriousness of science and the most solemnly printed truths. They wish to put into practice everything they read, and if success eludes them, as the images dissipate before Saint Anthony, it is not as a result of their initial gesture but of their persistent search. Their temptation arises from zealousness.

For these two simple men, to be tempted is to believe. It is to believe in the things they read, to believe in the things they overhear; it is to believe immediately and unquestioningly in the persistent flow of discourse. Their innocence is fully engaged in this domain of things already said. Those things that have been *read* and *heard* immediately became things *to do*. But their enterprise is so pure that no setback can alter their belief: they do not measure their truths by their success; they do not threaten their beliefs with the test of action. Possible disasters always remain outside the sovereign field of belief and their faith remains intact. When Bouvard and Pécuchet abandon their quest, they renounce not their faith but the possibility of applying their beliefs. They detach themselves from works to maintain the dazzling reality of their faith in faith. They repeat, for the modern world, the experiences of Job; stricken through their knowledge and not their possessions, abandoned by science and not by God, they persist, like him, in their fidelity—they are saints. For Saint Anthony, unlike these modern-day saints, temptation lies in the sight of the things without belief: it is to perceive error mixed with truth, the spectre of false gods resembling the true God, a nature abandoned without providence to the immensity of its spaces or the unleashing of its vital forces. And paradoxically, as these images are relegated to the shadows from which they emerged, they carry with them some of the belief that Saint Anthony had invested in them, if only for an instant— a part of the faith he had invested in the Christian God. The disappearance of those fantasies that seemed most inimical to his faith does not forcefully reinstate his religion, but gradually undermines it until it is completely taken from him. In their fanatical bloodshed, the heretics dissolve the truth; and the dying gods gather into their darkness part of the image of the true God. Anthony's saintliness was broken in the defeat of those things in which he had no faith; and that of Bouvard and Pécuchet triumphs in the downfall of their faith. They are the true elect. They were given the grace denied the saint.

The relationship between sainthood and stupidity was undoubtedly of fundamental importance for Flaubert; it can be found in Charles Bovary; it is visible in *Un coeur simple,* and perhaps as well, in the *Sentimental Education;* it is essential to *The Temptation* and *Bouvard,* but it adopts symmetrically opposite forms in these books. Bouvard and Pécuchet link sainthood to stupidity on the basis of the will-to-act, the dimension where they activate their desires: they had dreamed of being rich, of being men of leisure and independent means, men of property, but in achieving these goals, they discover that these new roles necessitate an endless cycle of tasks and not a pure and simple existence; the books that should have taught them how to exist dissipated their energies by telling them what they must do. Such is the stupidity and virtue, the sanctity and simple-mindedness of those who zealously undertake to make of themselves what they already are, who put into practice received ideas, and who silently endeavor throughout their lives to achieve union with their inner selves in a blind and desperate eagerness. On the other hand, Saint Anthony links simplemindedness to sainthood on the basis of a will-to-be: he wished to be a saint through a total deadening of his senses, intelligence, and emotions, and by dissolving himself into the images that come to him through the mediation of the Book. It is from this that the temptations increase their hold upon him: he refuses to be a heretic, but takes pity on the gods; he recognizes himself in the temptations of Buddha, secretly shares the raptures of Cybele, and weeps with Isis. But his desire to identify with the things he sees triumphs when faced with pure matter: he wishes to be blind, drowsy, greedy, and as stupid as the "Catoblepas";[19] he wishes that he were unable to lift his head higher than his stomach and that his eyelids would become so heavy that no light could possibly reach his eyes. He wishes to be a dumb creature—an animal, a plant, a cell. He wishes to be pure matter. Through this sleep of reason and in the innocence of desires that have

19. *The Temptation,* p. 159.

become pure movement, he could at least be reunited to the saintly stupidity of things.

As Anthony is about to accomplish his desire, the day returns and the face of Christ shines in the sun: the saint kneels and returns to his prayers. Has he triumphed over his temptations; has he been defeated and, as a punishment, must the same cycle be indefinitely repeated? Or has he achieved purity through the dumbness of matter; is this the moment when he achieves a true saintliness by discovering, through the dangerous space of books, the pulsation of innocent things; is he now able to *perform,* through his prayers, prostrations, and readings, this mindless sanctity he has become?

Bouvard and Pécuchet also make a new start: having been put to the test, they are now made to abandon the performance of those actions they had undertaken to become what they were initially. They can now be purely and simply themselves: they commission the construction of a large double desk to reestablish the link to their essential nature, to begin anew the activity which had occupied them for over ten years, to begin their copying. They will occupy themselves by copying books, copying their own books, copying every book; and unquestionably they will copy *Bouvard et Pécuchet.* Because to copy is *to do* nothing; it is *to be* the books being copied. It is to be this tiny protrusion of redoubled language, of discourse folded upon itself; this invisible existence transforms fleeting words into an enduring and distant murmur.[20] Saint Anthony was able to triumph over the Eternal Book in becoming the languageless movement of pure matter; Bouvard and Pécuchet triumph over everything alien to books, all that resists the book, by transforming themselves into the continuous movement of the book. The book opened by Saint Anthony, the book that initiated the flight of all possible temptations is indefinitely extended by these two simple men; it is prolonged without end, without illusion, without greed, without sin, without desire.

20. See above, "Language to Infinity," p. 55.

PART II

🌿

COUNTER-MEMORY:
THE PHILOSOPHY
OF DIFFERENCE

What Is an Author?

In proposing this slightly odd question, I am conscious of the need for an explanation. To this day, the "author" remains an open question both with respect to its general function within discourse and in my own writings; that is, this question permits me to return to certain aspects of my own work which now appear ill-advised and misleading. In this regard, I wish to propose a necessary criticism and reevaluation.

For instance, my objective in *The Order of Things* had been to analyse verbal clusters as discursive layers which fall outside the familiar categories of a book, a work, or an author. But while I considered "natural history," the "analysis of wealth," and "political economy" in general terms, I neglected a similar analysis of the author and his works; it is perhaps due to this omission that I employed the names of authors throughout this book in a naive and often crude fashion. I spoke of Buffon, Cuvier, Ricardo,

This essay originally appeared in the *Bulletin de la Société française de Philosophie*, 63, No. 3 (1969), 73–104. It was delivered as a lecture before the Society at the Collège de France on February 22, 1969, with Jean Wahl presiding. We have omitted Professor Wahl's introductory remarks and also Foucault's response and the debate that followed his lecture. Foucault's initial statement, however, has been interpolated in the first paragraph of the translation. The interest of the discussion that followed Foucault's paper lies in its preoccupation—especially as voiced by Lucien Goldmann—with Foucault's supposed affinity with the structuralist enterprise. As in the conclusion of *The Archaeology of Knowledge* (esp. pp. 200–201), Foucault forcefully denies this connection. This essay is reproduced here by permission of the Society. (All footnotes supplied by the editor.)

and others as well, but failed to realize that I had allowed their names to function ambiguously. This has proved an embarassment to me in that my oversight has served to raise two pertinent objections.

It was argued that I had not properly described Buffon or his work and that my handling of Marx was pitifully inadequate in terms of the totality of his thought.[1] Although these objections were obviously justified, they ignored the task I had set myself: I had no intention of describing Buffon or Marx or of reproducing their statements or implicit meanings, but, simply stated, I wanted to locate the rules that formed a certain number of concepts and theoretical relationships in their works.[2] In addition, it was argued that I had created monstrous families by bringing together names as disparate as Buffon and Linnaeus or in placing Cuvier next to Darwin in defiance of the most readily observable family resemblances and natural ties.[3] This objection also seems inappropriate since I had never tried to establish a genealogical table of exceptional individuals, nor was I concerned in forming an intellectual daguerreotype of the scholar or naturalist of the seventeenth and eighteenth century. In fact, I had no intention of forming any family, whether holy or perverse. On the contrary, I wanted to determine—a much more modest task—the functional conditions of specific discursive practices.

Then why did I use the names of authors in *The Order of*

1. See "Entretiens sur Michel Foucault" (directed by J. Proust), *La Pensée*, No. 137 (1968), pp. 6–7 and 11; and also Sylvie le Bon, "Un Positivisme désesperée," *Esprit*, No. 5 (1967), pp. 1317–1319.

2. Foucault's purpose, concerned with determining the "codes" of discourse, is explicitly stated in the Preface to *The Order of Things*, p. xx. These objections—see "Entretiens sur Michel Foucault"—are obviously those of specialists who fault Foucault for his apparent failure to appreciate the facts and complexities of their theoretical field.

3. For an appreciation of Foucault's technique, see Jonathan Culler, "The Linguistic Basis of Structuralism," *Structuralism: An Introduction*, ed. David Robey (Oxford: Clarendon Press, 1973), pp. 27–28.

Things? Why not avoid their use altogether, or, short of that, why not define the manner in which they were used? These questions appear fully justified and I have tried to gauge their implications and consequences in a book that will appear shortly.[4] These questions have determined my effort to situate comprehensive discursive units, such as "natural history" or "political economy," and to establish the methods and instruments for delimiting, analyzing, and describing these unities. Nevertheless, as a privileged moment of individualization in the history of ideas, knowledge, and literature, or in the history of philosophy and science, the question of the author demands a more direct response. Even now, when we study the history of a concept, a literary genre, or a branch of philosophy, these concerns assume a relatively weak and secondary position in relation to the solid and fundamental role of an author and his works.

For the purposes of this paper, I will set aside a sociohistorical analysis of the author as an individual and the numerous questions that deserve attention in this context: how the author was individualized in a culture such as ours; the status we have given the author, for instance, when we began our research into authenticity and attribution; the systems of valorization in which he was included; or the moment when the stories of heroes gave way to an author's biography; the conditions that fostered the formulation of the fundamental critical category of "the man and his work." For the time being, I wish to restrict myself to the singular relationship that holds between an author and a text, the manner in which a text apparently points to this figure who is outside and precedes it.

Beckett supplies a direction: "What matter who's speaking, someone said, what matter who's speaking."[5] In an indifference

4. *The Archaeology of Knowledge,* trans. A. M. Sheridan Smith (London: Tavistock, 1972) was published in France in 1969; for discussion of the author, see esp. pp. 92–6, 122.
5. Samuel Beckett, *Texts for Nothing,* trans. Beckett (London: Calder & Boyars, 1974), p. 16.

such as this we must recognize one of the fundamental ethical principles of contemporary writing. It is not simply "ethical" because it characterizes our way of speaking and writing, but because it stands as an immanent rule, endlessly adopted and yet never fully applied. As a principle, it dominates writing as an ongoing practice and slights our customary attention to the finished product.[6] For the sake of illustration, we need only consider two of its major themes. First, the writing of our day has freed itself from the necessity of "expression"; it only refers to itself, yet it is not restricted to the confines of interiority. On the contrary, we recognize it in its exterior deployment.[7] This reversal transforms writing into an interplay of signs, regulated less by the content it signifies than by the very nature of the signifier. Moreover, it implies an action that is always testing the limits of its regularity, transgressing and reversing an order that it accepts and manipulates. Writing unfolds like a game that inevitably moves beyond its own rules and finally leaves them behind. Thus, the essential basis of this writing is not the exalted emotions related to the act of composition or the insertion of a subject into language. Rather, it is primarily concerned with creating an opening where the writing subject endlessly disappears.[8]

The second theme is even more familiar: it is the kinship between writing and death. This relationship inverts the age-old

6. Cf. Edward Said, "The Ethics of Language," *Diacritics*, 4 (1974), 32.

7. On "expression" and writing as self-referential, see Jean-Marie Benoist, "The End of Structuralism," *Twentieth Century Studies*, 3 (1970), 39; and Roland Barthes, *Critique et vérité* (Paris: Collection Tel Quel, 1966). As the following sentence implies, the "exterior deployment" of writing relates to Ferdinand de Saussure's emphasis of the acoustic quality of the signifier, an external phenomena of speech which, nevertheless, responds to its own internal and differential articulation.

8. On "transgression," see above, "A Preface to Transgression," p. 42; and "Language to Infinity," p. 56. Cf. Blanchot, *L'Espace littéraire* (Paris, 1955), p. 58; and David P. Funt, "Newer Criticism and Revolution," *Hudson Review*, 22 (1969), 87–96.

conception of Greek narrative or epic, which was designed to guarantee the immortality of a hero. The hero accepted an early death because his life, consecrated and magnified by death, passed into immortality; and the narrative redeemed his acceptance of death. In a different sense, Arabic stories, and *The Arabian Nights* in particular, had as their motivation, their theme and pretext, this strategy for defeating death. Storytellers continued their narratives late into the night to forestall death and to delay the inevitable moment when everyone must fall silent. Scheherazade's story is a desperate inversion of murder; it is the effort, throughout all those nights, to exclude death from the circle of existence.[9] This conception of a spoken or written narrative as a protection against death has been transformed by our culture. Writing is now linked to sacrifice and to the sacrifice of life itself; it is a voluntary obliteration of the self that does not require representation in books because it takes place in the everyday existence of the writer. Where a work had the duty of creating immortality, it now attains the right to kill, to become the murderer of its author. Flaubert, Proust, and Kafka are obvious examples of this reversal.[10] In addition, we find the link between writing and death manifested in the total effacement of the individual characteristics of the writer; the quibbling and confrontations that a writer generates between himself and his text cancel out the signs of his particular individuality. If we wish to know the writer in our day, it will be through the singularity of his absence and in his link to death, which has transformed him into a victim of his own writing. While all of this is familiar in philosophy, as in literary criticism, I am not certain that the consequences derived from the disappearance or death of the author have been fully explored or that the importance of this event has been appreciated. To be specific, it

9. See above, "Language to Infinity," p. 58.
10. The recent stories of John Barth, collected in *Lost in the Funhouse* and *Chimera*, supply interesting examples of Foucault's thesis. The latter work includes, in fact, a novelistic reworking of *Arabian Nights*.

seems to me that the themes destined to replace the privileged position accorded the author have merely served to arrest the possibility of genuine change. Of these, I will examine two that seem particularly important.

To begin with, the thesis concerning a work. It has been understood that the task of criticism is not to reestablish the ties between an author and his work or to reconstitute an author's thought and experience through his works and, further, that criticism should concern itself with the structures of a work, its architectonic forms, which are studied for their intrinsic and internal relationships.[11] Yet, what of a context that questions the concept of a work? What, in short, is the strange unit designated by the term, work? What is necessary to its composition, if a work is not something written by a person called an "author?" Difficulties arise on all sides if we raise the question in this way. If an individual is not an author, what are we to make of those things he has written or said, left among his papers or communicated to others? Is this not properly a work? What, for instance, were Sade's papers before he was consecrated as an author? Little more, perhaps, than roles of paper on which he endlessly unravelled his fantasies while in prison.

Assuming that we are dealing with an author, is everything he wrote and said, everything he left behind, to be included in his work? This problem is both theoretical and practical. If we wish to publish the complete works of Nietzsche, for example, where do we draw the line? Certainly, everything must be published, but can we agree on what "everything" means? We will, of course, include everything that Nietzsche himself published, along with the drafts of his works, his plans for aphorisms, his marginal notations and corrections. But what if, in a notebook filled with aphorisms, we find a reference, a reminder of an appointment, an address, or a laundry bill, should this be included

11. Plainly a prescription for criticism as diverse as G. Wilson Knight's *The Wheel of Fire* (London, 1930) and Roland Barthes' *On Racine*, trans. Richard Howard (New York: Hill & Wang, 1964).

in his works? Why not? These practical considerations are endless once we consider how a work can be extracted from the millions of traces left by an individual after his death. Plainly, we lack a theory to encompass the questions generated by a work and the empirical activity of those who naively undertake the publication of the complete works of an author often suffers from the absence of this framework. Yet more questions arise. Can we say that *The Arabian Nights,* and *Stromates* of Clement of Alexandria, or the *Lives* of Diogenes Laertes constitute works? Such questions only begin to suggest the range of our difficulties, and, if some have found it convenient to bypass the individuality of the writer or his status as an author to concentrate on a work, they have failed to appreciate the equally problematic nature of the word "work" and the unity it designates.

Another thesis has detained us from taking full measure of the author's disappearance. It avoids confronting the specific event that makes it possible and, in subtle ways, continues to preserve the existence of the author. This is the notion of *écriture.*[12] Strictly speaking, it should allow us not only to circumvent references to an author, but to situate his recent absence. The conception of *écriture,* as currently employed, is concerned with neither the act of writing nor the indications, as symptoms or signs within a text, of an author's meaning; rather, it stands for a remarkably profound attempt to elaborate the conditions of any text, both the conditions of its spatial dispersion and its temporal deployment.

It appears, however, that this concept, as currently employed,

12. We have kept the French, *écriture,* with its double reference to the act of writing and to the primordial (and metaphysical) nature of writing as an entity in itself, since it is the term that best identifies the program of Jacques Derrida. Like the theme of a self-referential writing, it too builds on a theory of the sign and denotes writing as the interplay of presence and absence in that "signs represent the present in its absence" ("Differance," in *Speech and Phenomena,* trans. David B. Allison [Evanston Ill.: Northwestern Univ. Press, 1973], p. 138). See J. Derrida, *De la grammatologie* (Paris: Editions de Minuit, 1967).

has merely transposed the empirical characteristics of an author to a transcendental anonymity. The extremely visible signs of the author's empirical activity are effaced to allow the play, in parallel or opposition, of religious and critical modes of characterization. In granting a primordial status to writing, do we not, in effect, simply reinscribe in transcendental terms the theological affirmation of its sacred origin or a critical belief in its creative nature? To say that writing, in terms of the particular history it made possible, is subjected to forgetfulness and repression, is this not to reintroduce in transcendental terms the religious principle of hidden meanings (which require interpretation) and the critical assumption of implicit significations, silent purposes, and obscure contents (which give rise to commentary)? Finally, is not the conception of writing as absence a transposition into transcendental terms of the religious belief in a fixed and continuous tradition or the aesthetic principle that proclaims the survival of the work as a kind of enigmatic supplement of the author beyond his own death?[13]

This conception of *écriture* sustains the privileges of the author through the safeguard of the a priori; the play of representations that formed a particular image of the author is extended within a gray neutrality. The disappearance of the author—since Mallarmé, an event of our time—is held in check by the transcendental. Is it not necessary to draw a line between those who believe that we can continue to situate our present discontinuities within the historical and transcendental tradition of the nineteenth century and those who are making a great effort to liberate themselves, once and for all, from this conceptual framework?[14]

13. On "supplement," see *Speech and Phenomena*, pp. 88–104.
14. This statement is perhaps the polemical ground of Foucault's dissociation from phenomenology (and its evolution through Sartre into a Marxist discipline) on one side and structuralism on the other. It also marks his concern that his work be judged on its own merits and not on its reputed relationship to other movements. This insistence informs his appreciation of Nietzsche in "Nietzsche, Genealogy, History" as well as his sense of his own position in the Conclusion of *The Archaeology of Knowledge*.

꙾

It is obviously insufficient to repeat empty slogans: the author has disappeared; God and man died a common death.[15] Rather, we should reexamine the empty space left by the author's disappearance; we should attentively observe, along its gaps and fault lines, its new demarcations, and the reapportionment of this void; we should await the fluid functions released by this disappearance. In this context we can briefly consider the problems that arise in the use of an author's name. What is the name of an author? How does it function? Far from offering a solution, I will attempt to indicate some of the difficulties related to these questions.

The name of an author poses all the problems related to the category of the proper name. (Here, I am referring to the work of John Searle,[16] among others.) Obviously not a pure and simple reference, the proper name (and the author's name as well) has other than indicative functions. It is more than a gesture, a finger pointed at someone; it is, to a certain extent, the equivalent of a description. When we say "Aristotle," we are using a word that means one or a series of definite descriptions of the type: "the author of the *Analytics*," or "the founder of ontology," and so forth.[17] Furthermore, a proper name has other functions than that of signification: when we discover that Rimbaud has not written *La Chasse spirituelle*, we cannot maintain that the meaning of the proper name or this author's name has been altered. The proper name and the name of an author oscillate between the poles of description and designation, and, granting that they are linked to what they name, they are not totally determined either by their descriptive or designative functions.[18] Yet—and it is here that the specific difficulties attend-

15. Nietzsche, *The Gay Science*, III, 108.
16. John Searle, *Speech Acts: An Essay in the Philosophy of Language* (Cambridge: Cambridge University Press, 1969), pp. 162–174.
17. Ibid., p. 169.
18. Ibid., p. 172.

ing an author's name appear—the link between a proper name and the individual being named and the link between an author's name and that which it names are not isomorphous and do not function in the same way; and these differences require clarification.

To learn, for example, that Pierre Dupont does not have blue eyes, does not live in Paris, and is not a doctor does not invalidate the fact that the name, Pierre Dupont, continues to refer to the same person; there has been no modification of the designation that links the name to the person. With the name of an author, however, the problems are far more complex. The disclosure that Shakespeare was not born in the house that tourists now visit would not modify the functioning of the author's name, but, if it were proved that he had not written the sonnets that we attribute to him, this would constitute a significant change and affect the manner in which the author's name functions. Moreover, if we establish that Shakespeare wrote Bacon's *Organon* and that the same author was responsible for both the works of Shakespeare and those of Bacon, we would have introduced a third type of alteration which completely modifies the functioning of the author's name. Consequently, the name of an author is not precisely a proper name among others.

Many other factors sustain this paradoxical singularity of the name of an author. It is altogether different to maintain that Pierre Dupont does not exist and that Homer or Hermes Trismegistes have never existed. While the first negation merely implies that there is no one by the name of Pierre Dupont, the second indicates that several individuals have been referred to by one name or that the real author possessed none of the traits traditionally associated with Homer or Hermes. Neither is it the same thing to say that Jacques Durand, not Pierre Dupont, is the real name of X and that Stendhal's name was Henri Beyle. We could also examine the function and meaning of such statements as "Bourbaki is this or that person," and "Victor Eremita, Climacus, Anticlimacus, Frater Taciturnus, Constantin Constantius, all of these are Kierkegaard."

These differences indicate that an author's name is not simply an element of speech (as a subject, a complement, or an element that could be replaced by a pronoun or other parts of speech). Its presence is functional in that it serves as a means of classification. A name can group together a number of texts and thus differentiate them from others. A name also establishes different forms of relationships among texts. Neither Hermes not Hippocrates existed in the sense that we can say Balzac existed, but the fact that a number of texts were attached to a single name implies that relationships of homogeneity, filiation, reciprocal explanation, authentification, or of common utilization were established among them. Finally, the author's name characterizes a particular manner of existence of discourse. Discourse that possesses an author's name is not to be immediately consumed and forgotten; neither is it accorded the momentary attention given to ordinary, fleeting words. Rather, its status and its manner of reception are regulated by the culture in which it circulates.

We can conclude that, unlike a proper name, which moves from the interior of a discourse to the real person outside who produced it, the name of the author remains at the contours of texts—separating one from the other, defining their form, and characterizing their mode of existence. It points to the existence of certain groups of discourse and refers to the status of this discourse within a society and culture. The author's name is not a function of a man's civil status, nor is it fictional; it is situated in the breach, among the discontinuities, which gives rise to new groups of discourse and their singular mode of existence.[19] Con-

19. This is a particularly important point and brings together a great many of Foucault's insights concerning the relationship of an author (subject) to discourse. It reflects his understanding of the traditional and often unexamined unities of discourse whose actual discontinuities are resolved in either of two ways: by reference to an originating subject or to a language, conceived as plenitude, which supports the activities of commentary or interpretation. But since Foucault rejects the belief in the presumed fullness of language that underlies discourse, the author is subjected to the same fragmenta-

sequently, we can say that in our culture, the name of an author is a variable that accompanies only certain texts to the exclusion of others: a private letter may have a signatory, but it does not have an author; a contract can have an underwriter, but not an author; and, similarly, an anonymous poster attached to a wall may have a writer, but he cannot be an author. In this sense, the function of an author is to characterize the existence, circulation, and operation of certain discourses within a society.

In dealing with the "author" as a function of discourse, we must consider the characteristics of a discourse that support this use and determine its difference from other discourses. If we limit our remarks to only those books or texts with authors, we can isolate four different features.

First, they are objects of appropriation; the form of property they have become is of a particular type whose legal codification was accomplished some years ago. It is important to notice, as well, that its status as property is historically secondary to the penal code controlling its appropriation. Speeches and books were assigned real authors, other than mythical or important religious figures, only when the author became subject to punishment and to the extent that his discourse was considered transgressive. In our culture—undoubtedly in others as well—discourse was not originally a thing, a product, or a possession, but an action situated in a bipolar field of sacred and profane, lawful and unlawful, religious and blasphemous. It was a gesture charged with risks long before it became a possession caught in a circuit of property values.[20] But it was at the moment when a

---

tion which characterizes discourse and he is delineated as a discontinuous series; for example, see *L'Ordre du discours*, pp. 54–55 and 61–62.

20. In a seminar entitled "L'Epreuve et l'enquête," which Foucault conducted at the University of Montreal in the spring of 1974, he centered the debate around the following question: is the general conviction that truth derives from and is sustained by knowledge

system of ownership and strict copyright rules were established (toward the end of the eighteenth and beginning of the nineteenth century) that the transgressive properties always intrinsic to the act of writing became the forceful imperative of literature.[21] It is as if the author, at the moment he was accepted into the social order of property which governs our culture, was compensating for his new status by reviving the older bipolar field of discourse in a systematic practice of transgression and by restoring the danger of writing which, on another side, had been conferred the benefits of property.

Not just the state

Secondly, the "author-function"[22] is not universal or constant in all discourse. Even within our civilization, the same types of texts have not always required authors; there was a time when those texts which we now call "literary" (stories, folk tales, epics, and tragedies) were accepted, circulated, and valorized without any question about the identity of their author. Their anonymity was ignored because their real or supposed age was a sufficient guarantee of their authenticity. Texts, however, that we now call "scientific" (dealing with cosmology and the heavens, medicine or illness, the natural sciences or geography) were only considered

---

not simply a recent phenomenon, a limited case of the ancient and widespread belief that truth is a function of events? In an older time and in other cultures, the search for truth was hazardous in the extreme and truth resided in a danger zone, but if this was so and if truth could only be approached after a long preparation or through the details of a ritualized procedure, it was because it represented power. Discourse, for these cultures, was an active appropriation of power and to the extent that it was successful, it contained the power of truth itself, charged with all its risks and benefits.

21. Cf. *The Order of Things*, p. 300; and above, "A Preface to Transgression, pp. 30–33.

22. Foucault's phrasing of the "author-function" has been retained. This concept should not be confused (as it was by Goldmann in the discussion that followed Foucault's presentation) with the celebrated theme of the "death of man" in *The Order of Things* (pp. 342 and 386). On the contrary, Foucault's purpose is to revitalize the debate surrounding the subject by situating the subject, as a fluid function, within the space cleared by archaeology.

truthful during the Middle Ages if the name of the author was indicated. Statements on the order of "Hippocrates said . . ." or "Pliny tells us that . . ." were not merely formulas for an argument based on authority; they marked a proven discourse. In the seventeenth and eighteenth centuries, a totally new conception was developed when scientific texts were accepted on their own merits and positioned within an anonymous and coherent conceptual system of established truths and methods of verification. Authentification no longer required reference to the individual who had produced them; the role of the author disappeared as an index of truthfulness and, where it remained as an inventor's name, it was merely to denote a specific theorem or proposition, a strange effect, a property, a body, a group of elements, or pathological syndrome.

At the same time, however, "literary" discourse was acceptable only if it carried an author's name; every text of poetry or fiction was obliged to state its author and the date, place, and circumstance of its writing. The meaning and value attributed to the text depended on this information. If by accident or design a text was presented anonymously, every effort was made to locate its author. Literary anonymity was of interest only as a puzzle to be solved as, in our day, literary works are totally dominated by the sovereignty of the author. (Undoubtedly, these remarks are far too categorical. Criticism has been concerned for some time now with aspects of a text not fully dependent on the notion of an individual creator; studies of genre or the analysis of recurring textual motifs and their variations from a norm other than the author. Furthermore, where in mathematics the author has become little more than a handy reference for a particular theorem or group of propositions, the reference to an author in biology and medicine, or to the date of his research has a substantially different bearing. This latter reference, more than simply indicating the source of information, attests to the "reliability" of the evidence, since it entails an appreciation of the techniques and experimental materials available at a given time and in a particular laboratory.)

The third point concerning this "author-function" is that it is not formed spontaneously through the simple attribution of a discourse to an individual. It results from a complex operation whose purpose is to construct the rational entity we call an author. Undoubtedly, this construction is assigned a "realistic" dimension as we speak of an individual's "profundity" or "creative" power, his intentions or the original inspiration manifested in writing. Nevertheless, these aspects of an individual, which we designate as an author (or which comprise an individual as an author), are projections, in terms always more or less psychological, of our way of handling texts: in the comparisons we make, the traits we extract as pertinent, the continuities we assign, or the exclusions we practice. In addition, all these operations vary according to the period and the form of discourse concerned. A "philosopher" and a "poet" are not constructed in the same manner; and the author of an eighteenth-century novel was formed differently from the modern novelist. There are, nevertheless, transhistorical constants in the rules that govern the construction of an author.

In literary criticism, for example, the traditional methods for defining an author—or, rather, for determining the configuration of the author from existing texts—derive in large part from those used in the Christian tradition to authenticate (or to reject) the particular texts in its possession. Modern criticism, in its desire to "recover" the author from a work, employs devices strongly reminiscent of Christian exegesis when it wished to prove the value of a text by ascertaining the holiness of its author. In *De Viris Illustribus,* Saint Jerome maintains that homonymy is not proof of the common authorship of several works, since many individuals could have the same name or someone could have perversely appropriated another's name. The name, as an individual mark, is not sufficient as it relates to a textual tradition.

How, then, can several texts be attributed to an individual author? What norms, related to the function of the author, will disclose the involvement of several authors? According to Saint Jerome, there are four criteria: the texts that must be eliminated from the list of works attributed to a single author are those inferior to the others (thus, the author is defined as a standard level of quality); those whose ideas conflict with the doctrine expressed in the others (here the author is defined as a certain field of conceptual or theoretical coherence); those written in a different style and containing words and phrases not ordinarily found in the other works (the author is seen as a stylistic uniformity); and those referring to events or historical figures subsequent to the death of the author (the author is thus a definite historical figure in which a series of events converge). Although modern criticism does not appear to have these same suspicions concerning authentication, its strategies for defining the author present striking similarities. The author explains the presence of certain events within a text, as well as their transformations, distortions, and their various modifications (and this through an author's biography or by reference to his particular point of view, in the analysis of his social preferences and his position within a class or by delineating his fundamental objectives). The author also constitutes a principle of unity in writing where any unevenness of production is ascribed to changes caused by evolution, maturation, or outside influence. In addition, the author serves to neutralize the contradictions that are found in a series of texts. Governing this function is the belief that there must be—at a particular level of an author's thought, of his conscious or unconscious desire—a point where contradictions are resolved, where the incompatible elements can be shown to relate to one another or to cohere around a fundamental and originating contradiction. Finally, the author is a particular source of expression who, in more or less finished forms, is manifested equally well, and with similar validity, in a text, in letters, fragments, drafts,

and so forth. Thus, even while Saint Jerome's four principles of
authenticity might seem largely inadequate to modern critics,
they, nevertheless, define the critical modalities now used to
display the function of the author.[23]

However, it would be false to consider the function of the
author as a pure and simple reconstruction after the fact of a
text given as passive material, since a text always bears a number
of signs that refer to the author. Well known to grammarians,
these textual signs are personal pronouns, adverbs of time and
place, and the conjugation of verbs.[24] But it is important to note
that these elements have a different bearing on texts with an
author and on those without one. In the latter, these "shifters"
refer to a real speaker and to an actual deictic situation, with
certain exceptions such as the case of indirect speech in the first
person. When discourse is linked to an author, however, the role
of "shifters" is more complex and variable. It is well known that
in a novel narrated in the first person, neither the first person
pronoun, the present indicative tense, nor, for that matter, its
signs of localization refer directly to the writer, either to the
time when he wrote, or to the specific act of writing; rather,
they stand for a "second self"[25] whose similarity to the author is
never fixed and undergoes considerable alteration within the
course of a single book. It would be as false to seek the author in
relation to the actual writer as to the fictional narrator; the
"author-function" arises out of their scission—in the division and
distance of the two. One might object that this phenomenon only

23. See Evaristo Arns, *La Technique du livre d'après Saint Jerome*
(Paris, 1953).
24. On personal pronouns ("shifters"), see R. Jakobson, *Selected
Writings* (Paris: Mouton, 1971), II, 130–32; and *Essais de linguistique
générale* (Paris, 1966), p. 252. For its general implications, see
Eugenio Donato, "Of Structuralism and Literature," *MLN*, 82 (1967),
556–58. On adverbs of time and place, see Emile Benveniste,
Problèmes de la linguistique générale (Paris, 1966), pp. 237–50.
25. Cf. Wayne C. Booth, *The Rhetoric of Fiction* (Chicago: Univ.
of Chicago Press, 1961), pp. 67–77.

applies to novels or poetry, to a context of "quasi-discourse," but, in fact, all discourse that supports this "author-function" is characterized by this plurality of egos. In a mathematical treatise, the ego who indicates the circumstances of composition in the preface is not identical, either in terms of his position or his function, to the "I" who concludes a demonstration within the body of the text. The former implies a unique individual who, at a given time and place, succeeded in completing a project, whereas the latter indicates an instance and plan of demonstration that anyone could perform provided the same set of axioms, preliminary operations, and an identical set of symbols were used. It is also possible to locate a third ego: one who speaks of the goals of his investigation, the obstacles encountered, its results, and the problems yet to be solved and this "I" would function in a field of existing or future mathematical discourses. We are not dealing with a system of dependencies where a first and essential use of the "I" is reduplicated, as a kind of fiction, by the other two. On the contrary, the "author-function" in such discourses operates so as to effect the simultaneous dispersion of the three egos.[26]

Further elaboration would, of course, disclose other characteristics of the "author-function," but I have limited myself to the four that seemed the most obvious and important. They can be summarized in the following manner: the "author-function" is tied to the legal and institutional systems that circumscribe, determine, and articulate the realm of discourses; it does not operate in a uniform manner in all discourses, at all times, and in any given culture; it is not defined by the spontaneous attribution of a text to its creator, but through a series of precise and complex procedures; it does not refer, purely and simply, to an

26. This conclusion relates to Foucault's concern in developing a "philosophy of events" as described in L'Ordre du discours, pp. 60–61: "I trust that we can agree that I do not refer to a succession of moments in time, nor to a diverse plurality of thinking subjects; I refer to a caesura which fragments the moment and disperses the subject into a plurality of possible positions and functions."

actual individual insofar as it simultaneously gives rise to a variety of egos and to a series of subjective positions that individuals of any class may come to occupy.

I am aware that until now I have kept my subject within unjustifiable limits; I should also have spoken of the "author-function" in painting, music, technical fields, and so forth. Admitting that my analysis is restricted to the domain of discourse, it seems that I have given the term "author" an excessively narrow meaning. I have discussed the author only in the limited sense of a person to whom the production of a text, a book, or a work can be legitimately attributed. However, it is obvious that even within the realm of discourse a person can be the author of much more than a book—of a theory, for instance, of a tradition or a discipline within which new books and authors can proliferate. For convenience, we could say that such authors occupy a "transdiscursive" position.

Homer, Aristotle, and the Church Fathers played this role, as did the first mathematicians and the originators of the Hippocratic tradition. This type of author is surely as old as our civilization. But I believe that the nineteenth century in Europe produced a singular type of author who should not be confused with "great" literary authors, or the authors of canonical religious texts, and the founders of sciences. Somewhat arbitrarily, we might call them "initiators of discursive practices."

The distinctive contribution of these authors is that they produced not only their own work, but the possibility and the rules of formation of other texts. In this sense, their role differs entirely from that of a novelist, for example, who is basically never more than the author of his own text. Freud is not simply the author of *The Interpretation of Dreams* or of *Wit and its Relation to the Unconscious* and Marx is not simply the author of the *Communist Manifesto* or *Capital:* they both established the endless possibility of discourse. Obviously, an easy objection can be made. The author of a novel may be responsible for more than his own text; if he acquires some "importance" in the literary world, his influence can have significant ramifications. To take a very simple example, one could say that Ann Radcliffe did not simply write *The Mysteries of Udolpho* and a few other novels, but also made possible the appearance of Gothic Romances at the beginning of the nineteenth century. To this extent, her function as an author exceeds the limits of her work. However, this objection can be answered by the fact that the possibilities disclosed by the initiators of discursive practices (using the examples of Marx and Freud, whom I believe to be the first and the most important) are significantly different from those suggested by novelists. The novels of Ann Radcliffe put into circulation a certain number of resemblances and analogies patterned on her work—various characteristic signs, figures, relationships, and structures that could be integrated into other books. In short, to say that Ann Radcliffe created the Gothic Romance means that there are certain elements common to her works and to the nineteenth-century Gothic romance: the heroine ruined by her own innocence, the secret fortress that functions as a counter-city, the outlaw-hero who swears revenge on the world that has cursed him, etc. On the other hand, Marx and Freud, as "initiators of discursive practices," not only made possible a certain number of analogies that could be adopted by future texts, but, as importantly, they also made possible a certain number of differences. They cleared a space for the introduction of elements other than their own, which, nevertheless, remain within the field of discourse they initiated. In saying that Freud founded psychoanalysis, we do not simply mean that the concept of libido or the techniques of dream analysis reappear in the writings of Karl Abraham or Melanie Klein, but that he made possible a certain number of differences with respect to his books, concepts, and hypotheses, which all arise out of psychoanalytic discourse.

Is this not the case, however, with the founder of any new science or of any author who successfully transforms an existing science? After all, Galileo is indirectly responsible for the texts of those who mechanically applied the laws he formulated, in addition to having paved the way for the production of statements far different from his own. If Cuvier is the founder of biology and Saussure of linguistics, it is not because they were imitated or that an organic concept or a theory of the sign was uncritically integrated into new texts, but because Cuvier, to a certain extent, made possible a theory of evolution diametrically opposed to his own system and because Saussure made possible a generative grammar radically different from his own structural analysis. Superficially, then, the initiation of discursive practices appears similar to the founding of any scientific endeavor, but I believe there is a fundamental difference.

In a scientific program, the founding act is on an equal footing with its future transformations: it is merely one among the many modifications that it makes possible. This interdependence can take several forms. In the future development of a science, the founding act may appear as little more than a single instance of a more general phenomenon that has been discovered. It might be questioned, in retrospect, for being too intuitive or empirical and submitted to the rigors of new theoretical operations in order to situate it in a formal domain. Finally, it might be thought a hasty generalization whose validity should be restricted. In other words, the founding act of a science can always be rechanneled through the machinery of transformations it has instituted.[27]

On the other hand, the initiation of a discursive practice is heterogeneous to its ulterior transformations. To extend psychoanalytic practice, as initiated by Freud, is not to presume a formal generality that was not claimed at the outset; it is to explore a number of possible applications. To limit it is to isolate in the original texts a small set of propositions or statements that are recognized as having an inaugurative value and that mark other Freudian concepts or theories as derivative. Finally, there are no

27. Cf. the discussion of disciplines in *L'Ordre du discours*, pp. 31–38.

"false" statements in the work of these initiators; those statements considered inessential or "prehistoric," in that they are associated with another discourse, are simply neglected in favor of the more pertinent aspects of the work. The initiation of a discursive practice, unlike the founding of a science, overshadows and is necessarily detached from its later developments and transformations. As a consequence, we define the theoretical validity of a statement with respect to the work of the initiator, whereas in the case of Galileo or Newton, it is based on the structural and intrinsic norms established in cosmology or physics. Stated schematically, the work of these initiators is not situated in relation to a science or in the space it defines; rather, it is science or discursive practice that relate to their works as the primary points of reference.

In keeping with this distinction, we can understand why it is inevitable that practitioners of such discourses must "return to the origin." Here, as well, it is necessary to distinguish a "return" from scientific "rediscoveries" or "reactivations." "Rediscoveries" are the effects of analogy or isomorphism with current forms of knowledge that allow the perception of forgotten or obscured figures. For instance, Chomsky in his book on Cartesian grammar[28] "rediscovered" a form of knowledge that had been in use from Cordemoy to Humboldt. It could only be understood from the perspective of generative grammar because this later manifestation held the key to its construction: in effect, a retrospective codification of an historical position. "Reactivation" refers to something quite different: the insertion of discourse into totally new domains of generalization, practice, and transformations. The history of mathematics abounds in examples of this phenomenon as the work of Michel Serres on mathematical anamnesis shows.[29]

The phrase, "return to," designates a movement with its proper

---

28. Noam Chomsky, *Cartesian Linguistics* (New York: Harper & Row, 1966).

29. *La Communication: Hermes I* (Paris: Editions de Minuit, 1968), pp. 78–112.

specificity, which characterizes the initiation of discursive practices. If we return, it is because of a basic and constructive omission, an omission that is not the result of accident or incomprehension.[30] In effect, the act of initiation is such, in its essence, that it is inevitably subjected to its own distortions; that which displays this act and derives from it is, at the same time, the root of its divergences and travesties. This nonaccidental omission must be regulated by precise operations that can be situated, analysed, and reduced in a return to the act of initiation. The barrier imposed by omission was not added from the outside; it arises from the discursive practice in question, which gives it its law. Both the cause of the barrier and the means for its removal, this omission—also responsible for the obstacles that prevent returning to the act of initiation—can only be resolved by a return. In addition, it is always a return to a text in itself, specifically, to a primary and unadorned text with particular attention to those things registered in the interstices of the text, its gaps and absences. We return to those empty spaces that have been masked by omission or concealed in a false and misleading plenitude. In these rediscoveries of an essential lack, we find the oscillation of two characteristic responses: "This point was made—you can't help seeing it if you know how to read"; or, inversely, "No, that point is not made in any of the printed words in the text, but it is expressed through the words, in their relationships and in the distance that separates them." It follows naturally that this return, which is a part of the discursive mechanism, constantly introduces modifications and that the return to a text is not a historical supplement that would come to fix itself upon the primary discursivity and redouble it in the form of an ornament which, after all, is not essential. Rather, it is an effective and necessary means of transforming discursive practice. A study of Galileo's works could alter our knowledge

30. For a discussion of the recent reorientation of the sign, see Foucault's "Nietzsche, Freud, Marx." On the role of repetition, Foucault writes in L'Ordre du discours: "The new is not found in what is said, but in the event of its return" (p. 28); see also below, "Theatrum Philosophicum," pp. 186–196.

of the history, but not the science, of mechanics; whereas, a re-examination of the books of Freud or Marx can transform our understanding of psychoanalysis or Marxism.

A last feature of these returns is that they tend to reinforce the enigmatic link between an author and his works. A text has an inaugurative value precisely because it is the work of a par-ticular author, and our returns are conditioned by this knowledge. The rediscovery of an unknown text by Newton or Cantor will not modify classical cosmology or group theory; at most, it will change our appreciation of their historical genesis. Bringing to light, however, *An Outline of Psychoanalysis,* to the extent that we recognize it as a book by Freud, can transform not only our historical knowledge, but the field of psychoanalytic theory—if only through a shift of accent or of the center of gravity. These returns, an important component of discursive practices, form a relationship between "fundamental" and mediate authors, which is not identical to that which links an ordinary text to its im-mediate author.

These remarks concerning the initiation of discursive practices have been extremely schematic, especially with regard to the opposition I have tried to trace between this initiation and the founding of sciences. The distinction between the two is not readily discernible; moreover, there is no proof that the two procedures are mutually exclusive. My only purpose in setting up this opposition, however, was to show that the "author-function," sufficiently complex at the level of a book or a series of texts that bear a definite signature, has other determining factors when analysed in terms of larger entities—groups of works or entire disciplines.

Unfortunately, there is a decided absence of positive proposi-tions in this essay, as it applies to analytic procedures or direc-tions for future research, but I ought at least to give the reasons why I attach such importance to a continuation of this work.

Developing a similar analysis could provide the basis for a typology of discourse. A typology of this sort cannot be adequately understood in relation to the grammatical features, formal structures, and objects of discourse, because there undoubtedly exist specific discursive properties or relationships that are irreducible to the rules of grammar and logic and to the laws that govern objects. These properties require investigation if we hope to distinguish the larger categories of discourse. The different forms of relationships (or nonrelationships) that an author can assume are evidently one of these discursive properties.

This form of investigation might also permit the introduction of an historical analysis of discourse. Perhaps the time has come to study not only the expressive value and formal transformations of discourse, but its mode of existence: the modifications and variations, within any culture, of modes of circulation, valorization, attribution, and appropriation. Partially at the expense of themes and concepts that an author places in his work, the "author-function" could also reveal the manner in which discourse is articulated on the basis of social relationships.

Is it not possible to reexamine, as a legitimate extension of this kind of analysis, the privileges of the subject? Clearly, in undertaking an internal and architectonic analysis of a work (whether it be a literary text, a philosophical system, or a scientific work) and in delimiting psychological and biographical references, suspicions arise concerning the absolute nature and creative role of the subject. But the subject should not be entirely abandoned. It should be reconsidered, not to restore the theme of an originating subject, but to seize its functions, its intervention in discourse, and its system of dependencies. We should suspend the typical questions: how does a free subject penetrate the density of things and endow them with meaning; how does it accomplish its design by animating the rules of discourse from within? Rather, we should ask: under what conditions and through what forms can an entity like the subject appear in the order of discourse; what position does it occupy;

what functions does it exhibit; and what rules does it follow in each type of discourse? In short, the subject (and its substitutes) must be stripped of its creative role and analysed as a complex and variable function of discourse.

The author—or what I have called the "author-function"—is undoubtedly only one of the possible specifications of the subject and, considering past historical transformations, it appears that the form, the complexity, and even the existence of this function are far from immutable. We can easily imagine a culture where discourse would circulate without any need for an author. Discourses, whatever their status, form, or value, and regardless of our manner of handling them, would unfold in a pervasive anonymity. No longer the tiresome repetitions:

"Who is the real author?"

"Have we proof of his authenticity and originality?"

"What has he revealed of his most profound self in his language?"

New questions will be heard:

"What are the modes of existence of this discourse?"

"Where does it come from; how is it circulated; who controls it?"

"What placements are determined for possible subjects?"

"Who can fulfill these diverse functions of the subject?"

Behind all these questions we would hear little more than the murmur of indifference:

"What matter who's speaking?"

Nietzsche, Genealogy, History

1. Genealogy is gray, meticulous, and patiently documentary. It operates on a field of entangled and confused parchments, on documents that have been scratched over and recopied many times.

On this basis, it is obvious that Paul Ree[1] was wrong to follow the English tendency in describing the history of morality in terms of a linear development—in reducing its entire history and genesis to an exclusive concern for utility. He assumed that words had kept their meaning, that desires still pointed in a single direction, and that ideas retained their logic; and he ignored the fact that the world of speech and desires has known invasions, struggles, plundering, disguises, ploys. From these elements, however, genealogy retrieves an indispensable restraint: it must record the singularity of events outside of any monotonous finality; it must seek them in the most unpromising places, in what we tend to feel is without history—in sentiments, love, conscience, in-

This essay first appeared in *Hommage à Jean Hyppolite* (Paris: Presses Universitaires de France, 1971), pp. 145–72. Along with "Réponse au cercle d'épistémologie," which became the introductory chapter of *The Archaeology of Knowledge*, this essay represents Foucault's attempt to explain his relationship to those sources which are fundamental to his development. Its importance, in terms of understanding Foucault's objectives, cannot be exaggerated. It appears here by permission of Presses Universitaires de France.
1. See Nietzsche's Preface to *The Genealogy of Morals*, 4, 7—ED.

stincts; it must be sensitive to their recurrence, not in order to trace the gradual curve of their evolution, but to isolate the different scenes where they engaged in different roles. Finally, genealogy must define even those instances where they are absent, the moment when they remained unrealized (Plato, at Syracuse, did not become Mohammed).

Genealogy, consequently, requires patience and a knowledge of details and it depends on a vast accumulation of source material. Its "cyclopean monuments"[2] are constructed from "discreet and apparently insignificant truths and according to a rigorous method"; they cannot be the product of "large and well-meaning errors."[3] In short, genealogy demands relentless erudition. Genealogy does not oppose itself to history as the lofty and profound gaze of the philosopher might compare to the molelike perspective of the scholar; on the contrary, it rejects the metahistorical deployment of ideal significations and indefinite teleologies. It opposes itself to the search for "origins."

2. In Nietzsche, we find two uses of the word *Ursprung*. The first is unstressed, and it is found alternately with other terms such as *Entstehung, Herkunft, Abkunft, Geburt*. In *The Genealogy of Morals*, for example, *Entstehung* or *Ursprung* serve equally well to denote the origin of duty or guilty conscience;[4] and in the discussion of logic or knowledge in *The Gay Science*, their origin is indiscriminately referred to as *Ursprung, Entstehung*, or *Herkunft*.[5]

The other use of the word is stressed. On occasion, Nietzsche places the term in opposition to another: in the first paragraph of *Human, All Too Human* the miraculous origin (*Wunderursprung*) sought by metaphysics is set against the analyses of historical philosophy, which poses questions *über Herkunft und Anfang. Ursprung* is also used in an ironic and deceptive manner. In what, for instance, do we find the original basis (*Ursprung*)

2. *The Gay Science*, 7.
3. *Human, All Too Human*, 3.
4. *The Genealogy*, II, 6, 8.
5. *The Gay Science*, 110, 111, 300.

of morality, a foundation sought after since Plato? "In detestable, narrowminded conclusions. *Pudenda origo*."⁶ Or in a related context, where should we seek the origin of religion (*Ursprung*), which Schopenhauer located in a particular metaphysical sentiment of the hereafter? It belongs, very simply, to an invention (*Erfindung*), a sleight-of-hand, an artifice (*Kunststück*), a secret formula, in the rituals of black magic, in the work of the *Schwarzkünstler*.⁷

One of the most significant texts with respect to the use of all these terms and to the variations in the use of *Ursprung* is the preface to the *Genealogy*. At the beginning of the text, its objective is defined as an examination of the origin of moral preconceptions and the term used is *Herkunft*. Then, Nietzsche proceeds by retracing his personal involvement with this question: he recalls the period when he "calligraphied" philosophy, when he questioned if God must be held responsible for the origin of evil. He now finds this question amusing and properly characterizes it as a search for *Ursprung* (he will shortly use the same term to summarize Paul Ree's activity).⁸ Further on, he evokes the analyses that are characteristically Nietzschean and that began with *Human, All Too Human*. Here, he speaks of *Herkunfthypothesen*. This use of the word *Herkunft* cannot be arbitrary, since it serves to designate a number of texts, beginning with *Human, All Too Human*, which deal with the origin of morality, asceticism, justice, and punishment. And yet, the word used in all these works had been *Ursprung*.⁹ It would seem that at this point in the *Genealogy* Nietzsche wished to validate an opposition between *Herkunft* and *Ursprung* that did not exist ten years earlier. But immediately following the use of the two

6. *The Dawn*, 102 ("Shameful origin"—Ed.).
7. *The Gay Science*, 151, 353; and also *The Dawn*, 62; *The Genealogy*, I, 14; *Twilight of the Idols*, "The Great Errors," 7. (*Schwarzkünstler* is a black magician—Ed.)
8. Paul Ree's text was entitled *Ursprung der Moralischen Empfindungen*.
9. In *Human, All Too Human*, aphorism 92 was entitled *Ursprung der Gerechtigkeit*.

terms in a specific sense, Nietzsche reverts, in the final paragraphs of the preface, to a usage that is neutral and equivalent.[10]

Why does Nietzsche challenge the pursuit of the origin (*Ursprung*), at least on those occasions when he is truly a genealogist? First, because it is an attempt to capture the exact essence of things, their purest possibilities, and their carefully protected identities, because this search assumes the existence of immobile forms that precede the external world of accident and succession. This search is directed to "that which was already there," the image of a primordial truth fully adequate to its nature, and it necessitates the removal of every mask to ultimately disclose an original identity. However, if the genealogist refuses to extend his faith in metaphysics, if he listens to history, he finds that there is "something altogether different" behind things: not a timeless and essential secret, but the secret that they have no essence or that their essence was fabricated in a piecemeal fashion from alien forms. Examining the history of reason, he learns that it was born in an altogether "reasonable" fashion—from chance;[11] devotion to truth and the precision of scientific methods arose from the passion of scholars, their reciprocal hatred, their fanatical and unending discussions, and their spirit of competition—the personal conflicts that slowly forged the weapons of reason.[12] Further, genealogical analysis shows that the concept of liberty is an "invention of the ruling classes"[13] and not fundamental to man's nature or at the root of his attachment to being and truth. What is found at the historical beginning of things is not the inviolable identity of their origin; it is the dissension of other things. It is disparity.[14]

10. In the main body of *The Genealogy*, *Ursprung* and *Herkunpt* are used interchangeably in numerous instances (I, 2; II, 8, 11, 12, 16, 17).

11. *The Dawn*, 123.

12. *Human, All Too Human*, 34.

13. *The Wanderer and His Shadow*, 9.

14. A wide range of key terms, found in *The Archaeology of Knowledge*, are related to this theme of "disparity": the concepts of series, discontinuity, division, and difference. If the *same* is found in

History also teaches how to laugh at the solemnities of the origin. The lofty origin is no more than "a metaphysical extension which arises from the belief that things are most precious and essential at the moment of birth."[15] We tend to think that this is the moment of their greatest perfection, when they emerged dazzling from the hands of a creator or in the shadowless light of a first morning. The origin always precedes the Fall. It comes before the body, before the world and time; it is associated with the gods, and its story is always sung as a theogony. But historical beginnings are lowly: not in the sense of modest or discreet like the steps of a dove, but derisive and ironic, capable of undoing every infatuation. "We wished to awaken the feeling of man's sovereignty by showing his divine birth: this path is now forbidden, since a monkey stands at the entrance."[16] Man originated with a grimace over his future development; and Zarathustra himself is plagued by a monkey who jumps along behind him, pulling on his coattails.

The final postulate of the origin is linked to the first two in being the site of truth. From the vantage point of an absolute distance, free from the restraints of positive knowledge, the origin makes possible a field of knowledge whose function is to recover it, but always in a false recognition due to the excesses of its own speech. The origin lies at a place of inevitable loss, the point where the truth of things corresponded to a truthful discourse, the site of a fleeting articulation that discourse has obscured and finally lost. It is a new cruelty of history that compels a reversal of this relationship and the abandonment of "adolescent" quests: behind the always recent, avaricious, and measured truth, it posits the ancient proliferation of errors. It is now impossible to believe that "in the rending of the veil, truth

---

the realm and movement of dialectics, the *disparate* presents itself as an "event" in the world of chance. For a more detailed discussion, see below, "Theatrum Philosophicum," pp. 180, 193–196—ED.

15. *The Wanderer and His Shadow*, 3.
16. *The Dawn*, 49.

remains truthful; we have lived long enough not to be taken in."[17] Truth is undoubtedly the sort of error that cannot be refuted because it was hardened into an unalterable form in the long baking process of history.[18] Moreover, the very question of truth, the right it appropriates to refute error and oppose itself to appearance,[19] the manner in which it developed (initially made available to the wise, then withdrawn by men of piety to an unattainable world where it was given the double role of consolation and imperative, finally rejected as a useless notion, superfluous, and contradicted on all sides)—does this not form a history, the history of an error we call truth? Truth, and its original reign, has had a history within history from which we are barely emerging "in the time of the shortest shadow," when light no longer seems to flow from the depths of the sky or to arise from the first moments of the day.[20]

A genealogy of values, morality, asceticism, and knowledge will never confuse itself with a quest for their "origins," will never neglect as inaccessible the vicissitudes of history. On the contrary, it will cultivate the details and accidents that accompany every beginning; it will be scrupulously attentive to their petty malice; it will await their emergence, once unmasked, as the face of the other. Wherever it is made to go, it will not be reticent—in "excavating the depths," in allowing time for these elements to escape from a labyrinth where no truth had ever detained them. The genealogist needs history to dispel the chimeras of the origin, somewhat in the manner of the pious philosopher who needs a doctor to exorcise the shadow of his soul. He must be able to recognize the events of history, its jolts, its surprises, its unsteady victories and unpalatable defeats—

17. *Nietzsche contra Wagner*, p. 99.
18. *The Gay Science*, 265 and 110.
19. See "Theatrum Philosophicum" below, pp. 167–168, for a discussion of the development of truth; and also "History of Systems of Thought: Summary of a Course at the Collège de France—1970–1971," pp. 202–204—ED.
20. *Twilight of the Idols*, "How the world of truth becomes a fable."

the basis of all beginnings, atavisms, and heredities. Similarly, he must be able to diagnose the illnesses of the body, its conditions of weakness and strength, its breakdown and resistances, to be in a position to judge philosophical discourse. History is the concrete body of a development, with its moments of intensity, its lapses, its extended periods of feverish agitation, its fainting spells; and only a metaphysician would seek its soul in the distant ideality of the origin.

3. *Entstehung* and *Herkunft* are more exact than *Ursprung* in recording the true objective of genealogy; and, while they are ordinarily translated as "origin," we must attempt to reestablish their proper use.

Herkunft is the equivalent of stock or *descent;* it is the ancient affiliation to a group, sustained by the bonds of blood, tradition, or social class. The analysis of *Herkunft* often involves a consideration of race[21] or social type.[22] But the traits it attempts to identify are not the exclusive generic characteristics of an individual, a sentiment, or an idea, which permit us to qualify them as "Greek" or "English"; rather, it seeks the subtle, singular, and subindividual marks that might possibly intersect in them to form a network that is difficult to unravel. Far from being a category of resemblance, this origin allows the sorting out of different traits: the Germans imagined that they had finally accounted for their complexity by saying they possessed a double soul; they were fooled by a simple computation, or rather, they were simply trying to master the racial disorder from which they had formed themselves.[23] Where the soul pretends unification or the self fabricates a coherent identity, the genealogist sets out to study the beginning—numberless beginnings whose faint traces and hints of color are readily seen by an historical eye. The analysis of descent permits the dissociation of the self, its recognition

21. For example, *The Gay Science,* 135; *Beyond Good and Evil,* 200, 242, 244; *The Genealogy,* I, 5.
22. *The Gay Science,* 348–349; *Beyond Good and Evil,* 260.
23. *Beyond Good and Evil,* 244.

and displacement as an empty synthesis, in liberating a profusion of lost events.[24]

An examination of descent also permits the discovery, under the unique aspect of a trait or a concept, of the myriad events through which—thanks to which, against which—they were formed. Genealogy does not pretend to go back in time to restore an unbroken continuity that operates beyond the dispersion of forgotten things; its duty is not to demonstrate that the past actively exists in the present, that it continues secretly to animate the present, having imposed a predetermined form to all its vicissitudes. Genealogy does not resemble the evolution of a species and does not map the destiny of a people. On the contrary, to follow the complex course of descent is to maintain passing events in their proper dispersion; it is to identify the accidents, the minute deviations—or conversely, the complete reversals—the errors, the false appraisals, and the faulty calculations that gave birth to those things that continue to exist and have value for us; it is to discover that truth or being do not lie at the root of what we know and what we are, but the exteriority of accidents.[25] This is undoubtedly why every origin of morality from the moment it stops being pious—and *Herkunft* can never be—has value as a critique.[26]

Deriving from such a source is a dangerous legacy. In numerous instances, Nietzsche associates the terms *Herkunft* and *Erbschaft*. Nevertheless, we should not be deceived into thinking that this heritage is an acquisition, a possession that grows and solidifies; rather, it is an unstable assemblage of faults, fissures, and heterogeneous layers that threaten the fragile inheritor from within or from underneath: "injustice or instability in the minds of certain men, their disorder and lack of decorum, are the final consequences of their ancestors' numberless logical inaccuracies,

24. See below, "Theatrum Philosophicum," pp. 172–176—Ed.
25. *The Genealogy*, III, 17. The *abkunft* of feelings of depression.
26. *Twilight*, "Reasons for philosophy."

hasty conclusions, and superficiality."[27] The search for descent is not the erecting of foundations: on the contrary, it disturbs what was previously considered immobile; it fragments what was thought unified; it shows the heterogeneity of what was imagined consistent with itself. What convictions and, far more decisively, what knowledge can resist it? If a genealogical analysis of a scholar were made—of one who collects facts and carefully accounts for them—his *Herkunft* would quickly divulge the official papers of the scribe and the pleadings of the lawyer—their father[28]—in their apparently disinterested attention, in the "pure" devotion to objectivity.

Finally, descent attaches itself to the body.[29] It inscribes itself in the nervous system, in temperament, in the digestive apparatus; it appears in faulty respiration, in improper diets, in the debilitated and prostrate body of those whose ancestors committed errors. Fathers have only to mistake effects for causes, believe in the reality of an "afterlife," or maintain the value of eternal truths, and the bodies of their children will suffer. Cowardice and hypocrisy, for their part, are the simple offshoots of error: not in a Socratic sense, not that evil is the result of a mistake, not because of a turning away from an original truth, but because the body maintains, in life as in death, through its strength or weakness, the sanction of every truth and error, as it sustains, in an inverse manner, the origin—descent. Why did men invent the contemplative life? Why give a supreme value to this form of existence? Why maintain the absolute truth of those fictions which sustain it? "During barbarous ages . . . if the strength of an individual declined, if he felt himself tired or sick, melancholy or satiated and, as a consequence, without desire or appetite for a short time, he became relatively a better man, that is, less dangerous. His pessimistic ideas could only take form as words

27. *The Dawn*, 247.
28. *The Gay Science*, 348–349.
29. Ibid., 200.

or reflections. In this frame of mind, he either became a thinker and prophet or used his imagination to feed his superstitions."[30] The body—and everything that touches it: diet, climate, and soil—is the domain of the *Herkunft*. The body manifests the stigmata of past experience and also gives rise to desires, failings, and errors. These elements may join in a body where they achieve a sudden expression, but as often, their encounter is an engagement in which they efface each other, where the body becomes the pretext of their insurmountable conflict.

The body is the inscribed surface of events (traced by language and dissolved by ideas), the locus of a dissociated Self (adopting the illusion of a substantial unity), and a volume in perpetual disintegration. Genealogy, as an analysis of descent, is thus situated within the articulation of the body and history. Its task is to expose a body totally imprinted by history and the process of history's destruction of the body.

4. *Entstehung* designates *emergence*, the moment of arising. It stands as the principle and the singular law of an apparition. As it is wrong to search for descent in an uninterrupted continuity, we should avoid thinking of emergence as the final term of an historical development; the eye was not always intended for contemplation, and punishment has had other purposes than setting an example. These developments may appear as a culmination, but they are merely the current episodes in a series of subjugations: the eye initially responded to the requirements of hunting and warfare; and punishment has been subjected, throughout its history, to a variety of needs—revenge, excluding an aggressor, compensating a victim, creating fear. In placing present needs at the origin, the metaphysician would convince us of an obscure purpose that seeks its realization at the moment it arises. Genealogy, however, seeks to reestablish the various systems of subjection: not the anticipatory power of meaning, but the hazardous play of dominations.

Emergence is always produced through a particular stage of

30. *The Dawn*, 42.

forces. The analysis of the *Entstehung* must delineate this inter-action, the struggle these forces wage against each other or against adverse circumstances, and the attempt to avoid degener-ation and regain strength by dividing these forces against them-selves. It is in this sense that the emergence of a species (animal or human) and its solidification are secured "in an extended battle against conditions which are essentially and constantly unfavorable." In fact, "the species must realize itself as a species, as something—characterized by the durability, uniformity, and simplicity of its form—which can prevail in the perpetual strug-gle against outsiders or the uprising of those it oppresses from within." On the other hand, individual differences emerge at another stage of the relationship of forces, when the species has become victorious and when it is no longer threatened from outside. In this condition, we find a struggle "of egoisms turned against each other, each bursting forth in a splintering of forces and a general striving for the sun and for the light."[31] There are also times when force contends against itself, and not only in the intoxication of an abundance, which allows it to divide itself, but at the moment when it weakens. Force reacts against its growing lassitude and gains strength; it imposes limits, inflicts torments and mortifications; it masks these actions as a higher morality, and, in exchange, regains its strength. In this manner, the ascetic ideal was born, "in the instinct of a decadent life which . . . struggles for its own existence."[32] This also describes the movement in which the Reformation arose, precisely where the church was least corrupt;[33] German Catholicism, in the six-teenth century, retained enough strength to turn against itself, to mortify its own body and history, and to spiritualize itself into a pure religion of conscience.

Emergence is thus the entry of forces; it is their eruption, the

31. *Beyond Good and Evil*, 262.
32. *The Genealogy*, III, 13.
33. *The Gay Science*, 148. It is also to an anemia of the will that one must attribute the *Entstehung* of Buddhism and Christianity, 347.

leap from the wings to center stage, each in its youthful strength. What Nietzsche calls the *Entstehungsherd*[34] of the concept of goodness is not specifically the energy of the strong or the reaction of the weak, but precisely this scene where they are displayed superimposed or face-to-face. It is nothing but the space that divides them, the void through which they exchange their threatening gestures and speeches. As descent qualifies the strength or weakness of an instinct and its inscription on a body, emergence designates a place of confrontation but not as a closed field offering the spectacle of a struggle among equals. Rather, as Nietzsche demonstrates in his analysis of good and evil, it is a "non-place," a pure distance, which indicates that the adversaries do not belong to a common space. Consequently, no one is responsible for an emergence; no one can glory in it, since it always occurs in the interstice.

In a sense, only a single drama is ever staged in this "non-place," the endlessly repeated play of dominations. The domination of certain men over others leads to the differentiation of values;[35] class domination generates the idea of liberty;[36] and the forceful appropriation of things necessary to survival and the imposition of a duration not intrinsic to them account for the origin of logic.[37] This relationship of domination is no more a "relationship" than the place where it occurs is a place; and, precisely for this reason, it is fixed, throughout its history, in rituals, in meticulous procedures that impose rights and obligations. It establishes marks of its power and engraves memories on things and even within bodies. It makes itself accountable for debts and gives rise to the universe of rules, which is by no means designed to temper violence, but rather to satisfy it. Following traditional beliefs, it would be false to think that total war exhausts itself in its own contradictions and ends by re-

34. *The Genealogy*, I, 2.
35. *Beyond Good and Evil*, 260; cf. also *The Genealogy*, II, 12.
36. *The Wanderer*, 9.
37. *The Gay Science*, 111.

nouncing violence and submitting to civil laws. On the contrary, the law is a calculated and relentless pleasure, delight in the promised blood, which permits the perpetual instigation of new dominations and the staging of meticulously repeated scenes of violence. The desire for peace, the serenity of compromise, and the tacit acceptance of the law, far from representing a major moral conversion or a utilitarian calculation that gave rise to the law, are but its result and, in point of fact, its perversion: "guilt, conscience, and duty had their threshold of emergence in the right to secure obligations; and their inception, like that of any major event on earth, was saturated in blood."[38] Humanity does not gradually progress from combat to combat until it arrives at universal reciprocity, where the rule of law finally replaces warfare; humanity installs each of its violences in a system of rules and thus proceeds from domination to domination.

The nature of these rules allows violence to be inflicted on violence and the resurgence of new forces that are sufficiently strong to dominate those in power. Rules are empty in themselves, violent and unfinalized; they are impersonal and can be bent to any purpose. The successes of history belong to those who are capable of seizing these rules, to replace those who had used them, to disguise themselves so as to pervert them, invert their meaning, and redirect them against those who had initially imposed them; controlling this complex mechanism, they will make it function so as to overcome the rulers through their own rules.

The isolation of different points of emergence does not conform to the successive configurations of an identical meaning; rather, they result from substitutions, displacements, disguised conquests, and systematic reversals. If interpretation were the slow exposure of the meaning hidden in an origin, then only metaphysics could interpret the development of humanity. But if interpretation is the violent or surreptitious appropriation of a system of rules, which in itself has no essential meaning, in

38. *The Genealogy*, II, 6.

order to impose a direction, to bend it to a new will, to force its participation in a different game, and to subject it to secondary rules, then the development of humanity is a series of interpretations. The role of genealogy is to record its history: the history of morals, ideals, and metaphysical concepts, the history of the concept of liberty or of the ascetic life; as they stand for the emergence of different interpretations, they must be made to appear as events on the stage of historical process.

5. How can we define the relationship between genealogy, seen as the examination of *Herkunft* and *Entstehung,* and history in the traditional sense? We could, of course, examine Nietzsche's celebrated apostrophes against history, but we will put these aside for the moment and consider those instances when he conceives of genealogy as "wirkliche Historie," or its more frequent characterization as historical "spirit" or "sense."[39] In fact, Nietzsche's criticism, beginning with the second of the *Untimely Meditations,* always questioned the form of history that reintroduces (and always assumes) a suprahistorical perspective: a history whose function is to compose the finally reduced diversity of time into a totality fully closed upon itself; a history that always encourages subjective recognitions and attributes a form of reconciliation to all the displacements of the past; a history whose perspective on all that precedes it implies the end of time, a completed development. The historian's history finds its support outside of time and pretends to base its judgments on an apocalyptic objectivity. This is only possible, however, because of its belief in eternal truth, the immortality of the soul, and the nature of consciousness as always identical to itself. Once the historical sense is mastered by a suprahistorical perspective, metaphysics can bend it to its own purpose and, by aligning it to the demands of objective science, it can impose its own "Egyptianism." On the other hand, the historical sense can evade metaphysics and become a privileged instrument of

39. *The Genealogy,* Preface, 7; and I, 2. *Beyond Good and Evil,* 224.

genealogy if it refuses the certainty of absolutes. Given this, it corresponds to the acuity of a glance that distinguishes, separates, and disperses, that is capable of liberating divergence and marginal elements—the kind of dissociating view that is capable of decomposing itself, capable of shattering the unity of man's being through which it was thought that he could extend his sovereignty to the events of his past.

Historical meaning becomes a dimension of "wirkliche Historie" to the extent that it places within a process of development everything considered immortal in man. We believe that feelings are immutable, but every sentiment, particularly the noblest and most disinterested, has a history. We believe in the dull constancy of instinctual life and imagine that it continues to exert its force indiscriminately in the present as it did in the past. But a knowledge of history easily disintegrates this unity, depicts its wavering course, locates its moments of strength and weakness, and defines its oscillating reign. It easily seizes the slow elaboration of instincts and those movements where, in turning upon themselves, they relentlessly set about their self-destruction.[40] We believe, in any event, that the body obeys the exclusive laws of physiology and that it escapes the influence of history, but this too is false. The body is molded by a great many distinct regimes; it is broken down by the rhythms of work, rest, and holidays; it is poisoned by food or values, through eating habits or moral laws; it constructs resistances.[41] "Effective" history differs from traditional history in being without constants. Nothing in man—not even his body—is sufficiently stable to serve as the basis for self-recognition or for understanding other men. The traditional devices for constructing a comprehensive view of history and for retracing the past as a patient and continuous development must be systematically dismantled. Necessarily, we must dismiss those tendencies that encourage the consoling play of recognitions. Knowledge, even under the banner of history,

40. *The Gay Science*, 7.
41. Ibid.

does not depend on "rediscovery," and it emphatically excludes the "rediscovery of ourselves."[42] History becomes "effective" to the degree that it introduces discontinuity into our very being— as it divides our emotions, dramatizes our instincts, multiplies our body and sets it against itself. "Effective" history deprives the self of the reassuring stability of life and nature, and it will not permit itself to be transported by a voiceless obstinacy toward a millenial ending. It will uproot its traditional foundations and relentlessly disrupt its pretended continuity. This is because knowledge is not made for understanding; it is made for cutting.[43]

From these observations, we can grasp the particular traits of historical meaning as Nietzsche understood it—the sense which opposes "wirkliche Historie" to traditional history. The former transposes the relationship ordinarily established between the eruption of an event and necessary continuity. An entire historical tradition (theological or rationalistic) aims at dissolving the singular event into an ideal continuity—as a teleological movement or a natural process. "Effective" history, however, deals with events in terms of their most unique characteristics, their most acute manifestations. An event, consequently, is not a decision, a treaty, a reign, or a battle, but the reversal of a relationship of forces, the usurpation of power, the appropriation of a vocabulary turned against those who had once used it, a feeble domination that poisons itself as it grows lax, the entry of a masked "other." The forces operating in history are not controlled by destiny or regulative mechanisms, but respond to haphazard conflicts.[44] They do not manifest the successive forms of a primordial intention and their attraction is not that of a conclusion, for they always appear through the singular random-

42. See "What Is an Author?" above, p. 134, on rediscoveries— ED.
43. This statement is echoed in Foucault's discussion of "differentiations" in *The Archaeology of Knowledge*, pp. 130–131, 206; or the use of the word "division" above in "A Preface to Transgression," p. 36—ED.
44. *The Genealogy*, II, 12.

ness of events. The inverse of the Christian world, spun entirely by a divine spider, and different from the world of the Greeks, divided between the realm of will and the great cosmic folly, the world of effective history knows only one kingdom, without providence or final cause, where there is only "the iron hand of necessity shaking the dice-box of chance."[45] Chance is not simply the drawing of lots, but raising the stakes in every attempt to master chance through the will to power, and giving rise to the risk of an even greater chance.[46] The world we know is not this ultimately simple configuration where events are reduced to accentuate their essential traits, their final meaning, or their initial and final value. On the contrary, it is a profusion of entangled events. If it appears as a "marvelous motley, profound and totally meaningful," this is because it began and continues its secret existence through a "host of errors and phantasms."[47] We want historians to confirm our belief that the present rests upon profound intentions and immutable necessities. But the true historical sense confirms our existence among countless lost events, without a landmark or a point of reference.

Effective history can also invert the relationship that traditional history, in its dependence on metaphysics, establishes between proximity and distance. The latter is given to a contemplation of distances and heights: the noblest periods, the highest forms, the most abstract ideas, the purest individualities. It accomplishes this by getting as near as possible, placing itself at the foot of its mountain peaks, at the risk of adopting the famous perspective of frogs. Effective history, on the other hand, shortens its vision to those things nearest to it—the body, the nervous system, nutrition, digestion, and energies; it unearths the periods of decadence and if it chances upon lofty epochs, it is with the suspicion—not vindictive but joyous—of finding a barbarous and shameful confusion. It has no fear of looking down, so long as it

45. *The Dawn*, 130.
46. *The Genealogy*, II, 12.
47. *Human, All Too Human*, 16.

is understood that it looks from above and descends to seize the various perspectives, to disclose dispersions and differences, to leave things undisturbed in their own dimension and intensity.[48] It reverses the surreptitious practice of historians, their pretension to examine things furthest from themselves, the grovelling manner in which they approach this promising distance (like the metaphysicians who proclaim the existence of an afterlife, situated at a distance from this world, as a promise of their reward). Effective history studies what is closest, but in an abrupt dispossession, so as to seize it at a distance (an approach similar to that of a doctor who looks closely, who plunges to make a diagnosis and to state its difference). Historical sense has more in common with medicine than philosophy; and it should not surprise us that Nietzsche occasionally employs the phrase "historically and physiologically,"[49] since among the philosopher's idiosyncracies is a complete denial of the body. This includes, as well, "the absence of historical sense, a hatred for the idea of development, Egyptianism," the obstinate "placing of conclusions at the beginning," of "making last things first."[50] History has a more important task than to be a handmaiden to philosophy, to recount the necessary birth of truth and values; it should become a differential knowledge of energies and failings, heights and degenerations, poisons and antidotes. Its task is to become a curative science.[51]

The final trait of effective history is its affirmation of knowledge as perspective. Historians take unusual pains to erase the elements in their work which reveal their grounding in a particular time and place, their preferences in a controversy—the un-

48. See "Theatrum Philosophicum" below, p. 183, for an analysis of Deleuze's thought as intensity of difference—ED.
49. *Twilight*, 44.
50. *Twilight*, "Reason within philosophy," 1 and 4.
51. *The Wanderer*, 188. (This conception underlies the task of *Madness and Civilization* and *The Birth of the Clinic* even though it is not found as a conscious formulation until *The Archaeology of Knowledge;* for a discussion of archaeology as "diagnosis," see especially p. 131—ED.)

avoidable obstacles of their passion. Nietzsche's version of historical sense is explicit in its perspective and acknowledges its system of injustice. Its perception is slanted, being a deliberate appraisal, affirmation, or negation; it reaches the lingering and poisonous traces in order to prescribe the best antidote. It is not given to a discreet effacement before the objects it observes and does not submit itself to their processes; nor does it seek laws, since it gives equal weight to its own sight and to its objects. Through this historical sense, knowledge is allowed to create its own genealogy in the act of cognition; and "wirkliche Historie" composes a genealogy of history as the vertical projection of its position.

6. In this context, Nietzsche links historical sense to the historian's history. They share a beginning that is similarly impure and confused, share the same sign in which the symptoms of sickness can be recognized as well as the seed of an exquisite flower.[52] They arose simultaneously to follow their separate ways, but our task is to trace their common genealogy.

The descent (*Herkunft*) of the historian is unequivocal: he is of humble birth. A characteristic of history is to be without choice: it encourages thorough understanding and excludes qualitative judgments—a sensitivity to all things without distinction, a comprehensive view excluding differences. Nothing must escape it and, more importantly, nothing must be excluded. Historians argue that this proves their tact and discretion. After all, what right have they to impose their tastes and preferences when they seek to determine what actually occurred in the past? Their mistake is to exhibit a total lack of taste, the kind of crudeness that becomes smug in the presence of the loftiest elements and finds satisfaction in reducing them to size. The historian is insensitive to the most disgusting things; or rather, he especially enjoys those things that should be repugnant to him. His apparent serenity follows from his concerted avoidance of the exceptional and his reduction of all things to the lowest common denominator.

52. *The Gay Science*, 337.

Nothing is allowed to stand above him; and underlying his desire for total knowledge is his search for the secrets that belittle everything: "base curiosity." What is the source of history? It comes from the plebs. To whom is it addressed? To the plebs. And its discourse strongly resembles the demagogue's refrain: "No one is greater than you and anyone who presumes to get the better of you—you who are good—is evil." The historian, who functions as his double, can be heard to echo: "No past is greater than your present, and, through my meticulous erudition, I will rid you of your infatuations and transform the grandeur of history into pettiness, evil, and misfortune." The historian's ancestry goes back to Socrates.

This demagogy, of course, must be masked. It must hide its singular malice under the cloak of universals. As the demagogue is obliged to invoke truth, laws of essences, and eternal necessity, the historian must invoke objectivity, the accuracy of facts, and the permanence of the past. The demagogue denies the body to secure the sovereignty of a timeless idea and the historian effaces his proper individuality so that others may enter the stage and reclaim their own speech.[53] He is divided against himself: forced to silence his preferences and overcome his distaste, to blur his own perspective and replace it with the fiction of a universal geometry, to mimic death in order to enter the kingdom of the dead, to adopt a faceless anonymity. In this world where he has conquered his individual will, he becomes a guide to the inevitable law of a superior will. Having curbed the demands of his individual will in his knowledge, he will disclose the form of an eternal will in his object of study. The objectivity of historians inverts the relationships of will and knowledge and it is, in the same stroke, a necessary belief in Providence, in final causes and teleology—the beliefs that place the historian in the family of ascetics. "I can't stand these lustful eunuchs of history, all the seductions of an ascetic ideal; I can't stand these whited sepulchres producing life or those tired and indifferent beings

53. See below, "Intellectuals and Power," p. 211—ED.

who dress up in the part of wisdom and adopt an objective point of view."[54]

The *Entstehung* of history is found in nineteenth-century Europe: the land of interminglings and bastardy, the period of the "man-of-mixture." We have become barbarians with respect to those rare moments of high civilization: cities in ruin and enigmatic monuments are spread out before us; we stop before gaping walls; we ask what gods inhabited these empty temples. Great epochs lacked this curiosity, lacked our excessive deference; they ignored their predecessors: the classical period ignored Shakespeare. The decadence of Europe presents an immense spectacle (while stronger periods refrained from such exhibitions), and the nature of this scene is to represent a theater; lacking monuments of our own making, which properly belong to us, we live among crowded scenes. But there is more. Europeans no longer know themselves; they ignore their mixed ancestries and seek a proper role. They lack individuality. We can begin to understand the spontaneous historical bent of the nineteenth century: the anemia of its forces and those mixtures that effaced all its individual traits produced the same results as the mortifications of asceticism; its inability to create, its absence of artistic works, and its need to rely on past achievements forced it to adopt the base curiosity of plebs.

If this fully represents the genealogy of history, how could it become, in its own right, a genealogical analysis? Why did it not continue as a form of demagogic or religious knowledge? How could it change roles on the same stage? Only by being seized, dominated, and turned against its birth. And it is this movement which properly describes the specific nature of the *Entstehung:* it is not the unavoidable conclusion of a long preparation, but a scene where forces are risked in the chance of confrontations, where they emerge triumphant, where they can also be confiscated. The locus of emergence for metaphysics was surely Athenian demagogy, the vulgar spite of Socrates and his belief

54. *The Genealogy,* III, 26.

in immortality, and Plato could have seized this Socratic philosophy to turn it against itself. Undoubtedly, he was often tempted to do so, but his defeat lies in its consecration. The problem was similar in the nineteenth century: to avoid doing for the popular asceticism of historians what Plato did for Socrates. This historical trait should not be founded upon a philosophy of history, but dismantled beginning with the things it produced; it is necessary to master history so as to turn it to genealogical uses, that is, strictly anti-Platonic purposes. Only then will the historical sense free itself from the demands of a suprahistorical history.

7. The historical sense gives rise to three uses that oppose and correspond to the three Platonic modalities of history. The first is parodic, directed against reality, and opposes the theme of history as reminiscence or recognition; the second is dissociative, directed against identity, and opposes history given as continuity or representative of a tradition; the third is sacrificial, directed against truth, and opposes history as knowledge. They imply a use of history that severs its connection to memory, its metaphysical and anthropological model, and constructs a counter-memory—a transformation of history into a totally different form of time.

First, the parodic and farcical use. The historian offers this confused and anonymous European, who no longer knows himself or what name he should adopt, the possibility of alternate identities, more individualized and substantial than his own. But the man with historical sense will see that this substitution is simply a disguise. Historians supplied the Revolution with Roman prototypes, romanticism with knight's armor, and the Wagnerian era was given the sword of a German hero—ephemeral props that point to our own unreality. No one kept them from venerating these religions, from going to Bayreuth to commemorate a new afterlife; they were free, as well, to be transformed into street-vendors of empty identities. The new historian, the genealogist, will know what to make of this masquerade. He will not be too serious to enjoy it; on the contrary, he will push the masquerade to its limit and prepare the great carnival of time where masks are constantly reappearing. No longer the identification of our faint individuality with the solid identities of the past, but our "unrealization" through the excessive choice of identities—Frederick of Hohenstaufen, Caesar, Jesus, Dionysus, and possibly Zarathustra. Taking up these masks, revitalizing the buffoonery of history, we adopt an identity whose unreality surpasses that of God who started the charade. "Perhaps, we can discover a realm where originality is again possible as parodists of history and buffoons of God."[55] In this, we recognize the parodic double of what the second of the *Untimely Meditations* called "monumental history": a history given to reestablishing the high points of historical development and their maintenance in a perpetual presence, given to the recovery of works, actions, and creations through the monogram of their personal essence. But in 1874, Nietzsche accused this history, one totally devoted to veneration, of barring access to the actual intensities and creations of life. The parody of his last texts serves to emphasize that "monumental history" is itself a parody. Genealogy is history in the form of a concerted carnival.

The second use of history is the systematic dissociation of identity. This is necessary because this rather weak identity, which we attempt to support and to unify under a mask, is in itself only a parody: it is plural; countless spirits dispute its possession; numerous systems intersect and compete. The study of history makes one "happy, unlike the metaphysicians, to possess in oneself not an immortal soul but many mortal ones."[56] And in each of these souls, history will not discover a forgotten identity, eager to be reborn, but a complex system of distinct and multiple elements, unable to be mastered by the powers of synthesis: "it is a sign of superior culture to maintain, in a fully conscious way, certain phases of its evolution which lesser men pass through without thought. The initial result is that we can understand those who resemble us as completely determined systems and

55. *Beyond Good and Evil*, 223.
56. *The Wanderer* (Opinions and Mixed Statements), 17.

as representative of diverse cultures, that is to say, as necessary and capable of modification. And in return, we are able to separate the phases of our own evolution and consider them individually."[57] The purpose of history, guided by genealogy, is not to discover the roots of our identity but to commit itself to its dissipation. It does not seek to define our unique threshold of emergence, the homeland to which metaphysicians promise a return; it seeks to make visible all of those discontinuities that cross us. "Antiquarian history," according to the *Untimely Meditations*, pursues opposite goals. It seeks the continuities of soil, language, and urban life in which our present is rooted and, "by cultivating in a delicate manner that which existed for all time, it tries to conserve for posterity the conditions under which we were born."[58] This type of history was objected to in the *Meditations* because it tended to block creativity in support of the laws of fidelity. Somewhat later—and already in *Human, All Too Human*—Nietzsche reconsiders the task of the antiquarian, but with an altogether different emphasis. If genealogy in its own right gives rise to questions concerning our native land, native language, or the laws that govern us, its intention is to reveal the heterogenous systems which, masked by the self, inhibit the formation of any form of identity.

The third use of history is the sacrifice of the subject of knowledge. In appearance, or rather, according to the mask it bears, historical consciousness is neutral, devoid of passions, and committed solely to truth. But if it examines itself and if, more generally, it interrogates the various forms of scientific consciousness in its history, it finds that all these forms and transformations are aspects of the will to knowledge: instinct, passion, the inquisitor's devotion, cruel subtlety, and malice. It discovers the violence of a position that sides against those who are happy in their ignorance, against the effective illusions by which humanity protects itself, a position that encourages the dangers of

57. *Human, All Too Human*, 274.
58. *Untimely Meditations*, II, 3.

reserach and delights in disturbing discoveries.[59] The historical analysis of this rancorous will to knowledge[60] reveals that all knowledge rests upon injustice (that there is no right, not even in the act of knowing, to truth or a foundation for truth) and that the instinct for knowledge is malicious (something murderous, opposed to the happiness of mankind). Even in the greatly expanded form it assumes today, the will to knowledge does not achieve a universal truth; man is not given an exact and serene mastery of nature. On the contrary, it ceaselessly multiplies the risks, creates dangers in every area; it breaks down illusory defences; it dissolves the unity of the subject; it releases those elements of itself that are devoted to its subversion and destruction. Knowledge does not slowly detach itself from its empirical roots, the initial needs from which it arose, to become pure speculation subject only to the demands of reason; its development is not tied to the constitution and affirmation of a free subject; rather, it creates a progressive enslavement to its instinctive violence. Where religions once demanded the sacrifice of bodies, knowledge now calls for experimentation on ourselves,[61] calls us to the sacrifice of the subject of knowledge. "The desire for knowledge has been transformed among us into a passion which fears no sacrifice, which fears nothing but its own extinction. It may be that mankind will eventually perish from this passion for knowledge. If not through passion, then through weakness. We must be prepared to state our choice: do we wish humanity to end in fire and light or to end on the sands?"[62] We should now replace the two great problems of nineteenth-century philosophy, passed on by Fichte and Hegel (the reciprocal basis of truth and liberty and the possibility of absolute knowledge), with the theme that "to perish through absolute knowledge may well form a

59. Cf. *The Dawn*, 429 and 432; *The Gay Science*, 333; *Beyond Good and Evil*, 229–230.
60. "Vouloir-savoir": the phrase in French means both the will to knowledge and knowledge as revenge—ED.
61. *The Dawn*, 501.
62. Ibid., 429.

part of the basis of being."[63] This does not mean, in terms of a critical procedure, that the will to truth is limited by the intrinsic finitude of cognition, but that it loses all sense of limitations and all claim to truth in its unavoidable sacrifice of the subject of knowledge. "It may be that there remains one prodigious idea which might be made to prevail over every other aspiration, which might overcome the most victorious: the idea of humanity sacrificing itself. It seems indisputable that if this new constellation appeared on the horizon, only the desire for truth, with its enormous prerogatives, could direct and sustain such a sacrifice. For to knowledge, no sacrifice is too great. Of course, this problem has never been posed."[64]

The *Untimely Meditations* discussed the critical use of history: its just treatment of the past, its decisive cutting of the roots, its rejection of traditional attitudes of reverence, its liberation of man by presenting him with other origins than those in which he prefers to see himself. Nietzsche, however, reproached critical history for detaching us from every real source and for sacrificing the very movement of life to the exclusive concern for truth. Somewhat later, as we have seen, Nietzsche reconsiders this line of thought he had at first refused, but directs it to altogether different ends. It is no longer a question of judging the past in the name of a truth that only we can possess in the present; but risking the destruction of the subject who seeks knowledge in the endless deployment of the will to knowledge.

In a sense, genealogy returns to the three modalities of history that Nietzsche recognized in 1874. It returns to them in spite of the objections that Nietzsche raised in the name of the affirmative and creative powers of life. But they are metamorphosized; the veneration of monuments becomes parody; the respect for ancient continuities becomes systematic dissociation; the critique of the injustices of the past by a truth held by men in the present becomes the destruction of the man who maintains knowledge by the injustice proper to the will to knowledge.

63. *Beyond Good and Evil,* 39.
64. *The Dawn,* 45.

Theatrum Philosophicum

I must discuss two books of exceptional merit and importance: *Différence et répétition* and *Logique du sens*. Indeed, these books are so outstanding that they are difficult to discuss; this may explain, as well, why so few have undertaken this task. I believe that these works will continue to revolve about us in enigmatic resonance with those of Klossowski, another major and excessive sign,[1] and perhaps one day, this century will be known as Deleuzian.

One after another, I should like to explore the many paths which lead to the heart of these challenging texts. As Deleuze would say, however, this metaphor is misleading: there is no heart, but only a problem—that is, a distribution of notable points; there is no center, but always decenterings, series that register the halting passage from presence to absence, from excess to deficiency.[2] The circle must be abandoned as a faulty principle

This essay originally appeared in *Critique*, No. 282 (1970), pp. 885–908. It is a review of two books by Gilles Deleuze: *Différence et répétition* (Paris: P.U.F., 1969) and *Logique du sens* (Paris: Editions de Minuit, 1969). Neither of Deleuze's books have been translated into English, but this essay has been included here because of its importance in defining the nature of Foucault's *theater* and the kind of thought which has sustained his archaeological method from his earliest works. The essay is reprinted here by permission of *Critique*.

1. Foucault's essay on Klossowski, "La Prose d'Actéon," appeared in *Nouvelle Revue Française*, No. 135 (1964); for Deleuze's analysis of Klossowski, see *Logique du sens*, pp. 325–350—ED.

2. The concepts of series, sequence, and succession are explored throughout *The Archaeology of Knowledge*; on decenterings, see especially pp. 12–14—ED.

of return; we must abandon our tendency to organize everything into a sphere. All things return on the straight and narrow, by way of a straight and labyrinthine line. Thus, fibrils and bifurcation (Leiris' marvellous series would be well suited to a Deleuzian analysis).

What philosophy has not tried to overturn Platonism? If we defined philosophy at the limit as any attempt, regardless of its source, to reverse Platonism, then philosophy begins with Aristotle; or better yet, it begins with Plato himself, with the conclusion of the *Sophist* where it is impossible to distinguish Socrates from the crafty imitators; or it begins with the Sophists who were extremely vocal about the rise of Platonism and who ridiculed its future greatness with their perpetual play on words.

Are all philosophies individual species of the genus "anti-Platonic?" Does each begin with a declaration of this fundamental rejection? Can they be grouped around this desired and detestable center? Rather, the philosophical nature of a discourse is its Platonic differential, an element absent in Platonism but present in other philosophies. A better formulation would be: it is an element in which the effect of absence is induced in the Platonic series through a new and divergent series (consequently, its function in the Platonic series is that of a signifier that is both excessive and absent); and it is also an element in which the Platonic series produces a free, floating, and excessive circulation in that other discourse. Plato, then, is the excessive and deficient father. It is useless to define a philosophy by its anti-Platonic character (as a plant is distinguished by its reproductive organs); but a philosophy can be distinguished somewhat in the manner in which a phantasm is defined, by the effect of a lack when it is distributed into its two constituent series—the "archaic" and the "real";[3] and you will dream of a general history of philosophy, a Platonic phantasmatology, and not an architecture of systems.

3. See *Différence et répétition*, pp. 162–163—ED.

In any event, Deleuze's "reversed Platonism"[4] consists of displacing himself within the Platonic series in order to disclose an unexpected facet: division. Plato did not establish a weak separation between the genus "hunter," "cook," or "politician," as the Aristotelians said; neither was he concerned with the particular characteristics of the species "fisherman" or "one who hunts with snares";[5] he wished to discover the identity of the true hunter. *Who is?* and not *What is?* He searched for the authentic, the pure gold. Instead of subdividing, selecting, and pursuing a productive seam, he chose among the pretenders and ignored their fixed cadastral properties; he tested them with the strung bow which eliminates all but one (the nameless one, the nomad). But how does one distinguish the false (the simulators, the "so-called") from the authentic (the unadulterated and pure)? Certainly not by discovering a law of the true and false (truth is not opposed to error but to false appearances), but by looking beyond these manifestations to a model, a model so pure that the actual purity of the "pure" resembles it, approximates it, and measures itself against it; a model that exists so forcefully that in its presence the sham vanity of the false copy is immediately reduced to nonexistence. With the abrupt appearance of Ulysses, the eternal husband, the false suitors disappear. *Exeunt simulacra.*

Plato is said to have opposed essence to appearance, a higher world to this terrestrial world, the sun of truth to the shadows of the cave (and it becomes our duty to bring essences back into the world, to glorify the world, and to place the sun of truth within man). But Deleuze locates Plato's singularity in the delicate sorting operation which precedes the discovery of essence, because it necessitates the world of essences in its separation of false simulacra from the multitude of appearances. Thus, it is useless to attempt the reversal of Platonism by reinstating the

4. *Différence et répétition*, pp. 165–168 and 82–85; *Logique du sens*, pp. 292–300.
5. See the *Sophist*, 220–221—Ed.

rights of appearances, ascribing to them solidity and meaning, and bringing them closer to essential forms by lending them a conceptual backbone: these timid creatures should not be encouraged to stand upright. Neither should we attempt to rediscover the supreme and solemn gesture which established, in a single stroke, the inaccessible Idea. Rather, we should welcome the cunning assembly that simulates and clamors at the door. And what will enter, submerging appearance and breaking its engagement to essence, will be the event; the incorporeal will dissipate the density of matter; a timeless insistence will destroy the circle that imitates eternity; an impenetrable singularity will divest itself of its contamination by purity; the actual semblance of the simulacrum will support the falseness of false appearances. The sophist springs up, and challenges Socrates to prove that he is not the illegitimate usurper.

To reverse Platonism with Deleuze is to displace oneself insidiously within it, to descend a notch, to descend to its smallest gestures—discrete, but *moral*—which serve to exclude the simulacrum; it is also to deviate slightly from it, to encourage from either side the small talk it excluded; it is to initiate another disconnected and divergent series; it is to construct, by way of this small lateral leap, a dethroned para-Platonism. To convert Platonism (a serious task) is to increase its compassion for reality, for the world, and for time. To subvert Platonism is to begin at the top (the vertical distance of irony) and to grasp its origin. To pervert Platonism is to search out the smallest details, to descend (with the natural gravitation of humor) as far as its crop of hair or the dirt under its fingernails—those things that were never hallowed by an idea; it is to discover its initial decentering in order to recenter itself around the Model, the Identical, and the Same; it is the decentering of oneself with respect to Platonism so as to give rise to the play (as with every perversion) of surfaces at its border. Irony rises and subverts; humor falls and perverts.[6] To pervert Plato is to side with the Sophists'

6. On the rising of irony and the plunging of humor, cf. *Différence et répétition*, p. 12, and *Logique du sens*, pp. 159–166.

spitefulness, the rudeness of the Cynics, the arguments of the Stoics, and the fluttering visions of Epicurus. It is time to read Diogenes Laertius.

We should be alert to the surface effects in which the Epicurians take such pleasure:[7] emissions proceeding from deep within bodies and rising like the wisps of a fog—interior phantoms that are quickly reabsorbed into other depths by the sense of smell, by the mouth, by the appetites; extremely thin membranes, which detach themselves from the surfaces of objects and proceed to impose colors and contours deep within our eyes (floating epiderm, visual idols); phantasms created by fear or desire (cloud gods, the adorable face of the beloved, "miserable hope transported by the wind"). It is this expanding domain of intangible objects that must be integrated into our thought: we must articulate a philosophy of the phantasm that cannot be reduced to a primordial fact through the intermediary of perception or an image, but that arises between surfaces, where it assumes meaning, and in the reversal that causes every interior to pass to the outside and every exterior to the inside, in the temporal oscillation that always makes it precede and follow itself—in short, in what Deleuze would perhaps not allow us to call its "incorporeal materiality."

It is useless to seek a more substantial truth behind the phantasm, a truth to which it points as a rather confused sign (thus, the futility of "symptomatologizing"); it is also useless to contain it within stable figures and to construct solid cores of convergence where we might include, on the basis of their identical properties, all its angles, flashes, membranes, and vapors (no possibility of "phenomenalization"). Phantasms must be allowed to function at the limit of bodies; against bodies, because they stick to bodies and protrude from them, but also because they touch them, cut them, break them into sections, regionalize them, and multiply their surfaces; and equally,

7. *Logique du sens,* pp. 307–321.

outside of bodies, because they function between bodies according to laws of proximity, torsion, and variable distance—laws of
which they remain ignorant. Phantasms do not extend organisms
into an imaginary domain; they topologize the materiality of the
body. They should consequently be freed from the restrictions
we impose upon them, freed from the dilemmas of truth and
falsehood and of being and non-being (the essential difference
between simulacrum and copy carried to its logical conclusion);
they must be allowed to conduct their dance, to act out their
mime, as "extra-beings."

Logique du sens can be read as the most alien book imaginable
from *The Phenomenology of Perception*.[8] In this latter text, the
body-organism is linked to the world through a network of
primal significations, which arise from the perception of things,
while, according to Deleuze, phantasms form the impenetrable
and incorporeal surface of bodies; and from this process, simultaneously topological and cruel, something is shaped that falsely
presents itself as a centered organism and that distributes at its
periphery the increasing remoteness of things. More essentially,
however, *Logique du sens* should be read as the boldest and most
insolent of metaphysical treatises—on the basic condition that
instead of denouncing metaphysics as the neglect of being, we
force it to speak of extra-being. Physics: discourse dealing with
the ideal structure of bodies, mixtures, reactions, internal and
external mechanisms; metaphysics: discourse dealing with the
materiality of incorporeal things—phantasms, idols, and simulacra.

Illusion is certainly the source of every difficulty in metaphysics, but not because metaphysics, by its very nature, is
doomed to illusion, but because for the longest time it has been
haunted by illusion and because, in its fear of the simulacrum,
it was forced to hunt down the illusory. Metaphysics is not illusory—it is not merely another species of this particular genus—
but illusion is a metaphysics. It is the product of a particular

8. M. Merleau-Ponty, *The Phenomenology of Perception*, trans.
Colin Smith, (London: Routledge & Kegan Paul, 1962)—Ed.

metaphysics that designated the separation between the simulacrum on one side and the original and perfect copy on the other.
There was a critique whose task was to unearth metaphysical
illusion and to establish its necessity; Deleuze's metaphysics,
however, initiates the necessary critique for the disillusioning of
phantasms. With this grounding, the way is cleared for the
advance of the Epicurean and materialist series, for the pursuit
of their singular zig-zag. And it does not lead, in spite of itself,
to a shameful metaphysics; it leads joyously to metaphysics—a
metaphysics freed from its original profundity as well as from
a supreme being, but also one that can conceive of the phantasm
in its play of surfaces without the aid of models, a metaphysics
where it is no longer a question of the One Good, but of the
absence of God and the epidermic play of perversity. A dead
God and sodomy are the thresholds of the new metaphysical
ellipse. Where natural theology contained metaphysical illusion
in itself and where this illusion was always more or less related
to natural theology, the metaphysics of the phantasm revolves
around atheism and transgression. Sade and Bataille and somewhat later, the palm upturned in a gesture of defense and invita-
tion, Roberte.[9]

Moreover, this series of liberated simulacrum is activated, or
mimes itself, on two privileged stages: that of psychoanalysis,
which should eventually be understood as a metaphysical practice
since it concerns itself with phantasms; and that of the theater,
which is multiplied, polyscenic, simultaneous, broken into separate scenes that refer to each other, and where we encounter,
without any trace of representation (copying or imitating), the
dance of masks, the cries of bodies, and the gesturing of hands
and fingers. And throughout each of these two recent and
divergent series (the attempt to "reconcile" these series, to re-
duce them to either perspective, to produce a ridiculous "psycho-

9. In Klossowski's trilogy, *Les Lois de l'hospitalité* (Paris: Gallimard,
1965). For Deleuze's discussion of Roberte, see *Logique du sens*,
especially pp. 331–332—ED.

drama," has been extremely naive), Freud and Artaud exclude each other and give rise to a mutual resonance. The philosophy of representation—of the original, the first time, resemblance, imitation, faithfulness—is dissolving; and the arrow of the simulacrum released by the Epicureans is headed in our direction. It gives birth—rebirth—to a "phantasmaphysics."

❧

Occupying the other side of Platonism are the Stoics. Observing Deleuze in his discussion of Epicurus and Zeno, of Lucretius and Chrysippus, I was forced to conclude that his procedure was rigorously Freudian. He does not proceed—with a drum roll—toward the great Repression of Western philosophy; he registers, as if in passing, its oversights. He points out its interruptions, its gaps, those small things of little value that were neglected by philosophical discourse. He carefully reintroduces the barely perceptible omissions, knowing full well that they imply a fundamental negligence. Through the insistence of our pedagogical tradition, we are accustomed to reject the Epicurean simulacra as useless and somewhat puerile; and the famous battle of Stoicism, which took place yesterday and will reoccur tomorrow, has become cause for amusement in the schools. Deleuze did well to combine these tenuous threads and to play, in his own fashion, with this network of discourses, arguments, replies, and paradoxes, those elements that circulated for many centuries in Mediterranean cultures. We should not scorn Hellenistic confusion or Roman platitudes, but listen to those things said on the great surface of the empire; we should be attentive to those things that happened in a thousand instances, dispersed on every side: fulgurating battles, assassinated generals, burning triremes, queens poisoning themselves, victories that invariably led to further upheavals, the endlessly exemplary Actium, the eternal event.

To consider a pure event, it must first be given a metaphysical basis.[10] But we must be agreed that it cannot be the meta-physics of substances, which can serve as a foundation for accidents; nor can it be a metaphysical coherence, which situates these accidents in the entangled nexus of causes and effects. The event—a wound, a victory-defeat, death—is always an effect produced entirely by bodies colliding, mingling, or separating, but this effect is never of a corporeal nature; it is the intangible, inaccessible battle that turns and repeats itself a thousand times around Fabricius, above the wounded Prince Andrew.[11] The weapons that tear into bodies form an endless incorporeal battle. Physics concerns causes, but events, which arise as its effects, no longer belong to it. Let us imagine a stitched causality: as bodies collide, mingle, and suffer, they create events on their surfaces, events that are without thickness, mixture, or passion; for this reason, they can no longer be causes. They form, among themselves, another kind of succession whose links derive from a quasi-physics of incorporeals—in short, from metaphysics.

Events also require a more complex logic.[12] An event is not a state of things, something that could serve as a referent for a proposition (the fact of death is a state of things in relation to which an assertion can be true or false; dying is a pure event that can never verify anything). For a ternary logic, traditionally centered on the referent, we must substitute an interrelationship based on four terms. "Marc Antony is dead" *designates* a state of things; *expresses* my opinion or belief; *signifies* an affirmation; and, in addition, has a *meaning:* "dying." An intangible meaning with one side turned toward things because "dying" is something that occurs, as an event, to Antony, and the other toward the proposition because "dying" is what is said about Antony in a statement. To die: a dimension of the proposition; an incorporeal effect produced by a sword; a meaning and an

10. Cf. *Logique du sens*, pp. 13–21.
11. Fabricius was a Roman general and statesman (d. 250 B.C.); Prince Andrew is a main character in Tolstoi's *War and Peace*—ED.
12. Cf. *Logique du sens*, pp. 22–35.

event; a point without thickness or substance of which someone speaks and which roams the surface of things. We should not restrict meaning to the cognitive core that lies at the heart of a knowable object; rather, we should allow it to reestablish its flux at the limit of words and things, as what is said of a thing (not its attribute or the thing in itself) and as something that happens (not its process or its state). Death supplies the best example, being both the event of events and meaning in its purest state. Its domain is the anonymous flow of speech; it is that of which we speak as always past or about to happen and yet it occurs at the extreme point of singularity. A meaning-event is as neutral as death: "not the end, but the unending; not a particular death, but any death; not true death, but as Kafka said, the snicker of its devastating error."[13]

Finally, this meaning-event requires a grammar with a different form of organization,[14] since it cannot be situated in a proposition as an attribute (to be *dead,* to be *alive,* to be *red*) but is fastened to the verb (to die, to live, to redden). The verb, conceived in this fashion, has two principle forms around which the others are distributed: the present tense, which posits an event, and the infinitive, which introduces meaning into language and allows it to circulate as the neutral element to which we refer in discourse. We should not seek the grammar of events in temporal inflections; nor should we seek the grammar of meaning in the fictitious analyses of the type: to live = to be alive. The grammar of the meaning-event revolves around two asymmetrical and insecure poles: the infinitive mode and the present tense. The meaning-event is always both the displacement of the present and the eternal repetition of the infinitive. "To die" is never localized in the density of a given moment, but from its flux it infinitely divides the shortest moment. To die is even

13. Blanchot, *L'Espace littéraire,* cited in *Différence et répétition,* p. 149. Cf. also *Logique du sens,* pp. 175–179.
14. Cf. *Logique du sens,* pp. 212–216.

smaller than the moment it takes to think it and yet dying is indefinitely repeated on either side of this width-less crack. The eternal present? Only on the condition that we conceive the present as lacking plenitude and the eternal as lacking unity: the (multiple) eternity of the (displaced) present.

To summarize: at the limit of dense bodies, an event is incorporeal (a metaphysical surface); on the surface of words and things, an incorporeal event is the *meaning* of a proposition (its logical dimension); in the thread of discourse, an incorporeal meaning-event is fastened to the verb (the infinitive point of the present).

In the more or less recent past, there have been, I think, three major attempts at conceptualizing the event: neopositivism, phenomenology, and the philosophy of history. Neopositivism failed to grasp the distinctive level of the event; because of its logical error, the confusion of an event with a state of things, it had no choice but to lodge the event within the density of bodies, to treat it as a material process, and to attach itself more or less explicitly to a physicalism ("in a schizoid fashion," it reduced surfaces into depth); as for grammar, it transformed the event into an attribute. Phenomenology, on the other hand, reoriented the event with respect to meaning: either it placed the bare event before or to the side of meaning—the rock of facticity, the mute inertia of occurrences—and then submitted it to the active processes of meaning, to its digging and elaboration; or else it assumed a domain of primal significations, which always existed as a disposition of the world around the self, tracing its paths and privileged locations, indicating in advance where the event might occur and its possible form. Either the cat whose good sense precedes the smile or the common sense of the smile that anticipates the cat. Either Sartre or Merleau-Ponty. For them, meaning never coincides with an event; and from this evolves a logic of signification, a grammar of the first person, and a metaphysics of consciousness. As for the philosophy of history, it encloses the event in a cyclical pattern of time. Its error is grammatical;[15] it treats the present as framed by the past and future: the present is a former future where its form was prepared and the past, which will occur in the future, preserves the identity of its content. First, this sense of the present requires a logic of essences (which establishes the present in memory) and of concepts (where the present is established as a knowledge of the future), and then a metaphysics of a crowned and coherent cosmos, of a hierarchical world.

Thus, three systems that fail to grasp the event. The first, on the pretext that nothing can be said about those things which lie "outside" the world, rejects the pure surface of the event and attempts to enclose it forcibly—as a referent—in the spherical plenitude of the world. The second, on the pretext that signification only exists for consciousness, places the event outside and beforehand, or inside and after, and always situates it with respect to the circle of the self. The third, on the pretext that events can only exist in time, defines its identity and submits it to a solidly centered order. The world, the self, and God (a sphere, a circle, and a center): three conditions that invariably obscure the event and that obstruct the successful formulation of thought. Deleuze's proposals, I believe, are directed to lifting this triple subjection which, to this day, is imposed on the event: a metaphysics of the incorporeal event (which is consequently irreducible to a physics of the world), a logic of neutral meaning (rather than a phenomenology of signification based on the subject), and a thought of the present infinitive (and not the raising up of the conceptual future in a past essence).

We have arrived at the point where the two series of the event and the phantasm are brought into resonance—the resonance of the incorporeal and the intangible, the resonance of battles,

15. Cf. Nietzsche, *The Genealogy of Morals*, I, 13—ED.

of death that subsists and insists, of the fluttering and desirable idol: it subsists not in the heart of man but above his head, beyond the clash of weapons, in fate and desire. It is not that they converge in a common point, in some phantasmatic event, or in the primary origin of the simulacrum. The event is that which is invariably lacking in the series of the phantasm—its absence indicates its repetition devoid of any grounding in an original, outside of all forms of imitation, and freed from the constraints of similitude. Consequently, it is disguise of repetition, the always singular mask that conceals nothing, simulacra without dissimulation, incongrous finery covering a nonexistent nudity, pure difference.

As for the phantasm, it is "excessive" with respect to the singularity of the event, but this "excess" does not designate an imaginary supplement adding itself to the bare reality of facts; nor does it form a sort of embryonic generality from which the organization of the concept gradually emerges. To conceive of death or a battle as a phantasm is not to confuse them either with the old image of death suspended over a senseless accident or with the future concept of a battle secretly organizing the present disordered tumult; the battle rages from one blow to the next and the process of death indefinitely repeats the blow, always in its possession, which it inflicts once and for all. This conception of the phantasm as the play of the (missing) event and its repetition must not be given the form of individuality (a form inferior to the concept and therefore informal), nor must it be measured against reality (a reality which imitates an image); it presents itself as universal singularity: to die, to fight, to vanquish, to be vanquished.

Logique du sens shows us how to develop a thought capable of comprehending the event *and* the concept, their severed and double affirmation, their affirmation of disjunction. Determining an event on the basis of a concept, by denying any importance to repetition, is perhaps what might be called knowing; and measuring the phantasm against reality, by going in search of its origin, is judging. Philosophy tried to do both, it dreamed of itself as a science, and presented itself as a critique. Thinking, on the other hand, requires the release of a phantasm in the mime that produces it at a single stroke; it makes the event indefinite so that it repeats itself as a singular universal. It is this construction of the event *and* the phantasm that leads to thought in an absolute sense. A further clarification: if the role of thought is to produce the phantasm theatrically and to repeat the universal event in its extreme point of singularity, then what is thought itself if not the event that befalls the phantasm and the phantasmatic repetition of the absent event? The phantasm and the event, affirmed in disjunction, are the object of thought ("le pensé") and thought itself ("la pensée");[16] they situate extra-being at the surface of bodies where it can only be approached by thought and trace the topological event in which thought itself is formed. Thought must consider the process that forms it and form itself from these considerations. The critique-knowledge duality becomes absolutely useless as thought declares its nature.

This formulation, however, is dangerous. It implies equivalence and allows us once more to imagine the identification of an object and a subject. This would be entirely false. That the object of thought ("le pensé") forms thought ("la pensée") implies, on the contrary, a double dissociation: that of a central and founding subject to which events occur while it deploys meaning around itself; and of an object that is a threshold and point of convergence for recognizable forms and the attributes we affirm. We must conceive of an indefinite, straight line that (far from bearing events as a string supports its knots) cuts and recuts into each moment so many times that each event arises as both incorporeal and indefinitely multiple. We must imagine not the

16. The English word "thought" translates the French "le pensé" (meaning the thing being thought: the *object* of thought) and "la pensée" (thought itself). Where the meaning might be unclear, the original French word appears in brackets— ED.

synthesizing-synthesized subject, but an uncrossable fissure. Moreover, we must envisage a series lacking the primal appendages of simulacra, idols, and phantasms that always exist on either side of the gap in the temporal duality in which they form themselves and in which they signal to each other and come into existence as signs. The splitting of the self and the series of signifying points do not form a unity that permits thought to be both subject and object, but they are in themselves the event of thought ("la pensée") and the incorporeality of the object of thought ("le pensé"), the object of thought ("le pensé") as a problem (a multiplicity of dispersed points) and thought ("la pensée") as mime (repetition without a model).

This is why *Logique du sens* could have as a subtitle: *What is thinking?* This question always implies two different contexts throughout Deleuze's book: that of Stoic logic as it relates to the incorporeal and the Freudian analysis of the phantasm. What is thinking? The Stoics explain the operation of a thought concerning the objects of thought, and Freud tells us how thought is itself capable of thought. Perhaps, for the first time, this leads to a theory of thought that is completely freed from both the subject and the object. The thought-event is as singular as a throw of the dice; the thought-phantasm does not search for truth, but repeats thought.

In any case, we understand Deleuze's repeated emphasis of the mouth in *Logique du sens*. It is through this mouth, as Zeno recognized, that cartloads of food pass as well as carts of meaning ("If you say cart, a cart passes through your mouth."). The mouth, the orifice, the canal where the child intones the simulacra, the dismembered parts, and bodies without organs; the mouth in which depths and surfaces are articulated. Also the mouth from which falls the voice of the other giving rise to lofty idols that flutter above the child and form the superego. The mouth where cries are broken into phonemes, morphemes, semantemes: the mouth where the profundity of an oral body separates itself from incorporeal meaning. Through this open mouth, through this alimentary voice, the development of language, the formation of meaning, and the flash of thought extend their divergent series.[17] I would enjoy discussing Deleuze's rigorous phonocentrism were it not for the fact of a constant phonodecentering. Let Deleuze receive homage from the fantastic grammarian, from the dark precursor who nicely situated the remarkable facets of this decentering:

> Les dents, la bouche
> Les dents la bouchent
> L'aidant la bouche
> Laides en la bouche
> Lait dans la bouche, etc.[18]

Logique du sens causes us to reflect on matters that philosophy has neglected for many centuries: the event (assimilated in a concept, from which we vainly attempted to extract it in the form of a *fact*, verifying a proposition, of *actual experience*, a modality of the subject, of *concreteness*, the empirical content of history); and the phantasm (reduced in the name of reality and situated at the extremity, the pathological pole, of a normative sequence: perception–image–memory–illusion). After all, what most urgently needs thought in this century, if not the event and the phantasm.

We should thank Deleuze for his efforts. He did not revive the tiresome slogans: Freud with Marx, Marx with Freud, and both, if you please, with us. He developed a convincing analysis of the essential elements for establishing the thought of the event and the phantasm. His aim was not reconciliation (to expand

17. On this subject, see *Logique du sens*, pp. 217–267. My comments are, at best, an allusion to these splendid analyses.
18. Deleuze writes in *Logique du sens*, p. 111: "Artaud says that Being, which is non-sense, has teeth"; on "dark precursors," see *Différence et répétition*, pp. 156–158: "we call the *disparate* the dark precursor." Cf. above "Nietzsche, Genealogy, History," p. 143, for a discussion of the "disparate" as the "historical beginning of things"—ED.

the furthest reaches of an event with the imaginary density of a phantasm, or to ballast a floating phantasm by adding a grain of actual history); he discovered the philosophy which permits the disjunctive affirmation of both. Prior to *Logique du sens*, Deleuze formulated this philosophy with completely unguarded boldness in *Différence et répétition*, and we must now turn to this earlier work.

Instead of denouncing the fundamental omission that is thought to have inaugurated Western culture, Deleuze, with the patience of a Nietzschean genealogist, points to the variety of small impurities and paltry compromises.[19] He tracks down the miniscule, repetitive acts of cowardliness and all those features of folly, vanity, and complacency that endlessly nourish the philosophical mushroom, what Leiris might call "ridiculous rootlets." We all possess good sense; we all make mistakes, but no one is dumb (certainly, none of us). There is no thought without good will; every real problem has a solution, because our apprenticeship is to a master who has answers for the questions he poses; the world is our classroom. A whole series of insignificant beliefs. But in reality, we encounter the tyranny of goodwill, the obligation to think "in common" with others, the domination of a pedagogical model, and most importantly, the exclusion of stupidity—the disreputable morality of thought whose function in our society is easy to decipher. We must liberate ourselves from these constraints; and in perverting this morality, philosophy itself is disoriented.

Consider the handling of difference. It is generally assumed to be a difference *from* or *within* something; behind difference,

19. This entire section considers, in a different order from that of the text, some of the themes which intersect within *Différence et répétition*. I am, of course, aware that I have shifted accents and, far more important, that I have ignored its inexhaustible riches. I have reconstructed one of several possible models. Therefore, I will not supply specific references.

beyond it—but as its support, its site, its delimitation, and consequently as the source of its mastery—we pose, through the concept, the unity of a group and its breakdown into species in the operation of difference (the organic domination of the Aristotelian concept). Difference is transformed into that which must be specified within a concept, without overstepping its bounds. And yet above the species, we encounter the swarming of individualities. What is this boundless diversity, which eludes specification and remains outside the concept, if not the resurgence of repetition? Underneath the ovine species, we are reduced to counting sheep. This stands as the first form of subjection: difference as specification (within the concept) and repetition as the indifference of individuals (outside the concept). But subjection to what? To common sense which, turning away from the mad flux and anarchical difference, invariably recognises the identity of things (and this is at all times a general capacity). Common sense extracts the generality of an object while it simultaneously establishes the universality of the knowing subject through a pact of goodwill. But what if we gave free rein to ill will? What if thought freed itself from common sense and decided to function only in its extreme singularity? What if it adopted the disreputable bias of the paradox, instead of complacently accepting its citizenship in the *doxa?* What if it conceived of difference differentially, instead of searching out the common elements underlying difference? Then difference would disappear as a general feature that leads to the generality of the concept, and it would become—a different thought, the thought of difference—a pure event. As for repetition, it would cease to function as the dreary succession of the identical, and would become displaced difference. Thought is no longer committed to the construction of concepts once it escapes goodwill and the administration of common sense, concerned as it is with division and characterization. Rather, it produces a meaning-event by repeating a phantasm. The morality of goodwill, which assists common sense thought, had the fundamental role of protecting thought from its "genital" singularity.

But let us reconsider the functioning of the concept. For the concept to master difference, perception must apprehend global resemblances (which will then be decomposed into differences and partial identities) at the root of what we call diversity. Each new representation must be accompanied by those representations that display the full range of resemblances; and in this space of representation (sensation–image–memory), likenesses are put to the test of quantitative equalization and graduated quantities, and in this way the immense table of measurable differences is constructed. In the corner of this graph, on its horizontal axis where the smallest quantitative gap meets the smallest qualitative variation, at this zero point, we encounter perfect resemblance and exact repetition. Repetition, which functions within the concept as the impertinent vibration of identities, becomes, within a system of representation, the organizing principles for similarities. But *what* recognises these similarities, the exactly alike and the least similar—the greatest and the smallest, the brightest and the darkest—if not good sense? Good sense is the world's most effective agent of division in its recognitions, its establishment of equivalences, its sensitivity to gaps, its gauging of distances, as it assimilates and separates. And it is good sense that reigns in the philosophy of representation. Let us pervert good sense and allow thought to play outside the ordered table of resemblances; then it will appear as the vertical dimension of intensities, because intensity, well before its gradation by representation, is in itself pure difference: difference that displaces and repeats itself, that contracts and expands; a singular point that constricts and slackens the indefinite repetitions in an acute event. One must give rise to thought as intensive irregularity—disintegration of the subject.

A last consideration with respect to the table of representation. The meeting point of the axes is the point of perfect resemblance, and from this arises the scale of differences as so many lesser resemblances, marked identities: differences arise when representation can only partially present what was previously present, when the test of recognition is stymied. For a thing to be different, it must first no longer be the same; and it is on this negative basis, above the shadowy part that delimits the same, that contrary predicates are then articulated. In the philosophy of representation, the relationship of two predicates, like red and green, is merely the highest level of a complex structure: the *contradiction* between red and not-red (based on the model of *being* and *non-being*) is active on the lowest level; the non-identity of red and green (on the basis of the *negative* test of *recognition*) is situated above this; and this ultimately leads to the *exclusive* position of red and green (in the table where the *genus* color is *specified*). Thus for a third time, but in an even more radical manner, difference is held fast within an oppositional, negative, and contradictory system. For difference to exist, it was necessary to divide the "same" through contradiction, to limit its infinite identity through non-being, to transform its positivity which operates without specific determinations through the negative. Given the priority of similarity, difference could only arise through these mediations. As for repetition, it is produced precisely at the point where the barely launched mediation falls back on itself; when, instead of saying no, it twice pronounces the same yes, when it constantly returns to the same position, instead of distributing oppositions within a system of finite elements. Repetition betrays the weakness of similarity at the moment when it can no longer negate itself in the other, when it can no longer recapture itself in the other. Repetition, at one time pure exteriority and a pure figure of the origin, has been transformed into an internal weakness, a deficiency of finitude, a sort of stuttering of the negative: the neurosis of dialectics. For it was indeed toward dialectics that the philosophy of representation was headed.

And yet, how is it that we fail to recognize Hegel as the philosopher of the greatest differences and Leibniz as the thinker of the smallest differences? In actuality, dialectics does not liberate differences; it guarantees, on the contrary, that they can always be recaptured. The dialectical sovereignty of similarity consists in permitting differences to exist, but always under the rule of the negative, as an instance of non-being. They may appear as the successful subversion of the Other, but contradiction secretly assists in the salvation of identities. Is it necessary to recall the unchanging pedagogical origin of dialectics? The ritual in which it is activated, which causes the endless rebirth of the aporia of being and non-being, is the humble classroom interrogation, the student's fictive dialogue: "This is red; that is not red. At this moment, it is light outside. No, now it is dark." In the twilight of an October sky, Minerva's bird flies close to the ground: "Write it down, write it down," it croaks, "tomorrow morning, it will no longer be dark."

The freeing of difference requires thought without contradiction, without dialectics, without negation; thought that accepts divergence; affirmative thought whose instrument is disjunction; thought of the multiple—of the nomadic and dispersed multiplicity that is not limited or confined by the constraints of similarity; thought that does not conform to a pedagogical model (the fakery of prepared answers), but that attacks insoluble problems—that is, a thought that addresses a multiplicity of exceptional points, which are displaced as we distinguish their conditions and which insist and subsist in the play of repetitions. Far from being the still incomplete and blurred image of an Idea that eternally retains our answers in some upper region, the problem lies in the idea itself, or rather, the Idea exists only in the form of a problem: a distinctive plurality whose obscurity is nevertheless insistent and in which the question ceaselessly stirs. What is the answer to the question? The problem. How is the problem resolved? By displacing the question. The problem cannot be approached through the logic of the excluded third, because it is a dispersed multiplicity; it cannot be resolved by the clear distinctions of a Cartesian idea, because as an idea it is obscure-distinct; it does not respond to the seriousness of the Hegelian negative, because it is a multiple affirmation; it is not subjected to the contradiction of being and non-being, since it is being.

We must think problematically rather than question and answer dialectically.

The conditions for thinking of difference and repetition, as we have seen, have undergone a progressive expansion. First, it was necessary, along with Aristotle, to abandon the identity of the concept, to reject resemblance within representation, and simultaneously to free ourselves from the philosophy of representation; and finally, it was necessary to free ourselves from Hegel—from the opposition of predicates, from contradiction and negation, from all of dialectics. But there is yet a fourth condition and it is even more formidable than the others. The most tenacious subjection of difference is undoubtedly that maintained by categories. By showing the number of different ways in which being can express itself, by specifying its forms of attribution, by imposing in a certain way the distribution of existing things, categories create a condition where being maintains its undifferentiated repose at the highest level. Categories organize the play of affirmations and negations, establish the legitimacy of resemblances within representation, and guarantee the objectivity and operation of concepts. They suppress the anarchy of difference, divide differences into zones, delimit their rights, and prescribe their task of specification with respect to individual beings. On one side, they can be understood as the a priori forms of knowledge, but, on the other, they appear as an archaic morality, the ancient decalogue that the identical imposed upon difference. Difference can only be liberated through the invention of an acategorical thought. But perhaps invention is a misleading word, since in the history of philosophy there have been at least two radical formulations of the univocity of being, those given by Duns Scotus and Spinoza. In Duns Scotus' philosophy, however, being is neutral, while for Spinoza it is based on substance; in both contexts, the elimination of categories and the affirmation that being is expressed for all things in the same way had the single objective of maintaining the unity of being. Let us imagine, on the contrary, an ontology where being would be expressed in the same fashion for every difference, but could only express differences. Consequently, things could no longer be completely covered over, as in Duns Scotus, by the great monochrome abstraction of being, and Spinoza's forms would no longer revolve around the unity of substance. Differences would revolve of their own accord, being would be expressed in the same fashion for all these differences, and being would no longer be a unity that guides and distributes them, but their repetition as difference. For Deleuze, the noncategorical univocity of being does not directly attach the multiple to a unity (the universal neutrality of being, or the expressive force of substance); it allows being to function as that which is repetitively expressed as difference. Being is the recurrence of difference, without any difference in the form of its expression. Being does not distribute itself into regions; the real is not subordinated to the possible; and the contingent is not opposed to the necessary. Whether the battle of Actium or the death of Antony were necessary or not, the being of both these pure events—to fight, to die—is expressed in the same manner, in the same way that it is expressed with respect to the phantasmatic castration that occurred and did not occur. The suppression of categories, the affirmation of the univocity of being, and the repetitive revolution of being around difference—these are the final conditions for the thought of the phantasm and the event.

We have not quite reached the conclusion. We must return to this "recurrence," but let us pause a moment.

Can it be said that Bouvard and Pécuchet make mistakes? Do they commit blunders whenever an opportunity presents itself? If they make mistakes, it is because there are rules that underlie their failures and under certain definable conditions they might have succeeded. Nevertheless, their failure is constant, whatever their action, whatever their knowledge, whether or not they follow the rules, whether the books they consulted were good or bad. Everything befalls their undertaking—errors, of course, but also fires, frost, the foolishness and perversity of men, a dog's anger. Their efforts were not wrong; they were totally botched. To be wrong is to mistake a cause for another; it is not to foresee accidents; it may derive from a faulty knowledge of substances or from the confusion of necessities with possibilities. We are mistaken if we apply categories carelessly and inopportunely. But it is altogether different to ruin a project completely: it is to ignore the framework of categories (and not simply their points of application). If Bouvard and Pécuchet are reasonably certain of precisely those things which are largely improbable, it is not that they are mistaken in their discrimination of the possible but that they confuse all aspects of reality with every form of possibility (this is why the most improbable events conform to the most natural of their expectations). They confuse, or rather are confused by, the necessity of their knowledge and the contingency of the seasons, the existence of things and the shadows found in books: an accident, for them, possesses the obstinacy of a substance and those substances seized them by the throat in their experimental accidents. Such is their grand and pathetic stupidity, and it is incomparable to the meager foolishness of those who surround them and make mistakes, the others whom they rightfully disdain. Within categories, one makes mistakes; outside of them, beyond or beneath them, one is stupid. Bouvard and Pécuchet are acategorical beings.

These comments allow us to isolate a use of categories that may not be immediately apparent; by creating a space for the operation of truth and falsity, by situating the free supplement of error, categories silently reject stupidity. In a commanding voice, they instruct us in the ways of knowledge and solemnly alert us to the possibilities of error, while in a whisper they guarantee our intelligence and form the a priori of excluded stupidity. Thus, we court danger in wanting to be freed from categories; no sooner do we abandon their organizing principle than we face the magma of stupidity. At a stroke we risk being surrounded not by a marvellous multiplicity of differences, but by equivalences, ambiguities, the "it all comes down to the same thing," a levelling uniformity, and the thermodynamism of every miscarried effort. To think within the context of categories is to know the truth so that it can be distinguished from the false; to think "acategorically" is to confront a black stupidity and, in a flash, to distinguish oneself from it. Stupidity is contemplated: sight penetrates its domain and becomes fascinated; it carries one gently along and its action is mimed in the abandonment of oneself; we support ourselves upon its amorphous fluidity; we await the first leap of an imperceptible difference, and blankly, without fever, we watch to see the glimmer of light return. Error demands rejection—we can erase it; we accept stupidity—we see it, we repeat it, and softly, we call for total immersion.

This is the greatness of Warhol with his canned foods, sense-less accidents, and his series of advertising smiles: the oral and nutritional equivalence of those half-open lips, teeth, tomato sauce, that hygiene based on detergents; the equivalence of death in the cavity of an eviscerated car, at the top of a tele-phone pole and at the end of a wire, and between the glistening, steel blue arms of the electric chair. "It's the same either way," stupidity says, while sinking into itself and infinitely extending its nature with the things it says of itself; "Here or there, it's always the same thing; what difference if the colors vary, if they're darker or lighter. It's all so senseless—life, women, death! How ridiculous this stupidity!" But in concentrating on this boundless monotony, we find the sudden illumination of mul-tiplicity itself—with nothing at its center, at its highest point, or beyond it—a flickering of light that travels even faster than the eyes and successively lights up the moving labels and the captive snapshots that refer to each other to eternity, without ever saying anything: suddenly, arising from the background of the old inertia of equivalences, the striped form of the event tears through the darkness, and the eternal phantasm informs that soup can, that singular and depthless face.

Intelligence does not respond to stupidity, since it is stupidity already vanquished, the categorical art of avoiding error. The scholar is intelligent. But it is thought that confronts stupidity, and it is the philosopher who observes it. Their private conversation is a lengthy one, as the philosopher's sight plunges into this candleless skull. It is his death mask, his temptation, perhaps his desire, his catatonic theater. At the limit, thought would be the intense contemplation from close up—to the point of losing oneself in it—of stupidity; and its other side is formed by lassitude, immobility, excessive fatigue, obstinate muteness, and inertia— or rather, they form its accompaniment, the daily and thankless exercise which prepares it and which it suddenly dissipates. The philosopher must be sufficiently perverse to play the game of truth and error badly: this perversity, which operates in paradoxes, allows him to escape the grasp of categories. But aside from this, he must be sufficiently "ill humored" to persist in his confrontation with stupidity, to remain motionless to the point of stupefaction in order to approach it successfully and mime it, to let it slowly grow within himself (this is probably what we politely refer to as being absorbed in one's thoughts), and to await, in the always unpredictable conclusion to this elaborate preparation, the shock of difference. Once paradoxes have upset the table of representation, catatonia operates within the theater of thought.

We can easily see how LSD inverts the relationships of ill humor, stupidity, and thought: it no sooner eliminates the supremacy of categories than it tears away the ground of its indifference and disintegrates the gloomy dumbshow of stupidity; and it presents this univocal and acategorical mass not only as variegated, mobile, asymmetrical, decentered, spiraloid, and reverberating, but causes it to rise, at each instant, as a swarming of phantasm-events. As it slides upon this surface at once regular and intensely vibratory, as it is freed from its catatonic chrysalis, thought invariably contemplates this indefinite equivalence transformed into an acute event and a sumptuous, appareled repetition. Opium produces other effects: thought gathers unique differences into a point, eliminates the background and deprives immobility of its task of contemplating and soliciting stupidity through its mime. Opium ensures a weightless immobility, the stupor of a butterfly that differs from catatonic rigidity; and far beneath, it establishes a ground that no longer stupidly absorbs all differences, but allows them to arise and sparkle as so many minute, distanced, smiling, and eternal events. Drugs—if we can speak of them generally—have nothing at all to do with truth and falsity; only to fortunetellers do they reveal a world "more truthful than the real." In fact, they displace the relative positions of stupidity and thought by eliminating the old necessity for a theater of immobility. But perhaps, if it is given to thought to confront stupidity, the drugs, which mobilize it, which color, agitate, furrow, and dissipate it, which populate it with differences and substitute for the rare flash a continuous phosphorescence, are the source of a partial thought—perhaps.[20] At any rate, in a state deprived of drugs, thought possesses two horns: one is perversity (to baffle categories) and the other ill humor (to point to stupidity and transfix it). We are far from the sage who invests so much goodwill in his search for the truth that he can contemplate with equanimity the indifferent diversity of changing fortunes and things; far from the irritability of Schopenhauer who became annoyed with things that did not return to their indifference of their own accord. But we are also distant from the "melancholy" which makes itself indifferent to the world and whose immobility—alongside books and a globe— indicates the profundity of thought and the diversity of knowledge. Exercising its ill will and ill humor, thought awaits the outcome of this theater of perverse practices: the sudden shift of the kaleidoscope, signs that light up for an instant, the results of the thrown dice, the outcome of another game. Thinking does not

20. "What will people think of us?" (Note added by Gilles Deleuze.)

provide consolation or happiness. Like a perversion, it languidly drags itself out; it repeats itself with determination upon a stage; at a stroke, it flings itself outside the dice box. At the moment when chance, the theater, and perversions enter into resonance, when chance dictates a resonance among the three, then thought becomes a trance; and it becomes worthwhile to think.

The univocity of being, its singleness of expression, is paradoxically the principal condition which permits difference to escape the domination of identity, which frees it from the law of the Same as a simple opposition within conceptual elements. Being can express itself in the same way, because difference is no longer submitted to the prior reduction of categories; because it is not distributed inside a diversity that can always be perceived; because it is not organized in a conceptual hierarchy of species and genus. Being is that which is always said of difference; it is the *Recurrence* of difference.[21]

With this term, we can avoid the use of both *Becoming* and *Return*, because differences are not the elements—not even the fragmentary, intermingled, or monstrously confused elements—of an extended evolution that carries them along in its course and occasionally allows their masked or naked reappearance. The synthesis of Becoming might seem somewhat slack, but it nevertheless maintains a unity—not only and not especially that of an infinite container, but also the unity of fragments, of passing and recurring moments, and of floating consciousness where it achieves recognition. Consequently, we are led to mistrust Dionysus and his Bacchantes even in their state of intoxication. As for the Return, must it be the perfect circle, the well-oiled millstone, which turns on its axis and reintroduces things, forms, and men at their appointed time? Must there be a center and

21. On these themes, cf. *Différence et répétition,* pp. 52–61, 376–384; *Logique du sens,* pp. 190–197, 208–211.

must events occur on its periphery? Even Zarathustra could not tolerate this idea:

'Everything straight lies,' murmured the dwarf disdainfully. 'All truth is crooked, time itself is a circle.'
'Spirit of Gravity!' I said angrily, 'do not treat this too lightly.'[22]

And convalescing, he groans:

'Alas! Man will return eternally, abject man will return eternally.'[23]

Perhaps what Zarathustra is proclaiming is not the circle; or perhaps the intolerable image of the circle is the last sign of a higher form of thought; perhaps, like the young shepherd, we must break this circular ruse—like Zarathustra himself who bit off the head of a serpent and immediately spat it away.[24]

Chronos is the time of becoming and new beginnings. Piece by piece, Chronos swallows the things to which it gives birth and which it causes to be reborn in its own time. This monstrous and lawless becoming—the endless devouring of each instant, the swallowing up of the totality of life, the scattering of its limbs—is linked to the exactitude of re-beginning. Becoming leads into this great, interior labyrinth, a labyrinth no different in nature from the monster it contains. But from the depths of this convoluted and inverted architecture, a solid thread allows us to retrace our steps and to rediscover the same light of day. Dionysus with Ariadne: you have become my labyrinth. But Aeon is *recurrence* itself, the straight line of time, a splitting quicker than thought and narrower than any instant. It causes the same present to arise—on both sides of this indefinitely splitting arrow—as always existing, as indefinitely present, and as indefinite future. It is important to understand that this does not imply a succession of present instances that derive from a con-

22. *Thus Spoke Zarathustra*, Part III, "Of the Vision and the Riddle," Sec. 2—Ed.
23. Ibid., "The Convalescent," Sec. 2—Ed.
24. Ibid.—Ed.

tinuous flux and that, as a result of their plenitude, allow us to perceive the thickness of the past and the outline of a future in which they in turn become the past. Rather, it is the straight line of the future that repeatedly cuts the smallest width of the present, that indefinitely recuts it starting from itself. We can trace this schism to its limits, but we will never find the indivisible atom that ultimately serves as the minutely present unity of time (time is always more supple than thought). On both sides of the wound, we invariably find that the schism has already happened (and that it had already taken place, and that it had already happened that it had already taken place) and that it will happen again (and in the future, it will happen again): it is less a cut than a constant fibrillation. What repeats itself is time; and the present—split by this arrow of the future that carries it forward by always causing its swerving on both sides— endlessly recurs. But it recurs as singular difference; and the analogous, the similar, and the identical never return. Difference recurs; and being, expressing itself in the same manner with respect to difference, is never the universal flux of becoming; nor is it the well-centered circle of identities. Being is a return freed from the curvature of the circle; it is Recurrence. Consequently, the death of three elements: of Becoming, the devouring Father—mother in labor; of the circle, by which the gift of life passes to the flowers each springtime; of recurrence—the repetitive fibrillation of the present, the eternal and dangerous fissure fully given in an instant, universally affirmed in a single stroke.

By virtue of its splintering and repetition, the present is a throw of the dice. This is not because it forms part of a game in which it insinuates small contingencies or elements of uncertainty. It is at once the chance within the game and the game itself as chance; in the same stroke, both the dice and rules are thrown, so that chance is not broken into pieces and parcelled out, but is totally affirmed in a single throw. The present as the recurrence of difference, as repetition giving voice to difference, affirms at once the totality of chance. The univocity of being in Duns Scotus led to the immobility of an abstraction; and in Spinoza, it led to the necessity and eternity of substance, but here it leads to the single throw of chance in the fissure of the present. If being always declares itself in the same way, it is not because being is one, but because the totality of chance is affirmed in the single dice throw of the present.

Can we say that the univocity of being has been formulated on three different occasions in the history of philosophy, by Duns Scotus and Spinoza and finally by Nietzsche—the first to conceive of univocity as returning and not as an abstraction or a substance? Perhaps we should say that Nietzsche went as far as the thought of the Eternal Return; more precisely, he pointed to it as an intolerable thought. Intolerable, because as soon as its first signs are perceived, it fixes itself in this image of the circle that carries in itself the fatal threat that all things will return—the spider's reiteration. But this intolerable nature must be considered because it exists only as an empty sign, a passageway to be crossed, the formless voice of the abyss whose approach is indissociably both happiness and disgust, disgust. In relation to the Return, Zarathustra is the "Fürsprecher," the one who speaks for . . . , in the place of . . . , marking the spot of his absence. Zarathustra does not function as Nietzsche's image, but as his sign, the sign (and not at all a symptom) of rupture. Nietzsche left this sign, the sign closest to the intolerable thought of the eternal return, and it is our task to consider its consequences. For close to a century, the loftiest enterprise of philosophy has been directed to this task, but who has the arrogance to say that he had seen it through? Should the Return have resembled the nineteenth century's conception of the end of history, an end that circled menacingly about us as an apocalyptic fantasmagoria? Should we have ascribed to this empty sign, imposed by Nietzsche as an *excess*, a series of mythic contents that disarmed and reduced it? Should we have attempted, on the contrary, to refine it so that it could unashamedly assume its place within a particular discourse? Or should this excessive, this always misplaced and displaced sign have been accentuated;

and instead of finding an arbitrary meaning to correspond to it, instead of constructing an adequate word, should it have been made to enter into resonance with the supreme meaning which today's thought supports as an uncertain and controlled ballast? Should it have allowed recurrence to resound in unison with difference? We must avoid thinking that the return is the form of a content which is difference; rather, from an always nomadic and anarchical difference to the unavoidably excessive and displaced sign of recurrence, a lightning storm was produced which will, one day, be given the name of Deleuze: new thought is possible; thought is again possible.

This thought does not lie in the future, promised by the most distant of new beginnings. It is present in Deleuze's texts—springing forth, dancing before us, in our midst; genital thought, intensive thought, affirmative thought, acategorical thought— each of these an unrecognizable face, a mask we have never seen before; differences we had no reason to expect, but which nevertheless lead to the return, as masks of their masks, of Plato, Duns Scotus, Spinoza, Leibniz, Kant, and all other philosophers. This is philosophy not as thought, but as theater: a theater of mime with multiple, fugitive, and instantaneous scenes in which blind gestures signal to each other. This is the theater where the explosive laughter of the Sophists tears through the mask of Socrates; where Spinoza's methods conduct a wild dance in a decentered circle while substance revolves about it like a mad planet; where a limping Fichte announces "the fractured I $\neq$ the dissolved self;" where Leibniz, having reached the top of the pyramid, can see through the darkness that celestial music is in fact a *Pierrot lunaire*.[25] In the sentry box of the Luxembourg Gardens, Duns Scotus places his head through the circular window; he is sporting an impressive moustache; it belongs to Nietzsche, disguised as Klossowski.

25. Schoenberg's song cycle, transcribed from the poems of the Belgian poet Albert Giraud—ED.

PART III

❧

PRACTICE:

KNOWLEDGE AND POWER

History of Systems of Thought

Summary of a course given at
Collège de France—1970–1971

Our objective this past year was to initiate a series of individual analyses that will gradually form a "morphology of the will to knowledge." This theme was explored both in relation to specific historical investigations and in its own right in terms of its theoretical implications.

This past year we tried to situate this theme and to define its role within the history of systems of thought, to establish, at least in a provisional way, a working model for analysis and to test its effectiveness on an initial set of examples.

1. In earlier studies, we were able to isolate a distinctive level of investigation among all those approaches which permit the analysis of systems of thought: the analysis of discursive practices. This context discloses a systematic organization that cannot be reduced to the demands of logic or linguistics. Discursive practices are characterized by the delimitation of a field of objects, the definition of a legitimate perspective for the agent of knowledge, and the fixing of norms for the elaboration of concepts and theories. Thus, each discursive practice implies a play of prescriptions that designate its exclusions and choices.

Furthermore, these sets of "regularities" do not coincide with individual works; even if these "regularities" are manifested

This course description of Foucault's first year at Collège de France is reproduced here with Foucault's permission.

through individual works or announce their presence for the first time through one of them, they are more extensive and often serve to regroup a large number of individual works. But neither do they coincide with what we ordinarily call a science or a discipline even if their boundaries provisionally coincide on certain occasions; it is usually the case that a discursive practice assembles a number of diverse disciplines or sciences or that it crosses a certain number among them and regroups many of their individual characteristics into a new and occasionally unexpected unity.

Discursive practices are not purely and simply ways of producing discourse. They are embodied in technical processes, in institutions, in patterns for general behavior, in forms for transmission and diffusion, and in pedagogical forms which, at once, impose and maintain them.

Finally, they possess specific modes of transformation. These transformations cannot be reduced to precise and individual discoveries; and yet we cannot characterize them as a general change of mentality, collective attitudes, or a state of mind. The transformation of a discursive practice is linked to a whole range of usually complex modifications that can occur outside of its domain (in the forms of production, in social relationships, in political institutions), inside it (in its techniques for determining its object, in the adjustment and refinement of its concepts, in its accumulation of facts), or to the side of it (in other discursive practices). And it is linked to these modifications not as a simple result but as an effect that retains both its proper autonomy and the full range of its precise functions in relation to that which determines it.

These principles of exclusion and choice, whose presence is manifold, whose effectiveness is embodied in practices, and whose transformations are relatively autonomous, are not based on an agent of knowledge (historical or transcendental) who successively invents them or places them on an original footing; rather, they designate a will to knowledge that is anonymous, polymorphous, susceptible to regular transformations, and determined by the play of identifiable dependencies.

Empirical studies relating to psychopathology, clinical medicine, natural history, and so forth, have allowed us to isolate the distinctive level of discursive practices. Their general characteristics and the proper methods for their analysis were delineated under the heading of archaeology. Studies conducted in relation to the will to knowledge should now be able to supply the theoretical justification for these earlier investigations. For the moment, we can indicate in a very general way the direction in which this study should proceed: establishing a distinction between knowledge and the rules necessary to its acquisition;[1] the difference between the will to knowledge and the will to truth; the position of the subject and subjects in relation to this will.

2. To our time, few conceptual tools have been elaborated for analyzing the will to knowledge. The notions on hand are, at best, imprecise: "anthropological" or psychological notions like those of curiosity, the need for mastery or appropriation through knowledge, distress before the unknown, reactions to the threat of the undifferentiated; historical generalities such as the spirit of a period, its sensibility, its types of interests, its conception of the world, its system of values, its essential needs; philosophical themes such as a horizon of rationality that makes itself known through time. Finally, we have no reason to believe that the still rudimentary elaborations of psychoanalysis on the positions of the subject and object in the context of desire and knowledge can be readily applied to the study of history. We are faced with the unavoidable fact that the tools that permit the analysis of the will to knowledge must be constructed and defined as we proceed, according to the needs and possibilities that arise from a series of concrete studies.

1. In this passage, Foucault speaks of establishing a distinction between "savoir" and "connaissance." Unfortunately, both words translate as "knowledge" in English. For a discussion of the sense of both words, see *The Archaeology of Knowledge*, p. 15, note 2—ED.

The history of philosophy offers a number of theoretical models of the will to knowledge whose analysis can present us with initial coordinates. Among the many that should be studied and tested (Plato, Spinoza, Schopenhauer, Aristotle, Nietzsche, etc.), we concentrated on the last two during the past year, because they constitute two extreme and opposed forms.

The analysis of the Aristotelian model essentially derived from a study of the *Metaphysics,* the *Nicomachean Ethics,* and *De Anima.* It is approached on the level of sensation and establishes:

—the link between sensation and pleasure;
—the independence of this link with regard to the vital utility that might derive from sensation;
—a direct proportion between the intensity of pleasure and the knowledge derived from sensation;
—the incompatibility between the truth of pleasure and the error of sensation.

Visual perception, defined as the sensation of multiple objects given simultaneously at a distance and as a sensation that has no immediate connection to the needs of the body, reveals the link between knowledge, pleasure, and truth in the satisfaction it generates through its proper action. At the other extreme, this same relationship is transposed in the pleasure of theoretical contemplation. The desire for knowledge, given at the beginning of the *Metaphysics* as universal and natural, is based on the initial adherence already manifested by sensation; and it assures a smooth passage from this first type of knowledge to the ultimate knowledge that is formulated in philosophy. The intrinsic desire for knowledge in Aristotle relies upon and transposes a prior relationship between knowledge, truth, and pleasure.

In *The Gay Science,* Nietzsche defines an altogether different set of relationships:

—knowledge is an "invention" behind which lies something completely different from itself: the play of instincts, impulses, desires, fear, and the will to appropriate. Knowledge is produced on the stage where these elements struggle against each other;

—its production is not the effect of their harmony or joyful equilibrium, but of their hatred, of their questionable and provisional compromise, and of the fragile truce that they are always prepared to betray. It is not a permanent faculty, but an event or, at the very least, a series of events;

—knowledge is always in bondage, dependent, and interested[2] (not in itself, but to those things capable of involving an instinct or the instincts that dominate it);

—and if it gives itself as the knowledge of truth, it is because it produces truth through the play of a primary and always reconstituted falsification, which erects the distinction between truth and falsehood.

Thus, selfish interest is radically posed as coming before knowledge, which it subordinates to its needs as a simple instrument; a knowledge, which is dissociated from pleasure and happiness, is linked to the struggle, the hate, and the spitefulness directed against it until it arrives at its own rejection as an excess created by struggle, hate, and spitefulness: its original connection to truth is undone once truth becomes merely an effect—the effect of a falsification that we call the opposition of truth and falsehood. This model of a fundamentally selfish knowledge, produced by volition as an event and determining truth as an effect of falsification, is undoubtedly totally alien to the assumptions of classical metaphysics. This model, used in a variety of ways, was related, throughout the year, to a series of examples.

3. This series was drawn from the history and institutions of ancient Greece; and all of the examples derive from the domain of justice. We concerned ourselves with its evolution from the 7th to the 5th century. Concerned with the transformation of justice during this period, we examined its administration, its conceptions, and the social reactions to crime.

2. "Intéressé" in the French also carries the meaning of selfish—Ed.

We investigated the following areas:

—the practice of oaths in judicial disputes and its evolution from the oath-defiance of litigants who exposed themselves to the vengeance of the gods to the assertive oath of a witness who attests to the truth of an event in which he was involved or which he observed;

—the search for an equitable measure (not only in commercial exchanges but in the social relationships within a city) through the institution of money;

—the search for a "nomos," for a just law of distribution to guarantee order within the city, in establishing an order that is the order of the world;

—the purification rites after a murder.

Throughout this period, the distribution of justice served as an arena for important political struggles. These struggles ultimately created a form of justice linked to a form of knowledge which presupposes that truth is visible, ascertainable, and measurable, that it responds to laws similar to those which register the order of the world, and that to discover it is also to possess its value for purification. This type of affirmation of truth becomes fundamental in the history of Western knowledge.

The seminar during this past year set as its general framework the study of the penal system in France during the nineteenth century. It concerned itself with the early developments of prison psychiatry during the Restoration; a large part of its primary material derived from the medical and legal reports produced by the contemporaries and disciples of Esquirol.

(Papers were read by J.-P. Peter, R. Castel, and Fontana.)

❧

Intellectuals and Power

A conversation between
Michel Foucault and Gilles Deleuze

MICHEL FOUCAULT: A Maoist once said to me: "I can easily understand Sartre's purpose in siding with us; I can understand his goals and his involvement in politics; I can partially understand your position, since you've always been concerned with the problem of confinement. But Deleuze is an enigma." I was shocked by this statement because your position has always seemed particularly clear to me.

GILLES DELEUZE: Possibly we're in the process of experiencing a new relationship between theory and practice. At one time, practice was considered an application of theory, a consequence; at other times, it had an opposite sense and it was thought to inspire theory, to be indispensable for the creation of future theoretical forms. In any event, their relationship was understood in terms of a process of totalization. For us, however, the question is seen in a different light. The relationships between theory and practice are far more partial and fragmentary. On one side, a theory is always local and related to a limited field, and it is applied in another sphere, more or less distant from it. The relationship which holds in the application of a theory is

This discussion was recorded March 4, 1972; and it was published in a special issue of *L'Arc* (No. 49, pp. 3–10), dedicated to Gilles Deleuze. It is reprinted here by permission of *L'Arc*. (All footnotes supplied by the editor.)

never one of resemblance. Moreover, from the moment a theory
moves into its proper domain, it begins to encounter obstacles,
walls, and blockages which require its relay by another type of
discourse (it is through this other discourse that it eventually
passes to a different domain). Practice is a set of relays from one
theoretical point to another, and theory is a relay from one practice to another. No theory can develop without eventually en-
countering a wall, and practice is necessary for piercing this
wall. For example, your work began in the theoretical analysis
of the context of confinement, specifically with respect to the
psychiatric asylum within a capitalist society in the nineteenth
century. Then you became aware of the necessity for confined
individuals to speak for themselves, to create a relay (it's possible, on the contrary, that your function was already that of a
relay in relation to them); and this group is found in prisons—
these individuals are imprisoned. It was on this basis that you
organized the information group for prisons (G.I.P.),[1] the object
being to create conditions that permit the prisoners themselves
to speak. It would be absolutely false to say, as the Maoist implied, that in moving to this practice you were applying your
theories. This was not an application; nor was it a project for
initiating reforms or an enquiry in the traditional sense. The
emphasis was altogether different: a system of relays within a
larger sphere, within a multiplicity of parts that are both theoretical and practical. A theorising intellectual, for us, is no longer
a subject, a representing or representative consciousness. Those
who act and struggle are no longer represented, either by a
group or a union that appropriates the right to stand as their
conscience. Who speaks and acts? It is always a multiplicity,
even within the person who speaks and acts. All of us are
"groupuscules."[2] Representation no longer exists; there's only

1. "Groupe d'information de prisons": Foucault's two most recent
publications (*I, Pierre Rivière* and *Surveiller et punir*) result from
this association.
2. Cf. above "Theatrum Philosophicum," p. 185.

action—theoretical action and practical action which serve as relays and form networks.

FOUCAULT: It seems to me that the political involvement of the intellectual was traditionally the product of two different aspects of his activity: his position as an intellectual in bourgeois society, in the system of capitalist production and within the ideology it produces or imposes (his exploitation, poverty, rejection, persecution, the accusations of subversive activity, immorality, etc); and his proper discourse to the extent that it revealed a particular truth, that it disclosed political relationships where they were unsuspected. These two forms of politicization did not exclude each other, but, being of a different order, neither did they coincide. Some were classed as "outcasts" and others as "socialists." During moments of violent reaction on the part of the authorities, these two positions were readily fused: after 1848, after the Commune, after 1940. The intellectual was rejected and persecuted at the precise moment when the facts became incontrovertible, when it was forbidden to say that the emperor had no clothes. The intellectual spoke the truth to those who had yet to see it, in the name of those who were forbidden to speak the truth: he was conscience, consciousness, and eloquence.

In the most recent upheaval,[3] the intellectual discovered that the masses no longer need him to gain knowledge: they *know* perfectly well, without illusion; they know far better than he and they are certainly capable of expressing themselves. But there exists a system of power which blocks, prohibits, and invalidates this discourse and this knowledge, a power not only found in the manifest authority of censorship, but one that profoundly and subtly penetrates an entire societal network. Intellectuals are themselves agents of this system of power—the idea of their responsibility for "consciousness" and discourse forms part of the system. The intellectual's role is no longer to place himself "somewhat ahead and to the side" in order to express the stifled

3. May 1968, popularly known as the "events of May."

truth of the collectivity; rather, it is to struggle against the forms
of power that transform him into its object and instrument in
the sphere of "knowledge," "truth," "consciousness," and
"discourse."[4]

In this sense theory does not express, translate, or serve to
apply practice: it is practice. But it is local and regional, as you
said, and not totalizing. This is a struggle against power, a struggle aimed at revealing and undermining power where it is most
invisible and insidious. It is not to "awaken consciousness" that
we struggle (the masses have been aware for some time that
consciousness is a form of knowledge; and consciousness as the
basis of subjectivity is a prerogative of the bourgeoisie), but to
sap power, to take power; it is an activity conducted alongside
those who struggle for power, and not their illumination from a
safe distance. A "theory" is the regional system of this struggle.

DELEUZE: Precisely. A theory is exactly like a box of tools. It
has nothing to do with the signifier. It must be useful. It must
function. And not for itself. If no one uses it, beginning with the
theoretician himself (who then ceases to be a theoretician),
then the theory is worthless or the moment is inappropriate.
We don't revise a theory, but construct new ones; we have no
choice but to make others. It is strange that it was Proust, an
author thought to be a pure intellectual, who said it so clearly:
treat my book as a pair of glasses directed to the outside; if they
don't suit you, find another pair; I leave it to you to find your
own instrument, which is necessarily an instrument for combat.
A theory does not totalize; it is an instrument for multiplication
and it also multiplies itself. It is in the nature of power to
totalize and it is your position, and one I fully agree with, that
theory is by nature opposed to power. As soon as a theory is
enmeshed in a particular point, we realize that it will never
possess the slightest practical importance unless it can erupt in
a totally different area. This is why the notion of reform is so
stupid and hypocritical. Either reforms are designed by people

4. See *L'Ordre du discours*, pp. 47–53.

who claim to be representative, who make a profession of speaking for others, and they lead to a division of power, to a distribution of this new power which is consequently increased by a double repression; or they arise from the complaints and demands of those concerned. This latter instance is no longer a reform but revolutionary action that questions (expressing the full force of its partiality) the totality of power and the hierarchy that maintains it. This is surely evident in prisons: the smallest and most insignificant of the prisoners' demands can puncture Pleven's pseudoreform.[5] If the protests of children were heard in kindergarten, if their questions were attended to, it would be enough to explode the entire educational system. There is no denying that our social system *is totally without tolerance;* this accounts for its extreme fragility in all its aspects and also its need for a global form of repression. In my opinion, you were the first—in your books and in the practical sphere—to teach us something absolutely fundamental: the indignity of speaking for others. We ridiculed representation and said it was finished, but we failed to draw the consequences of this "theoretical" conversion—to appreciate the theoretical fact that only those directly concerned can speak in a practical way on their own behalf.

FOUCAULT: And when the prisoners began to speak, they possessed an individual theory of prisons, the penal system, and justice. It is this form of discourse which ultimately matters, a discourse against power, the counter-discourse of prisoners and those we call delinquents—and not a theory *about* delinquency. The problem of prisons is local and marginal: not more than 100,000 people pass through prisons in a year. In France at present, between 300,000 and 400,000 have been to prison. Yet this marginal problem seems to disturb everyone. I was surprised that so many who had not been to prison could become interested in its problems, surprised that all those who had never heard the discourse of inmates could so easily understand them. How do we explain this? Isn't it because, in a general way, the penal

5. René Pleven was the prime minister of France in the early 1950s.

system is the form in which power is most obviously seen as power? To place someone in prison, to confine him there, to deprive him of food and heat, to prevent him from leaving, from making love, etc.—this is certainly the most frenzied manifestation of power imaginable. The other day I was speaking to a woman who had been in prison and she was saying: "Imagine, that at the age of forty, I was punished one day with a meal of dry bread." What is striking about this story is not the childishness of the exercise of power but the cynicism with which power is exercised as power, in the most archaic, puerile, infantile manner. As children we learn what it means to be reduced to bread and water. Prison is the only place where power is manifested in its naked state, in its most excessive form, and where it is justified as moral force. "I am within my rights to punish you because you know that it is criminal to rob and kill. . . ." What is fascinating about prisons is that, for once, power doesn't hide or mask itself; it reveals itself as tyranny pursued into the tiniest details; it is cynical and at the same time pure and entirely "justified," because its practice can be totally formulated within the framework of morality. Its brutal tyranny consequently appears as the serene domination of Good over Evil, of order over disorder.

DELEUZE: Yes, and the reverse is equally true. Not only are prisoners treated like children, but children are treated like prisoners. Children are submitted to an infantilization which is alien to them. On this basis, it is undeniable that schools resemble prisons and that factories are its closest approximation. Look at the entrance to a Renault plant, or anywhere else for that matter: three tickets to get into the washroom during the day. You found an eighteenth-century text by Jeremy Bentham proposing prison reforms; in the name of this exalted reform, he establishes a circular system where the renovated prison serves as a model and where the individual passes imperceptibly from school to the factory, from the factory to prison and vice versa. This is the essence of the reforming impulse, of reformed representation. On the contrary, when people begin to speak and act on their own behalf, they do not oppose their representation (even as its reversal) to another; they do not oppose a new representativity to the false representativity of power. For example, I remember your saying that there is no popular justice against justice; the reckoning takes place at another level.

FOUCAULT: I think that it is not simply the idea of better and more equitable forms of justice that underlies the people's hatred of the judicial system, of judges, courts, and prisons, but—aside from this and before anything else—the singular perception that power is always exercised at the expense of the people. The antijudicial struggle is a struggle against power and I don't think that it is a struggle against injustice, against the injustice of the judicial system, or a struggle for improving the efficiency of its institutions. It is particularly striking that in outbreaks of rioting and revolt or in seditious movements the judicial system has been as compelling a target as the financial structure, the army, and other forms of power. My hypothesis—but it is merely an hypothesis—is that popular courts, such as those found in the Revolution, were a means for the lower middle class, who were allied with the masses, to salvage and recapture the initiative in the struggle against the judicial system. To achieve this, they proposed a court system based on the possibility of equitable justice, where a judge might render a just verdict. The identifiable form of the court of law belongs to the bourgeois ideology of justice.

DELEUZE: On the basis of our actual situation, power emphatically develops a total or global vision. That is, all the current forms of repression (the rascist repression of immigrant workers, repression in the factories, in the educational system, and the general repression of youth) are easily totalized from the point of view of power. We should not only seek the unity of these forms in the reaction to May '68, but more appropriately, in the concerted preparation and organization of the near future. French capitalism now relies on a "margin" of unemployment and has abandoned the liberal and paternal mask that promised full employment. In this perspective, we begin to see the unity of the forms of repression: restrictions on immigration, once it is acknowledged that the most difficult and thankless jobs go to immigrant workers—repression in the factories, because the French must reacquire the "taste" for increasingly harder work; the struggle against youth and the repression of the educational system, because police repression is more active when there is less need for young people in the work force. A wide range of professionals (teachers, psychiatrists, educators of all kinds, etc.) will be called upon to exercise functions that have traditionally belonged to the police. This is something you predicted long ago, and it was thought impossible at the time: the reinforcement of all the structures of confinement. Against this global policy of power, we initiate localized counter-responses, skirmishes, active and occasionally preventive defenses. We have no need to totalize that which is invariably totalized on the side of power; if we were to move in this direction, it would mean restoring the representative forms of centralism and a hierarchical structure. We must set up lateral affiliations and an entire system of networks and popular bases; and this is especially difficult. In any case, we no longer define reality as a continuation of politics in the traditional sense of competition and the distribution of power, through the so-called representative agencies of the Communist Party or the General Workers Union.[6] Reality is what actually happens in factories, in schools, in barracks, in prisons, in police stations. And this action carries a type of information which is altogether different from that found in newspapers (this explains the kind of information carried by the *Agence de Press Libération*).[7]

FOUCAULT: Isn't this difficulty of finding adequate forms of struggle a result of the fact that we continue to ignore the problem of power? After all, we had to wait until the nineteenth

6. "Confédération Générale de Travailleurs."
7. Liberation News Agency.

century before we began to understand the nature of exploitation, and to this day, we have yet to fully comprehend the nature of power. It may be that Marx and Freud cannot satisfy our desire for understanding this enigmatic thing which we call power, which is at once visible and invisible, present and hidden, ubiquitous. Theories of government and the traditional analyses of their mechanisms certainly don't exhaust the field where power is exercised and where it functions. The question of power remains a total enigma. Who exercises power? And in what sphere? We now know with reasonable certainty who exploits others, who receives the profits, which people are involved, and we know how these funds are reinvested. But as for power . . . We know that it is not in the hands of those who govern. But, of course, the idea of the "ruling class" has never received an adequate formulation, and neither have other terms, such as "to dominate," "to rule," "to govern," etc. These notions are far too fluid and require analysis. We should also investigate the limits imposed on the exercise of power—the relays through which it operates and the extent of its influence on the often insignificant aspects of the hierarchy and the forms of control, surveillance, prohibition, and constraint. Everywhere that power exists, it is being exercised. No one, strictly speaking, has an official right to power; and yet it is always exerted in a particular direction, with some people on one side and some on the other. It is often difficult to say who holds power in a precise sense, but it is easy to see who lacks power. If the reading of your books (from *Nietzsche* to what I anticipate in *Capitalism and Schizophrenia*)[8] has been essential for me, it is because they seem to go very far in exploring this problem: under the ancient theme of meaning, of the signifier and the signified, etc., you have developed the question of power, of the inequality of powers and their strug-

8. *Nietzsche et la philosophie* (Paris: P.U.F., 1962) and *Capitalisme et schizophrenie*, vol. I, *L'Anti-Oedipe*, in collaboration with F. Guattari (Paris: Editions de Minuit, 1972). Neither book has been translated into English.

gles. Each struggle develops around a particular source of power
(any of the countless, tiny sources—a small-time boss, the mana-
ger of "H.L.M.,"[9] a prison warden, a judge, a union representative, the editor-in-chief of a newspaper). And if pointing out
these sources—denouncing and speaking out—is to be a part of
the struggle, it is not because they were previously unknown.
Rather, it is because to speak on this subject, to force the institutionalized networks of information to listen, to produce
names, to point the finger of accusation, to find targets, is the
first step in the reversal of power and the initiation of new struggles against existing forms of power. If the discourse of inmates
or prison doctors constitutes a form of struggle, it is because
they confiscate, at least temporarily, the power to speak on
prison conditions—at present, the exclusive property of prison
administrators and their cronies in reform groups. The discourse
of struggle is not opposed to the unconscious, but to the secre-
tive. It may not seem like much; but what if it turned out to be
more than we expected? A whole series of misunderstandings
relates to things that are "hidden," "repressed," and "unsaid";
and they permit the cheap "psychoanalysis" of the proper objects
of struggle. It is perhaps more difficult to unearth a secret than
the unconscious. The two themes frequently encountered in the
recent past, that "writing gives rise to repressed elements" and
that "writing is necessarily a subversive activity," seem to betray
a number of operations that deserve to be severely denounced.

DELEUZE: With respect to the problem you posed: it is clear
who exploits, who profits, and who governs, but power nevertheless remains something more diffuse. I would venture the following hypothesis: the thrust of Marxism was to define the problem
essentially in terms of interests (power is held by a ruling class
defined by its interests). The question immediately arises: how
is it that people whose interests are not being served can strictly
support the existing power structure by demanding a piece of the
action? Perhaps, this is because in terms of *investments*, whether

9. "Habitations à loyer modéré": moderate rental housing.

economic or unconscious, interest is not the final answer; there are investments of desire that function in a more profound and diffuse manner than our interests dictate. But of course, we never desire against our interests, because interest always follows and finds itself where desire has placed it. We cannot shut out the scream of Reich: the masses were not deceived; at a particular time, they actually wanted a fascist regime! There are investments of desire that mold and distribute power, that make it the property of the policeman as much as of the prime minister; in this context, there is no qualitative difference between the power wielded by the policeman and the prime minister. The nature of these investments of desire in a social group explains why political parties or unions, which might have or should have revolutionary investments in the name of class interests, are so often reform oriented or absolutely reactionary on the level of desire.

FOUCAULT: As you say, the relationship between desire, power, and interest are more complex than we ordinarily think, and it is not necessarily those who exercise power who have an interest in its execution; nor is it always possible for those with vested interests to exercise power. Moreover, the desire for power establishes a singular relationship between power and interest. It may happen that the masses, during fascist periods, desire that certain people assume power, people with whom they are unable to identify since these individuals exert power against the masses and at their expense, to the extreme of their death, their sacrifice, their massacre. Nevertheless, they desire this particular power; they want it to be exercised. This play of desire, power, and interest has received very little attention. It was a long time before we began to understand exploitation; and desire has had and continues to have a long history. It is possible that the struggles now taking place and the local, regional, and discontinuous theories that derive from these struggles and that are indissociable from them stand at the threshold of our discovery of the manner in which power is exercised.

DELEUZE: In this context, I must return to the question: the present revolutionary movement has created multiple centers, and not as the result of weakness or insufficiency, since a certain kind of totalization pertains to power and the forces of reaction. (Vietnam, for instance, is an impressive example of localized counter-tactics). But how are we to define the networks, the transversal links between these active and discontinuous points, from one country to another or within a single country?

FOUCAULT: The question of geographical discontinuity which you raise might mean the following: as soon as we struggle against exploitation, the proletariat not only leads the struggle but also defines its targets, its methods, and the places and instruments for confrontation; and to ally oneself with the proletariat is to accept its positions, its ideology, and its motives for combat. This means total identification. But if the fight is directed against power, then all those on whom power is exercised to their detriment, all who find it intolerable, can begin the struggle on their own terrain and on the basis of their proper activity (or passivity). In engaging in a struggle that concerns their own interests, whose objectives they clearly understand and whose methods only they can determine, they enter into a revolutionary process. They naturally enter as allies of the proletariat, because power is exercised the way it is in order to maintain capitalist exploitation. They genuinely serve the cause of the proletariat by fighting in those places where they find themselves oppressed. Women, prisoners, conscripted soldiers, hospital patients, and homosexuals have now begun a specific struggle against the particularized power, the constraints and controls, that are exerted over them. Such struggles are actually involved in the revolutionary movement to the degree that they are radical, uncompromising and nonreformist, and refuse any attempt at arriving at a new disposition of the same power with, at best, a change of masters. And these movements are linked to the revolutionary movement of the proletariat to the extent that they fight against the controls and constraints which serve the same system of power.

In this sense, the overall picture presented by the struggle is certainly not that of the totalization you mentioned earlier, this theoretical totalization under the guise of "truth." The generality of the struggle specifically derives from the system of power itself, from all the forms in which power is exercised and applied.

DELEUZE: And which we are unable to approach in any of its applications without revealing its diffuse character, so that we are necessarily led—on the basis of the most insignificant demand—to the desire to blow it up completely. Every revolutionary attack or defense, however partial, is linked in this way to the workers' struggle.

Revolutionary Action: "Until Now"

A discussion with Michel Foucault
under the auspices of *Actuel*

MICHEL FOUCAULT: What is the most intolerable form of repression for those of you currently enrolled in a lycée [high school]: family authority, the impact of the police on ordinary life, the organization and discipline imposed by the lycée, or the passive role encouraged by the press (and this may include a journal like *Actuel*)?

SERGE: Repression in the schools is the most obvious, since it is aimed at those groups trying to be active; it seems most violent and we experience its effects in the most immediate way.

ALAIN: We shouldn't ignore the street scene—the raids in the Latin Quarter, the constant harassment of drug searches by the police. They seem to be everywhere: no sooner do I sit down than someone in uniform is telling me to stand. Aside from this, the schools may be worse: the obvious repression, biased information.

SERGE: We must make distinctions: first, there is the action of parents who force their children into schools, as a necessary step toward a particular professional goal and who discourage anything that gets in the way; second, there is the administration which prohibits all forms of free or collective action; and finally, the teaching itself, but this is more complicated.

This interview appeared in *Actuel,* No. 14 (Nov. 1971), pp. 42–47. It is reproduced here by permission of *Actuel.* (Footnotes supplied by the editor.)

JEAN-PIERRE: In most cases, our classes are not immediately experienced as repressive, even if they are.

FOUCAULT: You're right, of course, since the communication of knowledge is always positive. Yet, as the events of May showed convincingly, it functions as a double repression: in terms of those it excludes from the process and in terms of the model and the standard (the bars) it imposes on those receiving this knowledge.

PHILIPPE: It's your belief, then, that our educational system is not meant to convey real knowledge, that its main objective is to separate the good from the bad, and that it does this according to the standards of social conformity?

FOUCAULT: Knowledge initially implies a certain political conformity in its presentation. In a history course, you are asked to learn certain things and to ignore others: thus, certain things form the content of knowledge and its norms.[1] To give two examples: official knowledge has always represented political power as arising from conflicts within a social class (the dynastic disagreements within the aristocracy or parliamentary conflicts in the middle class) or, perhaps, as a conflict generated between the aristocracy and the middle class. Popular movements, on the other hand, are said to arise from famines, taxes, or unemployment; and they never appear as the result of a struggle for power, as if the masses could dream of a full stomach but never of exercising power. The history of this struggle for power and the manner in which power is exercised and maintained remain totally obscured. Knowledge keeps its distance: this should not be known! To take another example: the workers, at the beginning of the nineteenth century, carried out detailed investigations into their material conditions. This work served Marx for the bulk of his documentation; it led, in large part, to the political and trade-union practices of the proletariat throughout the nineteenth century; it maintains and develops itself through

1. A repetition of the theme of exclusion found in *L'Ordre du discours*, pp. 10–23.

continuing struggles. Yet this knowledge has never been allowed to function within official knowledge. It is not specific processes that have been excluded from knowledge, but a certain kind of knowledge. And if we become aware of it today, it is in a secondary sense: through the study of Marx and those elements in his texts that are most easily assimilated into official knowledge.

JEAN-FRANÇOIS: For the sake of argument, Alain, would you say that most students in your school are from working class families?

ALAIN: A little under fifty percent.

JEAN-FRANÇOIS: Were trade unions discussed in your history courses?

ALAIN: Not in those I attended.

SERGE: Nor in mine. Look at the way our studies are organized: only past history is discussed in the lower grades. You're sixteen or seventeen before you arrive at modern ideas or movements— the only ones that can be slightly subversive. Yet even in the third year of a lycée, teachers of French absolutely refuse to discuss contemporary authors; and of course, there is never a word about the actual problems of life. When we do touch on them in the last two years, it's probably too late, given the conditioning of our past education.

FOUCAULT: As a way of approaching texts—as a matter of choice and exclusion—this presentation affects everything that is said and done in the present. The system is telling you in effect: "If you wish to understand and perceive events in the present, you can only do so through the past, through an understanding—carefully derived from the past—which was specifically developed to clarify the present." We have employed a wide range of categories—truth, man, culture, writing, etc.—to dispel the shock of daily occurrences, to dissolve the event. The obvious intention of those famous historical continuities is to explain; the eternal "return" to Freud, Marx, and others is obviously to lay a foundation. But both function to exclude the radical break introduced by events.[2] In the broadest sense, both the nature of

2. Ibid., p. 59.

events and the fact of power are invariably excluded from knowledge as presently constituted in our culture. This is to be expected since the power of a certain class (which determines this knowledge) must appear inaccesible to events; and the event, in its dangerous aspect, must be dominated and dissolved in the continuity of power maintained by this class, by a class power which is never defined. On the other hand, the proletariat develops a form of knowledge which concerns the struggle for power, the manner in which they can give rise to an event, respond to its urgency, avoid it, etc.; this is a knowledge absolutely alien to the first kind because of its preoccupation with power and events. For this reason, we should not be fooled by the modernized educational program, its openness to the real world: it continues to maintain its traditional grounding in "humanism" while emphasizing the quick and efficient mastery of a certain number of techniques, which were neglected in the past. Humanism reinforces social organization and these techniques allow society to progress, but along its own lines.

JEAN-FRANÇOIS: What criticism do you direct against humanism; and what values, in another system for transmitting knowledge, can replace it?

FOUCAULT: By humanism I mean the totality of discourse through which Western man is told: "Even though you don't exercise power, you can still be a ruler. Better yet, the more you deny yourself the exercise of power, the more you submit to those in power, then the more this increases your sovereignty." Humanism invented a whole series of subjected sovereignties: the soul (ruling the body, but subjected to God), consciousness (sovereign in a context of judgment, but subjected to the necessities of truth), the individual (a titular control of personal rights subjected to the laws of nature and society), basic freedom (sovereign within, but accepting the demands of an outside world and "aligned with destiny"). In short, humanism is everything in Western civilization that restricts *the desire for power*: it prohibits the desire for power and excludes the possibility of power being seized. The theory of the subject (in the double sense of the word) is at the heart of humanism and this is why our culture has tenaciously rejected anything that could weaken its hold upon us. But it can be attacked in two ways: either by a "desubjectification" of the will to power (that is, through political struggle in the context of class warfare) or by the destruction of the subject as a pseudosovereign (that is, through an attack on "culture": the suppression of taboos and the limitations and divisions imposed upon the sexes; the setting up of communes; the loosening of inhibitions with regard to drugs; the breaking of all the prohibitions that form and guide the development of a normal individual). I am referring to all those experiences which have been rejected by our civilization or which it accepts only within literature.[3]

JEAN-FRANÇOIS: Since the Renaissance?

FOUCAULT: From the beginning of Roman law—the armature of our civilization that exists as a definition of individuality as subjected sovereignty. The system of private property implies this conception: the proprietor is fully in control of his goods; he can use or abuse them, but he must nevertheless submit to the laws that support his claim to property. The Roman system structured the government and established the basis of property. It controlled the will to power by fixing the "sovereign right of property" as the exclusive possession of those in power. Through this elegant exchange, humanism was institutionalized.

JEAN-PIERRE: Society forms an organized whole. It is repressive by nature because it seeks to reproduce itself and perpetuate its existence. How is struggle possible: are we dealing with a global and indissociable organism which responds to a general law of conservation and evolution, or is it a more differentiated entity where one class tries to maintain its interest against another, where one class profits by maintaining order and another is set

3. Cf. *The Order of Things*, p. 300.

on its destruction? The answer is far from obvious: I don't subscribe to the first hypothesis, but the second seems too simplistic. There is, in fact, interdependence within the social organism which perpetuates itself.

FOUCAULT: The movement of May suggests an initial response: the individuals who were subjected to the educational system, to the most constraining forms of conservatism and repetition, fought a revolutionary battle. In this sense, the intellectual crisis created by the events of May goes very deep. Society has been placed in an extremely perplexing and embarrassing position from which it has yet to extricate itself.

JEAN-PIERRE: But teaching is far from being the only instrument of humanism, the only tool for social repression—there are more essential mechanisms that operate before we enter school or outside of school.

FOUCAULT: It has always been a problem for someone like me, someone who has been teaching for a long time, to decide if I should act outside or inside the university. Should we decide that the question was settled in May, that the university has broken down, and that we can now move on to other concerns? (This is plainly the direction of some of the groups with whom I am working in the struggle against repression, in the penal system, in psychiatric hospitals, and in the police or judicial systems.) Or is this merely a way of evading a fact that continues to embarrass me: namely, that the university structure remains intact and that we must continue to fight in this arena?

JEAN-FRANÇOIS: Personally, I don't believe that the university was actually demolished. I think that the Maoists were wrong to dismiss the university—which might have served as a solid base—to cultivate the factory where their task was especially difficult and their position relatively artificial. The university was in the process of cracking: we should have widened the fissure; we should have created an irreparable rupture in the system that transmits knowledge. The school and the university remain decisive. Life doesn't end at the age of five, even if one does have an alcoholic father and a mother who does her ironing in the bedroom.

JEAN-PIERRE: The revolt in the universities immediately confronted a problem—always the same one: the revolutionaries, or those who had nothing practical to gain from their education, were blocked by the students who wanted to work and to learn a trade. What were we to do? Search for new methods? New content?

JEAN-FRANÇOIS: In the last analysis, this would only improve the present structure and train more students for the system.

PHILIPPE: That isn't so. We can learn different things and be exposed, in a different way, to a different knowledge without falling back into the system. If the university is abandoned after it's been shaken a bit, it will continue to function and to reproduce itself through inertia—unless we can propose concrete alternatives and gain the support of its victims.

FOUCAULT: The university stands for the institutional apparatus through which society ensures its uneventful reproduction, at the least cost to itself. The disorder within institutions of higher learning, their imminent demise (whether real or apparent), does not extend to the society's will for conservation, identity, and repetition. You are asking what can be done to disrupt the system's cycle of social reproduction; and it isn't enough to suppress or overturn the university. Other forms of repression must also be attacked.

JEAN-PIERRE: Unlike Philippe, I don't hold with this idea of a "different" education. What would interest me, on the other hand, would be the reversal of the university's functions under revolutionary pressure: undoing earlier conditioning and destroying established values and knowledge. An increasing number of teachers are prepared to attempt this.

FRÉDÉRIC: Experiences of this sort carried to their logical conclusion are very rare. Only Sénik comes to mind, a professor of philosophy at Bergson in 1969: he was actually able to demolish the status of the teacher and of knowledge in general. Of course, he was quickly isolated and excluded. Academic institutions still possess active mechanisms to defend themselves. They are still capable of integrating a great many things and of eliminating those foreign objects they cannot assimilate.

You speak as if French universities, before May 1968, were adapted to our industrial society. In my opinion, they were not particularly profitable or functional, but especially archaic. The events of May effectively fractured the old institutional framework of higher education. But did the ruling class suffer? It reconstructed the system and it is now far more functional. It preserved the best schools, those whose primary function was the selection of technocrats. It created a center like Dauphine, the first American-style business school in France. And finally, for the last three years, official opposition has been confined to Vincennes and to certain departments at Nanterre—university pockets that are irrelevant to the system, nets in which the small fish of the left have been trapped. The university eliminates its archaic structure and it effectively adapts itself to the needs of neocapitalism; it is now that we should return to the field of struggle.

FOUCAULT: I'm afraid I was referring to the "death of the university" in the most superficial way. The events of May effectively ended the form of higher education that began in the nineteenth century—the curious set of institutions that transformed a small proportion of the young into a social elite. This nevertheless leaves the full range of hidden mechanisms through which a society conveys its knowledge and ensures its survival under the mask of knowledge: newspapers, television, technical schools, and the lycée (even more than the university).

SERGE: Repression in the lycée continues unchecked. The educational system is sick, but only a minority are aware of this and dare to oppose it.

ALAIN: And the politicized minority of two or three years ago has disappeared from our school.

JEAN-FRANÇOIS: Does the fact of long hair continue to mean something?

ALAIN: Not anymore. Fashionable students now let their hair grow.

JEAN-FRANÇOIS: And drugs?

SERGE: Drug use has no meaning in itself. It largely means that a student has abandoned the idea of a career. The politicized students continue their studies; those who take drugs leave school altogether.

FOUCAULT: The campaign against drugs is a pretext for the reinforcement of social repression; not only through police raids, but also through the indirect exaltation of the normal, rational, conscientious, and well-adjusted individual. This prominent image can be found at every level. Read today's headlines in "France-Soir": fifty-three percent of the French population favors the death penalty, while only thirty-eight percent were supporting it a month ago.

JEAN-FRANÇOIS: Does this stem from the revolt at Clairvaux prison?

FOUCAULT: Evidently. We emphasize the fear of criminals: we brandish the threat of the monstrous so as to reinforce the ideology of good and evil, of the things that are permitted and prohibited—precisely those notions which teachers are now somewhat embarrassed to communicate. What the professor of philosophy no longer dares to say in his convoluted language, the journalist can now say in the most direct fashion. You might think that this has always been the case, that journalists and professors always existed to say the same things. But journalists are now expected, if not forced, to say these things in a loud and persistent voice, and at precisely the moment when professors no longer can. There is an interesting story in this: because of Clairvaux, a week of revenge was inflicted on the prisons. Inmates were indiscriminately beaten by the guards, especially at Fleury-Mérogis, the prison for juveniles. The mother of an inmate came to see us, and I went with her to R.T.L.[4] to find coverage for her report. A journalist agreed to see us and said: "You know, I'm not surprised by this; the guards are nearly as degenerate as the prisoners." A professor who spoke this way in a lycée would create a small riot and would have his ears boxed.

PHILIPPE: That's true; a teacher would never speak this way. Is it that he no longer can or that he would say it differently, in keeping with his role? In your opinion, how can we fight this ideology and its mechanisms of repression, apart from petitions and other actions of reform?

FOUCAULT: Local actions which are well-timed can be quite effective. Consider the actions of the G.I.P. (Information Group on Prisons) during the past year. The ultimate goal of its interventions was not to extend the visiting rights of prisoners to thirty minutes or to procure flush toilets for the cells, but to question the social and moral distinction between the innocent and the guilty. And if this goal was to be more than a philosophical statement or a humanist desire, it had to be pursued at the level of gestures, practical actions, and in relation to specific situations. Confronted by this penal system, the humanist would say: "The guilty are guilty and the innocent are innocent. Nevertheless, the convict is a man like any other and society must respect what is human in him: consequently, flush toilets!" Our action, on the contrary, isn't concerned with the soul or the man *behind* the convict, but it seeks to obliterate the deep division that lies between innocence and guilt. This was Genet's emphasis with relation to the judge at the Soledad trial or the plane hijacked by the Palestinians in Jordan; the newspapers decried the fate of the judge and the poor tourists being held in the middle of the desert for no apparent reason. Genet, for his part, was saying: "But is the judge innocent and what of an American lady who can afford to be a tourist in this way?"

PHILIPPE: Does this mean that your primary objective is to

4. Radio Luxembourg.

raise consciousness and that you can neglect, for the moment, the struggle against political and economic institutions?

FOUCAULT: You have badly misunderstood me. If it were a question of raising consciousness, we could simply publish newspapers and books, or attempt to win over a radio or television producer. We wish to attack an institution at the point where it culminates and reveals itself in a simple and basic ideology, in the notions of good and evil, innocence and guilt. We wish to change this ideology which is experienced through those dense institutional layers where it has been invested, crystallized, and reproduced. More simply, humanism is based on the desire to change the ideological system without altering institutions; and reformers wish to change the institution without touching the ideological system. Revolutionary action, on the contrary, is defined as the simultaneous agitation of consciousness and institutions; this implies that we attack the relationships of power through the notions and institutions that function as their instruments, armature, and armor. Do you think that the teaching of philosophy—and its moral code—would remain unchanged if the penal system collapsed?

JEAN-PIERRE: We can also reverse the question. Could we imprison people in the present way if we changed the educational system? Most of all, we should not restrict our actions to a single sector where the movement bogs down in individual reforms. We should move from the educational system to the prisons, from the prisons to the asylum. Isn't this your basic intention?

FOUCAULT: We have already started interventions in the asylum, using methods similar to those employed in the prisons: a kind of aggressive enquiry formulated, at least in part, by those who are being investigated. The repressive role of the asylum is well known: people are locked up and subjected to treatment—chemical or psychological—over which they have no control; or they are subjected to the nontreatment of a straitjacket. But the influence of psychiatry extends beyond this to the activity of social workers, professional guidance counsellors, school psychologists, and doctors who dispense psychiatric advice to their patients—all the psychiatric components of everyday life which form something like a third order of repression and policing. This infiltration is spreading throughout society, and this is not counting those psychiatrists who publish advice in the newspapers. The psychopathology of everyday life may reveal the unconscious facets of desire; the "psychiatrization" of everyday life, if it were closely examined, might reveal the invisible hand of power.

JEAN-FRANÇOIS: On what level do you plan to act? Can you address yourself to social workers?

FOUCAULT: No. We would like to work with students in the lycée, those whose education has been supervised, anyone who has been subjected to psychological or psychiatric repression in their choice of studies, in their relationships to their family, in their response to sexuality or drugs. We wish to know how they were divided, distributed, selected, and excluded in the name of psychiatry and of the normal individual, that is, in the name of humanism.

JEAN-FRANÇOIS: Aren't you interested in antipsychiatry, in working with psychiatrists in the asylum?

FOUCAULT: This is a task for psychiatrists, since entry into an asylum is restricted. We should, nevertheless, be careful that this movement directed against psychiatry, which opposes the idea of the asylum, does not ultimately serve to introduce psychiatry into the outside world by multiplying its interventions upon daily life.

FRÉDÉRIC: The situation in prisons is apparently worse, because the only relationships they sanction center on the conflict between the victims and the agents of repression: no "progressive" brutes will enlist in the movement. In the asylum, on the other hand, the struggle is being led by psychiatrists and not the victims: the agents of repression are fighting repression. Is this really an advantage?

FOUCAULT: I'm not sure. Unlike prison revolts, it is only with great difficulty that a patient's rejection of the psychiatric hospital can become a collective and political action. The problem is to know whether patients subjected to the segregation of the asylum can stand against the institution and finally denounce the very division that designates and excludes them as mentally ill. Basaglia, the psychiatrist, attempted some experiments of this kind in Italy: he brought together the patients, the doctors, and the hospital personnel, but not to stage a sociodrama where each could expose his fantasies and re-enact the primal scene. Rather, he posed this question: could the victims of the asylum initiate a political struggle against the social structure that denounces them as mad? These experiments were savagely prohibited.

FRÉDÉRIC: The distinction between the normal and the pathological is even stronger than that between innocence and guilt.

FOUCAULT: They reinforce each other. When a judgment cannot be framed in terms of good and evil, it is stated in terms of normal and abnormal. And when it is necessary to justify this last distinction, it is done in terms of what is good or bad for the individual. These are expressions that signal the fundamental duality of Western consciousness.

In more general terms, this also means that we can't defeat the system through isolated actions; we must engage it on all fronts—the university, the prisons, and the domain of psychiatry—one after another since our forces are not strong enough for a simultaneous attack. We strike and knock against the most solid obstacles; the system cracks at another point; we persist. It seems that we're winning, but then the institution is rebuilt; we must start again. It is a long struggle; it is repetitive and seemingly incoherent. But the system it opposes, as well as the power exercised through the system, supplies its unity.

ALAIN: This is a tiresome question, but it must be faced eventually: what replaces the system?

FOUCAULT: I think that to imagine another system is to extend our participation in the present system. This is perhaps what happened in the history of the Soviet Union: apparently, new institutions were in fact based on elements taken from an earlier system—the Red Army reconstituted on the model of the Czarist army, the return to realism in art, and the emphasis on traditional family morality. The Soviet Union returned to the standards of bourgeois society in the nineteenth century, and perhaps, more as a result of Utopian tendencies than a concern for realities.

FRÉDÉRIC: I don't accept that. Marxism defined itself as scientific socialism as opposed to Utopian socialism. It refused to declare itself on the possible forms of future society. Soviet society was besieged by concrete problems, by the problems generated by the civil war. The war must be won and the factories must operate: consequently, its recourse to the only available and immediately effective models—the military hierarchy and the Taylor system.[5] If the Soviet Union has progressively assimilated the standards of bourgeois society, it is probably because they were the only ones available. It is not utopianism, but its absence, that is in question. Utopianism might have a key role to play.

JEAN-FRANÇOIS: The present movement may require a utopian model and a theoretical elaboration that goes beyond the sphere of partial and repressed experiences.

FOUCAULT: Why not the opposite? Reject theory and all forms of general discourse. This need for theory is still part of the system we reject.

JEAN-FRANÇOIS: You feel that the simple fact of employing a theory still relates to the dynamic of bourgeois knowledge?

FOUCAULT: Maybe so. I would rather oppose actual experiences than the possibility of a utopia. It is possible that the rough outline of a future society is supplied by the recent experiences with drugs, sex, communes, other forms of consciousness, and other forms of individuality. If scientific socialism emerged from the *Utopias* of the nineteenth century, it is possible that a real socialization will emerge, in the twentieth century, from *experiences.*

5. Frederick W. Taylor, *The Principles of Scientific Management* (1911). Lenin, in a speech in 1919, advised the adoption of Taylor's time and study techniques.

JEAN-FRANÇOIS: The events of May were, of course, the experience of a certain power. But this experience essentially implied utopian discourse: May was a discourse occupying a space.

PHILIPPE: A discourse that was inadequate. The older ideas of the Left had only a marginal relationship to the aspirations liberated in May. The movement could have gone much further if it had been supported by an adequate theory, a thought capable of providing it with new perspectives.

FOUCAULT: I'm not convinced of this. But Jean-François has reason to speak of the experience of power. It is of the utmost importance that thousands of people exercised a power which did not assume the form of a hierarchical organization. Unfortunately, since power is by definition that which the ruling class abandons least readily and recaptures on the first occasion, it was impossible to maintain the experience for longer than a few weeks.

PHILIPPE: If I understand you correctly, you think that it's also useless or premature to create parallel circuits like the free universities in the United States that duplicate the institutions being attacked.

FOUCAULT: If you wish to replace an official institution by another institution that fulfills the same function—better and differently—then you are already being reabsorbed by the dominant structure.

JEAN-FRANÇOIS: I can't believe that the movement must remain at its present state, as this vague, unsubstantial, underground ideology that refuses to endorse any form of social work or community service, any action that requires going beyond the immediate group. It's unable to assume the responsibility for the whole of society, or it may be that it's incapable of conceiving of society as a whole.

FOUCAULT: You wonder if a global society could function without a general discourse on the basis of such divergent and dispersed experiences. I believe, on the contrary, that this particular idea of the "whole of society" derives from a utopian context.

This idea arose in the Western world, within this highly individualized historical development that culminates in capitalism.
To speak of the "whole of society" apart from the only form it
has ever taken is to transform our past into a dream. We readily
believe that the least we can expect of experiences, actions, and
strategies is that they take into account the "whole of society."
This seems absolutely essential for their existence. But I believe
that this is asking a great deal, that it means imposing impossible conditions on our actions because this notion functions in a
manner that prohibits the actualization, success, and perpetuation
of these projects. "The whole of society" is precisely that which
should not be considered except as something to be destroyed.
And then, we can only hope that it will never exist again.

FRÉDÉRIC: The social forms of Western culture were univer-
salized as a "social whole" that is embodied by the state, and
not necessarily because it stood as the best model, but because
it has material power and superior efficiency. Our problem is that
all successful revolts against the system succeeded by reinforcing
similar kinds of organization—under partisan or state control—
forms which exactly correspond to the dominant structure and
which pose the essential question of power. This includes
Leninism, but also the Maoist revolt: a popular organization and
army against a bourgeois organization and army, dictatorship
and the proletarian state. These instruments, initially conceived
for taking power, must disappear after the transition stage. Of
course, this is never the case as shown by the Bolshevik experience; and the cultural revolution in China was unable fully to
eliminate them. As a condition for victory, they maintain their
own dynamic which is quickly directed against the spontaneities
they helped to liberate. Plainly a contradiction, and it may be
the fundamental contradiction of revolutionary action.

FOUCAULT: What strikes me in your argument is that it takes
the form of "until now." However, a revolutionary undertaking
is directed not only against the present but against the rule of
"until now."

Index

Abraham, Karl, 32
absence, 31, 46, 48-49, 50, 81-86, 165-166; of historical sense, 156; of writer, 53-55, 116-117; *see also* writing
absence d'oeuvre (l'), 21, 85-86
Actuel, 218
affirmation: and limited being, 36-37; the thought of, 187-196
Apollonian, 22
Arabian Nights, The, 58, 117, 119
archaeology, 16-17, 25
Archaeology of Knowledge (Foucault), 25
Archipelago (Hölderlin), 68
Aristotle, 131, 166, 167, 182, 186; theory of knowledge, 202
art: limit of, 80; madness and, 74-76, 79, 80, 84-86; in the museum, 92-93; and representation, 73, 206-207
Artaud, A., 25, 172, 180n
artist: replaces epic hero, 72-75
author, 17, 19, 113-138; Aristotle as, 121; authority of, 126; death of, 117, 120; discursive function, 21, 115-120, 124-136; and *écriture*, 119, 120; meaning of name, 121-124; regularity, 127-131; role of "I," 129-130; Shakespeare as, 122; *see also* writing; transgression

Balzac, Honoré de, 123
Bataille, Georges, 25, 171; function of the eye, 44-49; the "inner experience," 32, 44-46, 49; limits of language, 39-40, 48, 52; *see also* language; transgression
Beck, Adolf, 69
Beckett, Samuel, 25, 115
Beissner, Friedrich, 69
Bentham, Jeremy, 210
Birth of the Clinic (Foucault), 16
Blanchot, Maurice, 25, 36, 38, 53, 84
Bleu du ciel (Bataille), 47
Borges, Jorges Luis, 25, 56, 61, 92
Bosch, Hieronymus, 88
Bouvard et Pécuchet (Flaubert), 88, 105-109; acategorical beings, 187-188; role of the book, 107-109
Breughel the Elder, 88
Buffon, G. L. L. de, 113, 114

Cantor, George, 136
Capital (Marx), 131
Capitalism and Schizophrenia (Deleuze), 213
Cartesian: grammar, 134; philosophy, 19, 44, 48, 185
Char, René, 86
Chomsky, Noam, 134
Chrysippus, 172
Cimabue (Cenno di Pepi), 72
Clement of Alexandria, 119
Coelina (or *The Child of Mystery*), 63
Communist Manifesto (Marx), 131
consciousness, 18, 23, 175, 208, 230; limit of, 30; and representation, 17; scientific, 162-164; *see also* history

Coppée, François, 89
Cordemoy, 134
Cuvier, Georges, 113, 114, 133
Cynics, 169

Danse des Morts (Flaubert), 88
Darwin, Charles, 114
Da Vinci, Leonardo, 73
De Anima (Aristotle), 202
death, 20, 21, 47-51; of God, 30-33,
    86, 121, 171; of God and the
    limit, 19, 32, 48-51; and language,
    47-48, 53-55, 59, 66; of the sub-
    ject, 51, 162-164; writing against,
    53-55, 116-117; see also trans-
    gression
Déjeuner sur l'herbe (Manet), 92
De la grammatologie (Derrida), 15
Deleuze, Gilles, 22-25, 165-196; the
    new thought of, 196; see also
    difference
Descartes, René, 48
De Viris Illustribus (Saint Jerome),
    127
diagnosis, 18; genealogy as, 145, 156-
    157
dialectic, 33-38, 40-41, 51; of pro-
    duction, 49-50; treatment of dif-
    ference, 184-185
Diderot, Denis, 57-58
difference: in Bataille, 36; definition
    of, 20, 23, 181-187; the form of
    time, 192-196; and identity, 182;
    liberation of, 186, 192; see also
    genealogy
Différence et répétition (Deleuze),
    22, 165, 181
Diogenes Laertes, 119, 169
Dionysus, 22, 83, 192, 193
Diotima, 70, 76, 80
discontinuity, 16, 17, 20; within his-
    tory, 154
discourse: author within, 124-136;
    initiators of practice, 21, 131-136;
    limits of language, 38, 39, 43;
    practice of, 24, 199-201; as prop-
    erty, 124-125; scientific, 125-126
Don Quixote (Cervantes), 69, 91
Du Camp, Maxime, 88
Duns Scotus, 186-187, 195-196

écriture, 119, 120
L'écriture et la différence (Derrida),
    15
Empedocles (Hölderlin), 19, 59, 82
Epicurus, 169, 172
Eponine (Bataille), 31
Eroticism (Bataille), 29n
eroticism, 33, 38, 47, 50
Esquirol, 204
event(s): death as pure event, 174;
    definition of, 172-176; grammar
    of, 174-175; in history, 144, 154-
    155, 220; logic of, 173-174; of
    May, 207, 211, 219, 223, 225;
    metaphysics of, 172-173, 175-176;
    philosophy of, 23, 154; related to
    phantasm, 176-181; related to
    thought, 177-179; and simulacrum,
    168
exteriority, 17, 32, 116

fantastic (the), 90
Faust (Tolstoi), 93
"The Fettered River" (Hölderlin),
    68
Fichte, Johann Gottlieb, 70, 163, 196
Filippo Lippi, 73, 74
Flaubert, Gustave, 18, 19, 87-109,
    117; experience of the fantastic,
    90; meaning of the library, 90-92;
    and stupidity, 107-109
Fretet, Jean, 76
Freud, Sigmund, 21, 23, 25, 29, 81,
    172, 180, 213, 220; as initiator of
    discursive practice, 131-136

Galileo, Galilei, 133, 134, 135
Ganymede (Hölderlin), 69
Gay Science (Nietzsche), 140, 202
genealogy, 17, 22, 24, 25, 181;
    curative science, 156-157; dissocia-
    tion of identity, 146-148, 154,
    160-162, 164; and knowledge, 140,
    144, 153-154, 157, 159, 162-164;
    recorded on the body, 147-148,
    153, 155, 156, 163; records domi-
    nations, 148-151, 154; recovery
    within, 18, 146; reevaluation of
    history, 140-144, 159-160; sin-
    gularity of its object, 139, 181

Genealogy of Morals (Nietzsche), 18, 22, 40, 141
Genet, Jean, 227
George, Stefan, 68
Ghirlandaio, Domenico, 73
Giorgione, 92
Giotto, 72, 74
G.I.P., 206, 227
Gontard, Suzette, 70, 76, 79, 80
Gothic Romance, 132
Goya, Francisco, 88
Grund Zum Empedokles (Hölderlin), 69
Gundolf, Friedrich, 68

Hegel, G. W. F., 80, 163, 184, 185, 186
Hippolyte, Jean, 81
Histoire de l'oeil (Bataille), 52
history, 16, 22, 23, 103, 115; for analysis of discourse, 137; effective ("wirkliche"), 154-157; events within, 175-176; form of demagogy, 158-160; parodic, 160-161, 164; and philosophy, 140, 143-144, 151-153, 155-156, 175-176; of philosophy, 202; role of historian, 152, 155-160; source of identity, 17, 20, 42, 144, 145, 151, 154, 160-162; in *The Temptation*, 104
Hölderlin, Friedrich, 18, 25, 68-86; at Jena, 69, 70, 77-78, 85; language of, 19, 59, 71, 86; madness of, 69, 71; transformed the work of art, 74-76, 84-86
Hölderlin Jahrbuch, 68, 71
Homer, 22, 42, 53, 55, 122, 131
Hugo, Victor, 89
Human, All Too Human (Nietzsche), 140, 141, 162
humanism, 221-222, 228
human sciences, 15-18
Humboldt, Alexander von, 134
Hyperion (Hölderlin), 78, 79, 80

identity, 20, 23, 184; related to history, 17, 142, 145, 151, 154, 160-162
interpretation, 21-22
Interpretation of Dreams (Freud), 131

Jaspers, Karl, 71
Joyce, James, 92

Kafka, Franz, 60, 92, 117
Kalb, Charlotte von, 70
Kant, Immanuel, 36, 38, 40, 49, 85, 196
Kierkegaard, Soren, 122
Klein, Melanie, 81, 132
Klossowski, Pierre, 25, 38, 165, 196
knowledge, 18, 20, 50, 99, 102, 105, 153, 188, 208; absolute, 21, 163-164; in Aristotle and Nietzsche, 202-204; creates phantasm, 90; for cutting, 154; and desire, 24-25, 158, 201; discourse regulates, 200; genealogical attitude toward, 140, 153-154, 157, 159, 162-164; as "invention," 202-203; of the origin, 143; as perspective, 156-157; politics of, 219-221

Lacan, Jacques, 81
Lange, Heinrich, 69
language, 18, 19, 21, 25, 41, 55, 86; of Bataille, 39-40, 44; and death, 19, 47-49, 53-55, 59, 66; and the death of God, 30-31, 33, 49, 86; discursive, 17, 19, 21, 38-39, 43, 60; of Hölderlin, 71, 79, 83-84, 86; infinite, 60, 66; within the library, 66-67; limit of, 21, 30, 33, 40-41, 48, 51, 53-55, 61, 65, 69, 79, 84; loss of, 19, 32, 42-44, 48, 51, 59, 71, 79, 86, 116; philosophical, 19, 41-42, 44; related to madness, 71-72; representative, 19, 21, 60, 206-208; self-reflexive, 19-20, 44, 49, 50, 54-60, 109; sovereignty of experience, 86; *see also* sexuality; transgression
Laplanche, Jean, 72, 76, 80, 84
Larmes d'Eros (Bataille), 44
Leibniz, G. W. von, 184, 196
Leigler, L., 69
Leiris, M., 51, 166, 181
library, 90-91, 92, 105; space of language, 66-67
"Library of Babel" (Borges), 66

limit, 30, 32-33, 36-37, 40, 46, 49, 50, 79-80, 83, 86, 116; and the death of God, 32, 48-49, 50; in language, 39-40, 43-44, 48, 51, 79, 83-84, 86; and transgression, 33-35, 40; in the work of art, 79-80

literature, 19, 20, 23, 57, 60, 64, 66, 86, 92; and imagination, 91-92; ontology of, 57; *see also* language; transgression

Livre, Le (Mallarmé), 92

Logique du sens (Deleuze), 22, 23, 165, 170, 177, 179, 181

Lucretius, 172

Madame Bovary (Flaubert), 87, 88

madness, 18, 20, 21; *see also* art; Hölderlin, Friedrich

Madness and Civilization (Foucault), 16, 20, 24

Mallarmé, Stéphane, 92

Manet, Edouard, 92-93

Marx, Karl, 21, 23, 25, 114, 180, 213, 219, 220; initiator of discursive practice, 131-136

Mémoires d'un Fou (Flaubert), 88

Merleau-Ponty, Maurice, 175

Metaphysics (Aristotle), 202

Michelangelo, 73

Michelet, Jules, 91

Müller, Andreas, 69

Mysteries of Udolpho (Ann Radcliffe), 132

neopositivism, 175-176

Newton, Isaac, 134, 136

Nicomachean Ethics (Aristotle), 202

Nietzsche (Deleuze), 213

Nietzsche, Friedrich, 17-19, 21-25, 36-38, 42, 139-164, 181, 195, 196, 202; definition of "works," 118; eternal return in, 192-196; sense of history, 160–164; theory of knowledge, 202-204; *see also* genealogy; history

Nouvelle Justine (Sade), 91

Novalis (Friedrich von Hardenberg), 78, 85

Novum Organum (Bacon), 19

Nun, The (Diderot), 57-58

Odyssey, 53-55

Olympia (Manet), 92

Order of Discourse (Foucault), 24, 25

Order of Things (Foucault), 15-18, 113-115

origin, 22, 37, 143-144, 156; as *Entstehung*, 145, 148-152, 159; as *Herkunft*, 140-141, 145-148, 152, 157; as *Ursprung*, 140-142; of the work of art, 53-56, 60

Outline of Psychoanalysis (Freud), 136

phantasm: definition of, 166, 187; for the Epicureans, 169-170; and the event, 176-181, 187; in Flaubert, 90, 100; in history, 155

phenomenology, 175-176

Phenomenology of Perception (Merleau-Ponty), 170

philosophy, 22, 23, 37, 41, 50; as "anti-Platonic," 166; emergence of, 159-160; Epicurean, 169, 171-172; of history, 175-176; language of, 42, 43-44, 46, 48, 51; of representation, 172, 183, 186, 206-207; placement of subject within, 18-19, 41-44, 46, 51, 183; as theater, 25, 196; *see also* Deleuze, Gilles; history; Platonism; thought

Pierrot lunaire (Schoenberg), 196

Plato, 22, 42, 75, 141, 160, 166-169, 202

Platonism, 22-23; effect on history, 160; overturning of, 166-169

Pound, Ezra, 92

power: definition of, 211-217; and knowledge, 24-25; struggle against, 211

practice, 24; discursive, 131-136, 199-201; within the institution, 23, 223-225; role of intellectuals, 206-208

prisons, 209-211, 226-227, 229

Proust, Marcel, 117, 208

psychoanalysis, 15, 132-136, 171-172, 179, 201, 214

Quinet, Edgar, 91

Radcliffe, Ann, 132
Raphael, 92
Ree, Paul, 139, 141
regularity: of "author-function," 127-131; in discursive practice, 199-200; writing as, 116
Reich, W., 215
repetition, 186-196; of event, 177; as recurrence, 192-196; *see also* difference
Rêve d'Enfer (Flaubert), 88
reversal, 22; principle of writing, 17, 116, 117; in *The Temptation*, 98-99; *see also* genealogy
revolutionary action, 209-212, 228-230, 232-233
rhetoric, 66-67
Ricardo, David, 113
Roussel, Raymond, 92
rupture, 21, 36, 71, 84-85

Sade, Marquis de, 18, 25, 29, 30, 33, 40, 50, 60, 62, 91, 118, 171; language of, 19, 39-40; works, 60-63, 65-66
sadism, 19, 62
Saint Augustine, 89
Saint Jerome, 127-129
Salammbô (Flaubert), 87, 88
Sand, Georges, 96
Sartre, Jean Paul, 175
Saussure, Ferdinand de, 133
Schiller, J. C. F. von, 70, 76, 77-78
Schlegel, Friedrich, 85
Schopenhauer, Arthur, 141, 202
Searle, John, 121
Sentimental Education (Flaubert), 87
series, 165-166, 180
Serres, Michel, 134
sexuality, 20, 21; denatured by language, 29, 50; and dialectics, 49-52; form of language, 30-31, 50-52; and the limit, 30; modern experience of, 31, 50; *see also* Bataille, Georges; Sade, Marquis de
Shakespeare, William, 159
simulacrum, 23, 167, 170-171
Smahr (Flaubert), 88
Socrates, 22, 43, 158-160, 166, 167, 196

Sophist (Plato), 166
Sophists, 22, 196
Sorcière (Michelet), 91
Spinoza, Benedict, 89, 186, 187, 195, 196, 202
Stoics, 169, 172, 179
structuralism, 15-18
surfaces, 17, 23; in genealogy, 148; phantasm arising from, 169-170, 179
Surveiller et punir (Foucault), 24-25

Taine, Hippolyte, 89
tales of terror, 60-61, 63-66
Taylor system, 231
Temptation of Saint Anthony (Flaubert), 19, 87-109; dreams every book, 91-93, 105; early drafts, 87-88, 103-104; erudite book, 89-93, 103; impression of first auditors, 88-89; multiple meaning of, 99-105; presence of books in, 93-99; product of library, 92-93, 105; related to *Bouvard*, 105-109; sources, 89-90; structure, 93-105
Thalia-Fragment (Hölderlin), 76, 78
theory and practice, 24-25, 205-209; serves struggle against power, 208
thought: "in common with others," 181; of Deleuze, 196; disjunctive, 185; and drugs, 190-192; intensive irregularity, 183; and knowledge, 176-179; as mime, 179; and stupidity, 187-192
Through the Looking Glass (Carroll), 23
Tintoretto, 74
Titian, 74
transgression, 30-31, 44, 50, 58; act of affirmation, 37; language of, 33, 39, 51, 83; and the limit, 33-35, 40, 50; of sight, 46; writing as, 125; *see also* Bataille, Georges; death

Uccello, Paolo, 73, 74
Ulysses, 53-55, 167

Untimely Meditations (Nietzsche), 152, 161, 162, 164

Vasari, Giorgio, (*Vite*), 72, 80
Velasquez, Diego, 92
Verrochio, Andrea del, 73
Vinchon, Jean, 76

Wanderer, The (Hölderlin), 69
Warhol, Andy, 189
will to power, 155
will to truth (knowledge), 22, 163, 164, 199-201

Wit and Its Relation to the Un-conscious (Freud), 131
writing: alphabetical, 55-56; and death, 53-55, 56, 59, 116-117; ethical principle of, 116; and "expression," 116; invention of, 55-56; limits of a work, 118-119; and transgression, 125, 214; *see also* author; language

Zarathustra, 42, 143, 193, 195
Zeno, 172, 179

8 4 3 7

CPSIA information can be obtained at www.ICGtesting.com
Printed in the USA
LVOW07s1028181016

509244LV00001B/79/P